Small, George L
The blue whale

DATE DUE

FEB 9 '72			
FEB 21 '73			
MAY 16 '73			
MAR 26 '75			
MAY 10 '78			
NOV 22 '79			
APR 22 '80			
DEC 11 '96			

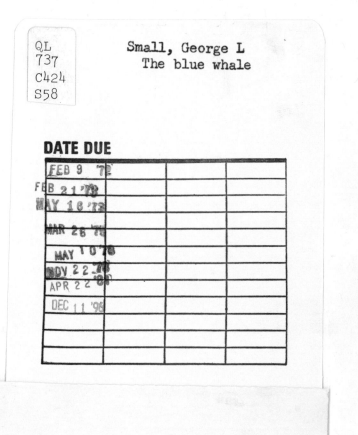

THE BLUE WHALE

GEORGE L. SMALL

THE BLUE WHALE

NEW YORK & LONDON

COLUMBIA UNIVERSITY PRESS

1971

George L. Small is Professor of Geography
at The City University of New York

Copyright © 1971 Columbia University Press
Library of Congress Catalog Card Number: 76-134986
International Standard Book Number: 0-231-03288-9
Printed in the United States of America

To the memory of my most patient teacher, my father
GEORGE ARTHUR SMALL

FOREWORD

THE PLIGHT OF THE BLUE WHALE came to my attention several
years ago when I was a student in a graduate seminar conducted
by Professor Herman F. Otte of Columbia University. His encour-
agement, incisive criticisms, and wise counsel were of inestimable
value and without them this book would not have been written.
Research into the conditions affecting the blue whale, which produced
a doctoral thesis and ultimately this book, was greatly facilitated by
the endless patience, cooperation, and sound advice of Professor William A. Hance, Chairman of the Department of Geography, Columbia University.

During the course of research valuable and generous help came
from many people in several countries. In some cases the individuals
are still employed by whaling companies and to spare them acute
embarrassment their names will not be divulged. In other cases the
individuals are, on occasion, members of their national delegations
to the International Whaling Commission and they too must remain
anonymous. There are even a few individuals in neither category
who have expressed the desire to remain anonymous because of the
controversial nature of this book. Nevertheless, in all cases I wish to
acknowledge here the gratitude that I have expressed privately.

On numerous occasions in this volume reference has been made to
the shortsightedness and rapaciousness of whalers. The term *whaler*
refers to owners, directors, and executives of whaling companies. The
men who manned the whaling ships—the gunners, flensers, and deck-
hands—are referred to as *whalingmen*. The distinction is important.
Unexpectedly, I found that the men who killed and butchered the
whales expressed, almost to a man, genuine compassion for their victims. In sharp contrast was the attitude of whaling company officials
who considered whales a mere industrial raw material, like iron ore,
valuable only for their contribution to production and corporate
profits.

The most valuable single source of information about whaling controls is the records of the annual meetings of the International Whaling Commission. Records of plenary sessions are verbatim but committees publish only final reports with an occasional minority opinion. Despite the value of Whaling Commission documents, not all of them are available to Americans. The documents are in the custody of the State Department where they have been carelessly handled. All documents of the Whaling Commission are mimeographed and stapled, and each annual meeting produces nearly 2 dozen documents. These vary in length from 2 pages for a financial report to 75 pages for a plenary session report. The State Department has not bound these documents and many have been lost. For example, there is almost nothing available about the first meeting of the Commission in 1949, and about 17 percent of all Whaling Commission documents are missing from the State Department files. Fortunately, several copies of all documents are available in Norway, bound by year. Canada is a member of the International Whaling Commission and complete records may exist there.

Finally, I must admit that help and inspiration have come from the blue whale. Few authors have been privileged to write about so magnificent an animal. During a few quiet moments, of discouragement as well as joy, I felt in some unknown way that the spirit of the great blue whale was present. I hope I have done him justice.

GEORGE L. SMALL

New York, 1970

CONTENTS

LIST OF ILLUSTRATIONS

PLATES

FIGURES

LIST OF TABLES

THE BLUE WHALE

And the fear of you and the dread of you shall be on every beast of the earth. . . .   GENESIS 9:2.

I

INTRODUCTION TO TRAGEDY

66"THAR SHE BLOWS!" was a jubilant cry from the lookout that to-day is a sad reminder of America's proud days as a great whaling and seafaring nation. A century ago America began to turn away from the sea to develop the far greater wealth within her borders. Petroleum eliminated the market for sperm-whale oil as an illuminating fuel. New and expanding industries offered greater fortunes to shipowners and an easier, richer life for the men who worked the whaling ships. The shipbuilding industry entered a long period of decline, and today for every 2 tons of shipping constructed in the United States, 3 are built by tiny Denmark. The fishing industry, remote from inland cities and unable to compete with cheaper animal products, suffered a similar decline. Today for every ton of fish caught by Americans 3 tons are caught by Peruvians. So far as most Americans are concerned the seas have become mere highways where steel-hulled giants carry ever increasing amounts of industrial and petroleum products and fewer and fewer passengers. The seas have even become an aquatic barrier that can best be overcome by more, bigger, and faster aircraft. America has all but abandoned the high seas; little remains but nostalgia.

America's maritime nostalgia, whether centered on *Old Ironsides*, clipperships, or whaling barks is unfortunately compounded with a good measure of ignorance. As a people we have the naïve idea that when our resources begin to run short, in the not too distant future, we can turn to the seas and their untapped riches. After all, we rationalize, as the world's industrial giant we have scarcely touched the wealth of the seas. No other nation has our sophisticated know-how or markets so that wealth must be waiting for us. Alas, the truth is quite different. Many nations lacking our resources have long been engaged in exploiting the riches of the seas, and in most cases they have used those riches no more wisely than we have used ours on land. On occasion their rapacious folly has even surpassed ours. The tale is a sad one. Today every major high-seas fishing ground in the world is showing declining yields. In addition, the coastal waters of all major industrial nations of the world are being polluted at an alarming rate with serious consequences for man's food supply. Coastal waters play an important role in the reproductive phase of the life cycle of many species of fish as well as shrimp, lobster, clams, and oysters. As these waters become more and more polluted fewer and fewer of those animals are able to reproduce. Unfortunately for man, the chemicals with which he pollutes the coastal waters are carried by currents far out onto the high seas and conditions there are frightening. The accumulation of *DDT* in the bodies of the Bermuda petrel is a direct cause of the declining ability of that handsome bird to reproduce. No corner of the world ocean escapes defilement. The livers of Antarctic penguins, seals, and fish are accumulating *DDT* and other persistent pesticides at a rapid rate. Every cubic yard of water in every ocean now contains man-made radioactive material. And the rate of destruction, depletion, and pollution is increasing. The harvest of the sea is ending, not beginning.

If man today is guilty of misuse of the seas through overfishing and pollution of the marine environment, his past record is not much better. The damage merely took a little longer to accomplish. This book is concerned with the blue whale, the largest living animal. It is interesting to examine briefly what man did in the past to other cetacean (whale) species before he developed the capacity to kill the mighty blue whale.

The history of the whaling industry can be divided into three periods: old style, from the twelfth century to 1868; modern land-based whaling, from 1868 to 1925; and modern pelagic whaling, 1926 to the present.

Old-style whaling began on a commercial scale in the twelfth century in the Bay of Biscay by the Basques. The methods and equipment used were rudimentary—small oar-driven boats and hand harpoons. Results, however, were initially most satisfactory, for the area was rich with an untouched stock of whales. The species found there was the Biscayan Right whale (*Balaena biscayensis*), and it existed then not in pods of 5 or 6 but in herds of up to a hundred individuals. According to tradition, the name Right whale was later given to the animal by English whalingmen because it was a slow swimmer and it floated when dead, hence it was the "right" species to pursue. The oil of the Biscayan Right whale was highly prized for lamps, and the animal was such a great source of wealth that man's pursuit of it soon surpassed the ability of the animal to survive locally. In about one century the local industry collapsed; there were no longer enough whales to be worth the killing.

A demand for whale products had been created in Europe, and ambitious men made ceaseless efforts to fill it. Local industries sprang up farther and farther north along the coast of Europe to hunt the stocks of whales offshore and to continue the process begun in the Bay of Biscay. The Right whale, now called the North Atlantic Right whale (*Balaena glacialis*), was so ruthlessly hunted that by the seventeenth century it had simply ceased to exist in the waters off France, Great Britain, Ireland, and Spitzbergen in the Arctic. A similar slaughter, or development if one is industrially minded, took place on the east coast of North America. By the early eighteenth century the Right whale was almost commercially extinct everywhere in the Atlantic. British whalers in the nineteenth century, operating with new steam-driven vessels, hunted the few remaining animals in such far northern waters as Baffin Land, with the result that by the twentieth century the Right whale was facing complete biological extinction in the Atlantic Ocean. It seems likely that a few individuals are still alive, since two were definitely sighted in the Gulf of Mexico in 1963.[1] The odds against the survival of the species, however, are probably hopeless. Aside from all the natural dangers they encounter, the few remaining Right whales, if they are to reproduce, have the great problem of simply finding each other in the vast spaces of the sea. Their survival would rival the miracle of their creation.

The Right whale existed under many names in many oceans and

it was hunted as ruthlessly in one as in another. The results were about the same everywhere: hunting ceased when there were so few individuals left alive that it didn't pay to hunt them. When that happened the poor animal was not far from biological extinction. And so today the Right whale is as rare in the South Atlantic as in the North Atlantic, in the Indian as in the North Pacific. Man's enterprise is a thing of wonder, his wisdom questionable, his greed frightful.

Old-style whaling was not limited to one species. When the Right whale became scarce in the North Atlantic whalers turned to the Greenland Right whale (*Balaena mysticetus*), a species famous for very long whalebone. The hunt was relentless and by the early eighteenth century there were no more to be found in the waters around Spitzbergen, and it was soon obliterated everywhere in the Arctic. The present status of the species is somewhat in doubt because the animal does not migrate to more southerly waters. It apparently spends its lifetime in and around the edge of the arctic ice where there is little opportunity for man to observe any apparent change in its population.[2] The Greenland Right whale may or may not survive its past association with the human race.

During the long history of old-style commercial whaling the nations most guilty of annihilating entire stocks of whales did not include America. The Yankees from New Bedford and Nantucket hunted mainly sperm whales (*Physeter catodon*), the most famous individual of which was the legendary Moby Dick. The species is still hunted today and is far from extinct, although its numbers are greatly depleted. The ability of the sperm whale to survive is due to several unique aspects of the species. It does not congregate in any one small area to feed or mate, but remains widely scattered throughout tropical and subtropical waters. The male of the species is larger than the female which makes possible a higher survival rate for the females. This factor is of special importance because the sperm whale is the only polygamous species of large whale. No, Americans did not drive the sperm whale to the verge of extinction; the country's escutcheon is clean or just a bit tarnished if one looks closely at the Right whales of the Bering Sea. That is part of the nostalgia and the ignorance.

There is the case of the California gray whale (*Eschrichtius gibbosus*), a slow-swimming species that had been unmolested for time immemorial. It was also called the Devilfish because the females when accompanied by a calf defended their offspring with particular ferocity. The Gold Rush of 1849 in California brought a great increase in the number of American ships sailing north from Cape Horn to San Francisco. Some of the captains, if not the gold seekers, had had experience with the whaling industry, and they soon learned that there was a mass migration of gray whales every winter. The animals usually appeared in December and for about three months could be seen very close to shore swimming southward. They were heading for the warm, shallow bays and lagoons of Baja California where they mated and where the females gave birth and nursed their calves. So numerous were the gray whales that on some days as many as a thousand could be seen passing the numerous promontories of southern California. Their population was estimated to be from 25,000 to 50,000.[3] The hunt began in 1851. One whaler, C. M. Scammon, found the narrow inlet to a large lagoon in Baja California (now called Scammon Lagoon) that was the most important nursery for the gray whale. For several years his secret source of whales yielded great wealth, but the secret was discovered when an off-shore breeze carried the stench of his tryworks out to sea. Soon there were dozens of whalers squabbling for a good spot in the narrow channel where they could intercept the whales entering with their calves. Scarcely a whale survived the gauntlet and the slaughter at times covered the entire surface of the water with blood. The motherless calves were left to starve. When the whales grew scarce in the lagoons, whaling stations were set up along the coast of southern California. Here the migrating whales were easily spotted since they passed very close to land. Many whalers adopted a ruthless tactic. The main weapon in use at the time was Greener's bomb lance, which was fired from a short-barreled weapon resembling a large-bore shotgun. The explosive lance was not large, had no line attached, and several were usually required to kill a whale. Wounded animals thrashed around furiously and often attacked the boats. Whalers found it simpler and safer to harpoon a calf and haul it quickly to shore where the bereaved mother followed. In the shallow water she could not defend herself and was effectively shot. Here, moreover, her carcass was not lost if it sank.[4]

Against such odds the gray whale could not long survive, and it did not. By 1880 most of the whalers were out of business. By 1890 all whaling ceased. The gray whale was no more. For the next couple of decades the animal was thought to be extinct, although a very small number was still being taken, unknown to the Americans, along the coast of Korea.[5] Eventually gray whales were again seen along the California coast, but it is not known whether they were offspring of a few that had managed to survive or part of the separate stock that inhabited the coast of Asia. In any event, their reappearance saved the United States from the guilt of cetacean genocide, at least temporarily.

In the mid-1920s the gray whale was seen migrating along the coast in fairly substantial numbers and temptation was too great. Whaling began again. This time the whalers had modern efficient equipment to match their determination and enterprise. A decade later the killing stopped. There were no more whales.

In 1936 Congress passed a law forbidding the killing of gray whales. With at most a hundred gray whales still alive the law was as much an epitaph as a protection. The gray whale, like many other cetacean species, needs far more than a hundred individuals to avoid the danger of biological extinction. If there were 100 adults there might have been 40 sexually mature females, but a gray whale needs nearly two years to produce one calf. Thus 20 or 25 calves at most were the species only hope for survival, and these had to face the dangers of birth, disease, stranding, killer whales, and Japanese and Eskimo whalers in the Bering and Chuckchi seas.

By 1947 there were about 250 gray whales in the annual migration. Their number continues to grow until today there may be as many as 10,000 in the annual swim-past that delights thousands of Californians.[6] For the second time the gray whale's successful struggle for life saved the United States from the guilt of cetacean genocide, at least temporarily.

The industrialization of the California coast is raising new problems for the gray whale. Sparsely populated Baja California is attractive for industrial development, and along that several hundred-mile arid coast man decided to build a giant, modern salt factory. Where did he put it? Right on the shore of the greatest gray whale nursery— Scammon Lagoon. If the gray whale abandoned San Diego Bay a century ago when a few small boats began using it, how will noise, ship traffic, altered temperature, and salinity conditions in Scammon Lagoon affect its rate of reproduction? If the species requires a lagoon for breeding where will it find one? How many gray whales will die of pollution by chemicals and by oil leaking from offshore wells? How long will it be before whalers again demand the right to harvest the gray whale? Twice the animal came back from the horrible brink of biological extinction. It does not deserve to be threatened a third time. Who will prevent it? Who can prevent it?

The whalers of the world were frustrated for centuries. Some had made fortunes, to be sure, but many had seen their industry collapse with the disappearance of individual species. Fortunes could have been greater and industrial collapse could have been long postponed if the whalers had found some way of killing the largest of all species—the rorquals of the family *Balaenopteridae* that include the sei, fin, and blue whales. These animals were such fast swimmers that no sailboat or oar-driven whaleboat could overtake them. Moreover they sank when dead and thus could not be towed to tryworks. For centuries the whalers of the world watched those giants, those fortunes, swim with impunity past their boats and tiny harpoons. But inevitably the Industrial Revolution brought technical advances that could be adapted to the needs of whaling.

In the mid-1860s Svend Foyn, a Norwegian sealing captain with long experience in the Arctic, began working on a new method of killing the large rorquals. He used a steam-driven vessel that could develop a speed of seven knots, not enough to overtake a rorqual but enough to permit successful stalking. He erected a small cannon high in the bow to fire a heavy harpoon tipped with an explosive head. The harpoon was connected to a heavy line that in turn fed back around a winch and a special block, called an accumulator, that was composed of a series of springs to take up the powerful strain. When the harpooned whale died its carcass could be hauled alongside by the winch. Finally a long tube was pushed into the body cavity of the carcass and compressed air was pumped in to keep it afloat. These techniques were perfected by 1868 and proved to be highly successful. The whaling industry got a new lease on life, but the blue whale and other rorquals were doomed to a slaughter unparalleled in the history of commercial whaling.

Captain Foyn first used his new techniques along the north coast of Norway, and he was so successful that he was quickly imitated. Soon over 30 new-type catcher boats were in use killing over a thousand whales a year of all species, fin and blue particularly. The stocks of whales in that restricted area could not support such depletion, and by 1903 the total kill of all species fell to less than 400. Declining yields combined with vociferous complaints from local fishermen induced the Norwegian government to close the area to whaling.

Long before coastal whaling ceased in North Norway the new techniques made it highly profitable to use Iceland as a base to intercept rorquals as they migrated northward in summer. Operations began in 1883 with one catcher that caught 8 whales. By 1893 there were 15 catchers operating, with an annual kill of over 500 whales. The number of catchers doubled by 1900, and in 1902 a total of 1,305 whales were killed, the highest on record for Iceland. A catch of that magnitude was a quick source of wealth. The number of catchers increased, but the annual kill began to drop precipitously. By 1915, 4 catchers produced only 54 whales. In 1916 no one bothered to try.[7]

The claim has often been made, particularly by whalers, that whaling does not cease because there are no more whales, but because the price of whale oil drops. When whaling stopped in Iceland in 1916 the price of whale oil was £32 per ton, the highest in history.[8] Clearly, there were so few whales left that it did not pay to go after them.

Many other coastal regions of the North Atlantic underwent a similar evolution: initial success with a few boats catching a large number of whales, rapid expansion of the industry, and inevitable decline in the catch until all whaling ceased. Among them were the Faroe Islands, the Shetlands, Hebrides Islands, Ireland, Svalbard, Newfoundland, and West Greenland. When whaling ceased in these areas there were some whales left, although they were the pitifully small remnants of their former populations. Unfortunately, few accurate records were kept on species and lengths, and it is impossible to arrive at any sound conclusions about the blue-whale population. It is safe to conclude, however, that the blue whale was hunted more heavily than other species because of its size and value. (One blue whale could produce 2 times the oil of a fin whale and 30 times that of a Minke whale.)

The whale populations of the various Atlantic coastal regions eventually showed some growth in total numbers, and in a few places some whaling was resumed in the 1930s. This renewed activity never reached the amplitude of the "old days" and became intermittent. In Newfoundland, for example, there have been many years with no whaling at all, as in the 1950s, but it has now been resumed, certainly only temporarily. This modern phase of Atlantic coastal whaling, carried on with ruthless efficiency, adopted one worthwhile practice, namely, the keeping of accurate statistics on the catch. Thus it is possible to formulate some idea on the size of the North Atlantic blue-whale population.

From 1935 through 1939 the North Atlantic and Arctic catch of all large whales was 4,752, of which 139, or about 3 percent, were blue whales. Clearly, the blue whales in the North Atlantic were headed for extinction, and in that year all but 2 Atlantic whaling nations agreed to stop killing them. The exceptions were Iceland and Denmark, which continued to hunt blue whales from bases in Iceland, the Faroe Islands, and West Greenland. During the period from 1956 to 1960, the year in which they agreed to stop killing blue whales, they caught a total of 2,370 large whales, of which 31, or just over 1 percent, were blues.[9] It is no wonder Denmark and Iceland agreed to stop the killing of blue whales: the poor animal was no more.

Are there any lonely members of that great species alive in all the North Atlantic? Yes, probably a few. On rare occasions a fisherman or sealer reports sighting a small pod of 1 or 2 blue whales. The total blue-whale population in all probability now numbers fewer than 100 individuals. The animal has such a low rate of reproduction that even if it numbered 100 individuals, it might not be able to survive as a species. (The reasons for this are explained in the next chapter.) Moreover, even if there were a "surplus" of blue whales in other oceans, no improvement in the Atlantic could be expected. The blue whale never crosses the Equator, and it cannot move from the Pacific to the Atlantic. If the animal does not become extinct in the Atlantic, it will be a miracle.

The fate of the blue whale in the North Pacific was distressingly similar to its fate in the Atlantic. The only significant differences were in chronology and in the nationality of the executioners. The techniques developed by Svend Foyn were quickly adopted by land-based whalers from California and British Columbia to Japan and the nearby Kuriles and Ryukyus. The rapidity of industrial expansion varied from place to place, but the decline in the blue-whale population in the North Pacific was no less serious. In 1966 the whaling nations agreed to give complete protection to the blue whale in the North Pacific because the species was in obvious danger of extinction. In the preceding five years land-based whalers on the periphery of the Pacific had killed a total of 22,707 large whales, of which 138 or 0.5 percent were blues.[10]

The North Pacific is a much larger ocean than the Atlantic, and the total cetacean resources were much greater. These resources were also largely inaccessible to land-based whalers. The Pacific Ocean, as a consequence, was the scene of extensive pelagic whaling, which consists of factory ships operating on the high seas with large fleets of catcher boats. These industrial armadas scoured northern Pacific waters for many years with ruthless efficiency, harvesting whales by the thousands. Their preference was the blue whale, the most valuable species. In 1965, the last season during which blue whales could be legally hunted there, they killed a total of 16,051 whales of which 121 were blues.

In all the vast North Pacific there might be a hundred blue whales left alive. This, as in the case of the Atlantic, is no guarantee that the animal can survive.

During the long centuries of commercial whaling that began with the Basques in the Bay of Biscay, the industry was to a large extent limited to the Northern Hemisphere and the subtropical regions of the Southern Hemisphere. During the late nineteenth and early twentieth centuries the cost of production of whale oil began to rise with the increasing scarcity of whales. Ambitious whalers began to seek out new, untouched whaling grounds. What they found was the

greatest whaling ground in all the history of commercial whaling—
the Antarctic. The story of that discovery is a modern saga of exploration in dangerous, uncharted seas by such courageous and highly
skilled Norwegians as Svend Foyn and Captains C. A. Larsen and C.
Christensen. The details of their exploits read like an epic, but they
are beyond the scope of this book. Hopefully they will someday become available to English readers through translation from numerous
Norwegian works.[11] The significant result of those explorations was
that the whalers of the world came to know that the Antarctic contained unbelievably rich stocks of whales. There were blue and fin
whales and humpbacks by the thousands that had never been shot at!
There were sperm whales and sei whales too. Here was untouched
wealth such as whalers had dreamed of for centuries. With this discovery there began a slaughter that would soon surpass anything
seen before.

The first land station in the Antarctic was begun in 1904 by Captain
Larsen on the island of South Georgia. The enterprise was started
with Argentinian capital, but with men and material from Larsen's
native Vestfold on the southeast coast of Norway. His station in the
harbor of Grytviken, South Georgia was well chosen. Whales were so
plentiful that catcher boats had only to go to the mouth of the small
harbor to get all they wanted. By 1909 there were 4 shore stations on
South Georgia operating with a total of 17 catchers; they killed 3,516
whales in just one season. The following season the South Georgia
catch rose to 6,535 whales. The record catch there was still many years
away. Industrial Europe had no problem consuming all the oil the
Antarctic could produce. The price of oil began to rise in 1906
and soared during World War I. The demand for whale oil and the
abundance of whales stimulated an industrial growth that was only
temporarily slowed by a shortage of materiel during the war.

Tiny South Georgia was not big enough to house all the rapacious
whalers. Soon bases were established on South Shetland, the Falk-
land, and Kerguelen islands. Some of the islands had a limited supply
of fresh water and a hostile climate that precluded year-round human
habitation. (The South Shetlands are only 300 miles north of the
Antarctic Circle.) The whalers were forced to convert large ships into
floating factories that could be anchored in sheltered bays during the

short Antarctic summer. Dead whales were towed alongside, the blubber peeled off and hoisted onboard for rendering, and the oil stored in the factory ships. By 1924, twenty years after Larsen established his first station, 6 shore stations, 13 factory ships, and 65 catcher boats were in operation in the Antarctic. During these years some Norwegian whaling companies were paying more in dividends than in wages. The cost was staggering only to the whales who were soon dying at the rate of over 10,000 a season.

The methods of operation in the early days of Antarctic whaling were wasteful to a degree that would shock modern whalers. For many years only the back and belly blubber of the whale was utilized; the thinner layers on the tail flukes, head, and jaws were ignored. The oil rich bones, the meat, and valuable organs were not used at all. In short, once the back and belly blubber had been flensed off, the entire whale carcass was cast adrift. On calm days many harbors in the Antarctic were cluttered with the stinking, decaying carcasses of dozens of half-skinned whales. Despite the waste, total production reached startling proportions. From 1910 to 1925, production totaled 6,498,771 barrels of whale oil, or 1,083,128 tons (1 metric ton equals 6 barrels). To supply such vast quantities of oil, 134,026 whales died— that is what the statistics say, but they tell only part of the story.

Under normal whaling conditions it is rare to encounter just one whale at a time. Often many will be sighted, and as one is shot it is cast adrift to be picked up later when the shooting is over. This inevitably results in lost whales whose carcasses are never seen again. In the early years of Antarctic whaling the rate of lost whales was very high. Catcher boats were small and slow and they had no radar and no radio direction transmitters to attach to carcasses to aid recovery. In addition, whales were so plentiful that it did not pay to spend much time looking for a lost carcass. Some writers suggest that as many as 25 percent of the whales shot in the early years of Antarctic whaling were lost. During the 1950s loss rates as high as 5 or 6 percent were recorded; therefore, a 20 percent estimate for the Antarctic does not seem exaggerated. That means that during the period of land-based whaling from 1909 to 1925, an additional 26,800 whales were lost and uncounted and never went into the steam kettles. They are the "missing-in-action" who died for nothing.

During the early years of Antarctic whaling about 90 percent of the catch was composed of humpback whales. This animal, rich in oil, was a slow swimmer and had the habit of migrating close to shore where catcher boats lay in wait. Some 8,500 humpbacks perished in 1911, but only 9 were to be had in 1922. With the disappearance of such easy targets the whalers had to go farther out to sea where they could prey on the blue whale. This they did with equal vengeance. In 1910 only 176 blue whales were killed; 5,700 died in 1925. The total kill of blue whales between those years was 47,200. This slaughter was a heavy burden for a species with an estimated population of 150,000 when whaling began. The blue whale could have recovered in time if the killing had ceased or even significantly declined. But the price of whale oil remained high for many years, and several European nations came to rely on it as their main source of margarine and cooking oils. The killing continued.

By the mid-1920s the whalers began to experience that old feeling of frustration: there were a lot more whales in the open Antarctic if they could reach them. From their sheltered anchorages on small islands they could intercept only a limited number of migrating whales whose numbers were declining. Once again, a Norwegian sea captain solved the problem. In 1925 Captain Sørlle of Vestfold fitted out a large factory ship, the S.S. *Lancing,* with a stern slipway: a long sloping ramp that led from a large hole in the stern up to the main deck. With the stern slipway whale carcasses could be hauled up to the deck by a steam winch and flensed even while the ship was on the open sea. Flensers no longer had to work on slippery carcasses floating alongside, a dangerous practice that could plunge them into freezing water. (This method of flensing is shown in Plate VIII.) Now the factory ship could go onto the high seas wherever there were whales. Another advantage was that on the high-seas whalers were subject to the laws of no nation. The old anchorages on South Georgia and other islands required a lease and the payment of fees to Great Britain, who owned them.

Captain Sørlle's slipway worked well and the S.S. *Lancing* had a successful whaling season. Other whalers, eager to increase their catches and avoid British controls, converted their ships to include a slipway. They moved out to the high seas and whaling in the Antarctic became pelagic. In 1930, only five years after Captain Sørlle's successful experiment, the number of pelagic factory ships with a slipway rose to 38 and the number of catcher boats accompanying them rose from 4 to 184.[12] This flotilla combined with the forces of the land-based whalers was a veritable armada. With its formation there began a period of cetacean slaughter that surpassed all that had gone before.

During the 1925 whaling season in the Antarctic 10,500 whales died. In 1930 the figure exceeded 30,000. In 1931 the blood ran thicker and 40,200 whales died. The worst was yet to come for the whales in general, but it had already arrived for the blue whales. Between 1910 and 1925 the blue whale suffered grievous losses with the deaths of 47,200. With the development of pelagic whaling the animal was exposed to even greater danger. Between 1926 and 1930 the total catch climbed to 49,800. In the 1931 season alone, the kill of blue whales reached an incredible 29,400, the highest ever recorded. Never again could man find so many blue whales in one year. The bloodletting continued for another eight years until World War II gave the poor beast a short respite. But even during those years another 118,300 blue whales died.

If such slaughter continued the blue whale would cease to exist. Were there any voices raised in warning? Not many. Few people knew what was happening. It was the Norwegians who led the development of modern whaling, and it was the Norwegians who led the struggle to keep it within reasonable bounds. As early as 1910 J. A. Mørch, a Norwegian engineer, warned British authorities of the possibility of exterminating all commercially hunted whales.[13] The warning resulted in the formation of several important government agencies, especially the British Discovery Committee that performed invaluable cetacean research. But the killing continued. Other voices, British, French, American, joined the Norwegians. Scientists and conservationists—even diplomats—became alarmed. International conferences were held and treaties were ratified to protect the whales. But the killing continued. After World War II the victorious allies made a major effort to protect the whales. They established the famous International Whaling Commission, which all the pelagic whaling nations of the world joined. Together, they would regulate the industry and, at last, would impose reason and restraint upon the whalers. But the killing continued. Why? Why were the nations of the world unable to restrain their own whalers? The answer to that question is a major aim of this book.

Why did the whalers of the world have to be restrained at all? Surely it would not be to their advantage to slaughter so many whales that there would not be enough left to support the industry. Every child knows the parable of the goose that laid the golden eggs. It seems such a simple truth. The whalers rejected it. Had they agreed to kill only the sustainable yield of each species, that is, the number that could be killed without permanently decreasing the population, the industry could have carried on forever. This they did not do. The killing continued. Company after company went out of business for lack of whales. Why did they continue killing when they knew it would lead inevitably to their own financial ruin? The answer to that question is another aim of this book.

And what of the blue whale? When did the whalers give in and stop killing this magnificent animal in order that it might survive? They didn't, really. The whalers of most nations, with a kind of sanctimonious perversity, agreed to stop killing whales when there were no more to be found. The year was 1965. A few nations still permit the killing of blue whales and one has even found a way to circumvent its agreement not to do so. There are precious few blue whales left, but the killing continues. Are there enough now alive to avert biological extinction? The answer to this question is still another aim of this book.

The ensuing chapters, which explore and answer these questions, concentrate on whaling activities in the Southern Hemisphere, particularly in the Antarctic. This approach avoids needless repetition since the problems facing the blue whale in its struggle for survival are the same in the Antarctic as in the North Pacific and North Atlantic. Indeed, the same companies that engaged in North Pacific whaling also worked the Antarctic. Finally, the blue whale was to a large extent a Southern Hemisphere animal. About 97 percent of all blue whales killed met death in the Antarctic, the same battleground where the species must now wage a fateful struggle ordained by man—survival or extinction.

And God created great whales, and every living creature that moveth, which
the waters brought forth abundantly. . . .   GENESIS 1:21.

II

THE BLUE WHALE

DURING THE MILLIONS OF YEARS that life has existed on earth
many exotic animals have appeared. People generally think
that the largest of them must have been some dinosaur of the Meso-
zoic Age. One of them, *Brachiosaurus*, was a giant that weighed an
estimated 50 tons. But such a giant was a runt compared to the blue
whale, which weighs 50 tons long before the age of puberty. Indeed,
a large female blue whale can lose 50 tons while nursing a calf and
still weigh twice as much as *Brachiosaurus*. Most dinosaurs were so
small that they could pass through the jawbone of a blue whale (see
Plate III). Even in terms of length the blue whale remains superlative.
Diplodocus, an herbivorous Jurassic dinosaur, reached an estimated
length of almost 100 feet; blue whales have exceeded that by many
feet. The blue whale, therefore, is the largest animal known to have
lived on land or sea since the beginning of time.

It is surprising that an animal as large as the blue whale presented
scientists with problems of taxonomy, that is, classification and identification by species. Such was the case with the blue and many other
members of the order Cetacea.

The blue whale is a member of the suborder *Mystacoceti,* which
includes all whales having baleen as distinct from the suborder
Odontoceti (sperm whales, porpoises, and dolphins) which has true
teeth. The *baleen,* erroneously called whalebone, is in the form of
long horny plates that hang down from the upper jaw bone. These
plates vary from 1 to 14 feet in length and from 2 to 18 inches in
width, depending on the species. They are about a half an inch apart

Plate II Blue-whale fetus, circa 21 feet, taken from a whale killed at South Georgia, 1925. The ventral pleats may be clearly seen. This specimen would have been a very large calf at birth, which normally would have taken place four to five months later. Part of a carcass with entrails may be seen in the background. Courtesy of the National Institute of Oceanography.

Plate I An 89-foot female blue whale killed at South Georgia, 1925 (dorsal view). Note the very small dorsal fin, the mottled color pattern on the flanks, and a few ventral pleats near the base of the jaw. Courtesy of the National Institute of Oceanography.

Plate III   Lower jawbone of a blue whale erected on the waterfront of Sandefjord, Norway. Photograph by the author.

and their inner edges have a hairy fringe that acts as a strainer. With a mouthful of zooplankton, a whale closes its jaws and raises its tongue to force out the seawater, and the fringed plates hold back the food that can then be swallowed. (A baleen plate of a blue whale is shown in Plate IV. The position of plates in the jaw of a baleen whale is shown in Plate V.)

The *Mystacoceti* are subdivided into three families, the most important of which is the *Balaenopteridae*. The outstanding characteristics of this family are: a small dorsal fin; short baleen, usually 3 feet or less; and ventral grooves or pleats that extend nearly half the length of the body, beginning just under the tip of the lower jaw. The term *rorqual* is the common name given to the *Balaenopteridae*, and *whalebone whales* or *baleen whales* are used as substitutes for *Mystacoceti*.

Several centuries passed before man could accurately classify the

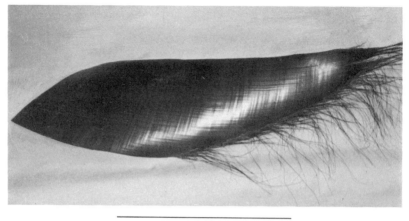

20 inches

Plate IV Baleen plate of a blue whale. The vertical ridges used by Ruud for age determination may be seen. The very thin horizontal ridges are formed by the portion of the fringes that are covered by the horny plate. Maximum thickness of this plate is just under 3/16 of an inch, and the longest individual fringe is 13 inches. Over-all length of plate minus fringes is 31 inches (20-inch rule gives scale). Photograph by the author.

rorquals by species. These animals were such fast swimmers and so large that they could not be killed by man until Svend Foyn mounted his harpoon gun on a steam-driven vessel. Prior to that rorquals were only dissected and studied when they were accidentally stranded. In such cases they were often sick, discolored through decomposition, and perhaps far from a trained anatomist. Thus the blue whale was first called "Sibbald's rorqual," for Robert Sibbald, a Scot, who described a blue whale stranded in the Firth of Forth in 1692. The name has tended to persist to the present day in English-speaking countries, as has its Latin equivalent, *Sibbaldus musculus*.[1]

A second factor that complicated the accurate subdivision of the rorqual family by species was their habit of migrating annually from their breeding grounds in warm tropical waters to their feeding grounds in cold polar waters. After about a month in plankton-rich polar oceans the whales begin to accumulate a film of diatoms, particularly on their ventral sides. On the blue whale this film differs markedly from the normal light greenish-blue color of the animal and is

Plate V   Close-up view of the head of a 27-foot Minke whale (Balaenoptera acutorostrata). *The outer, unfringed edges of the baleen plates may be seen in their typical position in a baleen whale, that is, hanging down side by side from the upper jaw. The tongue of this specimen was damaged during towing to the factory ship and is protruding onto the deck.* Courtesy of Crowell Collier and Macmillan, Inc.

distinctly yellow. The name *sulphur bottom* was given to such whales and for many years they were considered to be a separate species. Eventually the whalers learned the cause of this discoloration, but the name persists, although whalers know it is a blue whale and not a separate species.

For centuries the blue whale was called by many names, which led to the erroneous belief that there were many species of whales this large.[2] The scientific name for the blue whale that eventually gained universal acceptance is *Balaenoptera musculus,* a modification of Linnaeus's *Balaena musculus.* The second half of this binomial is a false cognate. *Musculus* in Latin is the diminutive form of *mouse,* meaning therefore "little mouse," and has nothing to do with muscle. The only plausible explanation for the choice of the term is that Linnaeus must have been in a jocular mood at the time.

The blue whale, *Balaenoptera musculus,* resembles the 5 other members of the genus *Balaenoptera* to a remarkable degree, especially in over-all body form. Its distinguishing features are: enormous size; a mottled color pattern particularly on the ventral side, gray or greenish-blue color; and an exceptionally small dorsal fin. These characteristics may be seen in Plate I.

After many decades of taxonomic peace the blue whale again became the center of a taxonomic dispute that remains unsolved to this day. Japanese whalers operating near the Kerguelen Islands during the 1960 season killed several hundred blue whales that they reported as being noticeably different from the regular blue whale. This new whale, they claimed, was about 10 feet shorter at sexual maturity and had proportionally a shorter tail and longer body than the regular blue whale. Soviet whalers subsequently visited the area and also reported finding a smaller blue whale that generally resembled the description given by the Japanese. This apparently new subspecies was given the colloquial name *pygmy blue whale*. There are, however, many cetologists and whalers in the Western world who doubt the existence of such a subspecies and are critical of their colleagues who do recognize it. The Latin name assigned to the pygmy blue whale, formulated by two Soviet writers, is *Balaenoptera musculus brevicaudatus*.[3] This taxonomic dispute, which was to have profound consequences for the blue whale, is treated in more detail in Chapter VII.

The blue whale, like other baleen species, is a monogamous, warm-blooded mammal. Over 99 percent of all pregnancies, and therefore births, involves a single fetus,[4] and the sex of the calves is almost exactly half male and half female.

The average length of a blue whale at birth has never been accurately determined. Probably it never will be. No man has ever seen the birth of a blue whale, and even the place of birth remains unknown. Presumably births take place in warm, low latitude waters because calves have no blubber and hence could probably not survive in frigid polar seas.

Most of man's knowledge of blue-whale fetuses comes from scientists working on factory ships where they could examine the carcasses of dead females. The most recent work on the subject was by a Dutch cetologist who obtained his data from material gathered on the Dutch factory ship *Willem Barendsz.* He was of the opinion that a blue whale is 24 or 25 feet long at birth.[5] Contemporary Norwegian cetologists disagreed and felt that the evidence pointed to a length of only 23 feet at birth.[6] An earlier Norwegian specialist, after extensive research in the Antarctic in the 1920s, concluded that blue whales must be 25 to 27 feet in length at birth.[7] This opinion was shared by an English cetologist, J. T. Jenkins, whose reasoning was based on statistical data and a rather interesting observation as well.

During the late summer in the Antarctic the weather becomes stormier than usual making it increasingly difficult to tow whale carcasses to factory ships. This is precisely the season when the fetuses are largest, the females having been feeding in the Antarctic prior to migrating equatorward to give birth. Normal muscle tonus ceases at death and a pregnant female carcass being towed backward, is very apt to lose the fetus, especially a large one. Numerous fetuses 27 feet long were recorded. Jenkins concluded: "In that way large foetuses may escape record, in fact some of the largest foetuses are probably not recorded at all."[8] A large, but not a term, blue-whale fetus is shown in Plate II.

Whether the average day-old, blue-whale calf is 23 or 27 feet long is of no great import. In either case, it is a true "baby"—curious, probably awkward, surely hungry. How wonderful it would be if someday one human being witnessed the entry of such a life into the world.

A blue-whale calf is nursed by its mother for about seven months, during which time it grows to a length of 53 feet. There is no doubt about the accuracy of this figure, because biologists could determine the time of weaning with precision by examining the stomach contents of the carcasses. If the contents were milk the calf was still nursing; if they were zooplankton, called *krill,* weaning was completed; and if there was a mixture of milk and krill weaning was in process at the time of death.

The growth of a baby blue whale from about 25 feet at birth to 53 feet at weaning seven months later requires a growth rate of over an inch and a half per day. That is astounding. Growth in terms of weight is equally astounding. At birth the baby blue weighs just under 3 tons but at weaning it has reached 23 tons. For seven months, therefore, a baby blue whale grows at the rate of 200 pounds a day. Such a growth rate can only be explained in terms of a copious supply of nutritious milk provided by the mother. Blue-whale milk has the consistency of loose, runny cheese, but its fishy odor discouraged most whalers from sampling it. While it has been impossible, for obvious reasons, to determine the daily milk production of a female it must have been enormous. In addition to the daily weight increment of 200 pounds the mother's milk had to furnish a calf with energy for youthful gamboling, and a migration of thousands of miles to the feeding grounds in the Antarctic. If natural losses and the efficiency rate of the milk as a fuel could be measured the daily milk production of a female would probably surpass 300 pounds.

Samples of blue-whale milk have been chemically analyzed on numerous occasions and typical results are shown in Table 1. It will be noted that in terms of fat content alone blue-whale milk is about 10 times more concentrated than cows' milk. Part of the explanation for the high fat content is the solution to a biochemical problem facing all whales. As mammals their life processes require a great quantity of water yet never once in their lives can they take a drink. They live in the world's "driest" climate—salt water. Their water comes from the chemical breakdown of blubber, and the supply of that is limited. Concentrating milk by reducing its water content is one successful measure all whales have adopted for living with a perpetual water shortage.

Table 1

Percentage composition of blue-whale milk by selected components

	Whale 1 (Length 88′)	Whale 2 (Length 83′)
Nonfat solids	13.21	16.38
Protein	10.76	13.56
Fat	49.85	34.79

Source: M. E. Gregory, *et al.,* "The Composition of the Milk of the Blue Whale," *The Journal of Dairy Research,* Cambridge, England, XXII (1955), 108–14.

When man must establish conservation measures for a commercially valuable animal specific information about its life cycle is necessary. The most important information usually concerns the age and the size of the animal at sexual maturity. In the case of the blue whale many years of research were required before such information was finally obtained.

The first study of the size of the blue whale at sexual maturity was carried out at Norwegian whaling stations and on factory ships in the Antarctic in the early 1920s. It was found to be extremely rare for a female blue whale under 70 feet to be gestating. When a length of 80 feet was attained there was a sudden increase in the pregnancy rate. From this the author of the study concluded that sexual maturity was reached when females were 79 feet in length. (The pertinent details of the research are shown in Table 2.) Research into the problem continued for another fifteen years and greater precision was obtained by examination of the ovaries.

In all mammals the ovum, or egg, is formed in an ovarian follicle that enlarges as the egg matures. After ovulation, if fertilization takes place, the follicle is transformed into a progestin-producing body known as a *corpus luteum*. After birth the *corpus luteum* diminishes in size, ceases production of progestin, and becomes a small, spherical *corpus albicans*. A *corpus albicans* is also produced soon after ovulation if fertilization does not take place. In all land mammals and some marine species as well the *corpus albicans* shrivels and eventually

Table 2

Pregnancy percentage rates of young female blue whales

Length (in feet)	Percentage pregnant Antarctic pelagic	Percentage pregnant South Georgia land stations
70	2.1	2.4
75	4.9	4.8
79	8.1	5.0
80	22.1	22.4

Source: S. Risting, "Whales and Whale Foetuses," *Rapports et Procès-Verbaux des Réunions,* Conseil Permanent International pour l'Exploration de la Mer, L (1928), 116–17.

disappears. In the blue whale, and all other rorquals, it never disappears. It shrivels to a diameter of half an inch or less and remains
throughout life imbedded in the ovary wall. Thus it is possible to
determine not only if sexual maturity has been reached but how often
a female has ovulated.

The examination and study of cetacean ovaries have never been
easy or pleasant tasks. Little imagination is required to understand the
problem of searching for and counting the *corpora albicantia* in the
midst of tons of stinking entrails steaming in the cold Antarctic air on
the busy deck of a factory ship. The Norwegian *Statens Institutt For
Hvalforskning* (Institute for Whale Research) undertook a research
program and trained several marine biologists at whaling stations
along the Norwegian coast. These men, with the cooperation of Norwegian pelagic whaling companies, carried out extensive research on
whale carcasses during the 1939/40 whaling season in the Antarctic.

They found that the largest sexually immature female was 84 feet
in length, while the smallest mature female was 72 feet. The mean
was 78 feet. All data worked to the nearest inch indicated a figure
of 77.6 feet.[9] Since that time cetologists have agreed that 78 feet is a
reasonably accurate figure for the average length of female blue
whales at sexually maturity.

The length of the male of the species at sexual maturity was determined with greater ease and precision. Greater precision was
possible because the male of all baleen species is shorter in
length than the female and consequently shows less variation in
length between individuals. The most recent and thorough study of
the matter was carried out just after World War II by scientists of
the Norwegian Institute for Whale Research. Histological examination of the testes, a somewhat inconvenient procedure, was necessary
to be certain that sexual maturity had been attained. However, it was
found that sexual maturity was reached when the testes reached a
weight of 10 kilograms, or 22 pounds. This proved to be a simple
method for examining hundreds of individual male blue whales, and
it was found that, on average, they reached sexual maturity at a
length of 74 feet.[10]

During the 1930s the first feeble attempts were made to regulate
whaling on a world-wide basis. It was evident that conservation mea-

sures were necessary if the blue and other whales in the Southern Hemisphere were to be protected from the virtual extinction suffered by other species in the Northern Hemisphere. One of the regulations adopted then by most whaling nations was minimum-length requirements. For the blue whale the minimum length was 65 feet for land-based whalers, and 70 feet for pelagic whalers. This meant that the animal was legal prey before it even had time to reproduce! It seems a bit stupid to list such a regulation under the rubric of conservation, but this is what it was supposed to be. If there had also been limits on the number of blue whales killed the adverse effects of insufficient length requirements might have been lessened. Such was not the case. Man's intelligence was no help to the blue whale. The ludicrous length requirements can in part be explained by two factors of a purely biological nature. In the first instance the blue whale even as it approached sexual maturity was larger than the second largest whale in the world and consequently a great source of wealth.[11] Even when sexually immature therefore the blue whale was simply too valuable an animal to be allowed to live. Second, minimum-length requirements were set low in the belief that the blue whale grew so rapidly that it reached sexual maturity at age two. If such had been the case the species would have had reasonably good powers of regeneration. But such was not the case.

The problem of determining age at sexual maturity was realy one of determining age itself. How does one learn the age of a wild animal or even a domesticated one like man if the date of birth is not recorded? In the case of the blue and other large whales the problem proved to be particularly difficult.

The first effort to determine the age of blue whales at sexual maturity was made by the famous Norwegian scientist Sigurd Risting. He worked on board Norwegian factory ships during the 1920s and was well aware of the very rapid growth of immature blue whales during their nursing period. He felt that since a calf could grow from 25 feet to 53 feet in six or seven months it could certainly grow 6 or 7 more feet during the next six months. By that time it would be back in warm tropical waters after having left the Antarctic in December or January when weaned. At that point in time the whale would be one-year old and 60 feet in length. Moreover, since some blue whales attained sexual maturity when only 70 feet long he felt that sexual maturity was reached at the end of the second year of life. It did seem logical to assume that the animal could grow 10 feet during its second year if it could grow over 25 feet during its first seven months.[12]

During those same years similar studies were being carried out at land stations in the Antarctic, particularly South Georgia. The funds obtained from whaling leases on these British-owned islands were used to support extensive research in many aspects of whaling and the findings were published in the now famous *Discovery Reports*. Two English cetologists, N. A. Mackintosh and J. F. E. Wheeler, conducted exhaustive studies on blue and fin whales taken by the land-based whalers. They began their study of the question of age at sexual maturity with the assumption that there is a positive relationship between age and length, especially for the younger animals. They plotted, therefore, the length-frequency distribution by meters and found two crests, or maxima, for immature blue whales. The first they interpreted as being the length attained when weaning was completed. The second they believed represented the growth attained by the whales at the end of their second summer in the Antarctic. The rate of growth was such that by the time the whales had returned to warm subtropical waters for the second time the males and females would be 78 and 77 respectively. Thus they would be sexually mature and could begin to mate at the age of about two years and two months. Mackintosh and Wheeler point out that their statistical approach was possibly open to question. They felt, however, that their conclusions, like Risting's, were sound in view of the phenomenal growth rate of very young blue whales.[13]

The reputation of the authors of these studies was such that the two-year figure for age at sexual maturity was universally accepted. Efforts were made by other scientists to find an accurate method of determining the age of baleen whales but these were all unsuccessful by the time of World War II. Wartime conditions made impossible pelagic expeditions to the Antarctic, and for lack of transports even the land-based whalers had to cease operations. For five years therefore the killing stopped, and the whales had an unexpected respite. It was widely assumed that such a long period of rest would have beneficial results on the stocks of whales, especially the blue that had shown unmistakable signs of depletion by 1939. When whaling was resumed in 1945 it was quite evident that the stock of blue whales had not increased significantly. There were fewer very young blue whales but evidently those born early in the war had made no contribution to the population. Sexual maturity at age two was obviously wrong.

This surprising discovery stimulated renewed research into the problems of age determination, and a major effort was begun by the Norwegian Institute for Whale Research under the direction of Professor Ruud of the University of Oslo. Two separate methods of investigation were employed.

It had long been known that the surface of the baleen plates of rorquals was composed of a horny layer of material similar to human fingernails and the hooves and horns of cattle. In cattle the annual rings in the horns had been used to determine age. Baleen plates have no rings but they are traversed by parallel ridges and grooves. These may be seen in Plate IV. Ruud felt that these differences in thickness of the baleen might hold the key to the problem of age determination, especially if they were caused by annual changes in metabolism resulting from feeding in the Antarctic and fasting during migrations and the mating season. He succeeded in developing an apparatus to trace on paper an enlarged profile reproduction of baleen ridges and grooves. Studying the tracings of plates from hundreds of blue whales Ruud was able to discern a series of growth steps. Each of these he interpreted as corresponding to a year's metabolic changes. Fortunately, one of the growth steps was distinctly different and was identified from very young whales as having been formed while on a diet of milk. This first growth step remained visible on the plate for six and, in some cases, seven years, but it eventually disappeared by being worn away at the baleen plate tip as new growth descended from the gums above. As long as this initial step remained visible on a baleen plate it was possible to determine the actual age of the blue whale from which it came. This method of age determination could not often be used much above the age of six, but it was sufficient to provide the answer to the problem of age at sexual maturity.[14]

The baleen plates from which Ruud made his tracings had each been taken from the carcass of a blue whale that had been measured for

Table 3

Age at sexual maturity of female blue whales
based on Ruud's system of baleen plate analysis

Age group	Approximate age (in years)	Length (in feet)	Percentage sexually mature
0	¾	63.5	0.0
i	1¾	67.7	0.0
ii	2¾	70.4	0.0
iii	3¾	74.4	5.6
iv	4¾	76.0	19.5
v	5¾	79.8	62.1
vi	6¾	82.3	94.5
vii	7¾	84.8	100.0

Source: J. T. Ruud, Å. Jonsgård, and P. Ottestad, "Age Studies on Blue Whales," *Hvalrådets Skrifter*, XXXIII (1950), 28–31, 37–39.

length and examined for sexual maturity. Correlating this information with his theory of baleen-plate profile-age determination he came up with startling new conclusions about the age of blue whales. These are summarized in Table 3. He concluded that most female blue whales do not attain sexual maturity until the age of five. Moreover, some were still immature at age six and could not mate until nearly seven years old. For males he found a tendency to reach sexual maturity somewhat earlier, usually between ages four and five.

While Ruud was working with baleen plates a colleague, P. Ottestad, was reexamining the statistical approach of Mackintosh and Wheeler. Like them, he assumed that whales of a given age group would center on some length value. In order that any such grouping might show up more clearly he worked with feet instead of meters. He also worked with whales taken during one-month periods rather than an entire whaling season. This was to obtain samples from a more homogeneous stock because migrating blue whales have a tendency to group themselves by size. His length-frequency plottings showed 4 rather than 2 maxima for whales that had not reached sexual maturity. He therefore agreed with Ruud tht sexual maturity was reached above the age of four.[15]

That new information about the blue whale was not widely accepted at the time for reasons unknown. Two years later a study by Japanese scientists confirmed Ruud's findings that sexual maturity was reached at age five rather than two.[16] At the time, 1952, it was clear to nearly everyone concerned with the industry that the blue-whale population was declining rapidly. It should have been logical therefore, indeed obligatory, for the International Whaling Commission to give the species increased protection. It did not. The matter was not even discussed. The Commission in that year increased the length of the whaling season, a move that virtually guaranteed that more rather than fewer blue whales would be killed! (Much of Chapter VIII is devoted to the functioning of the International Whaling Commission.) The point to be emphasized here is the length of time it took man to determine one simple but important biological fact about the blue whale. The animal was so remote and so unmanageable that it could not be studied by direct observation during any stage of its life cycle. Only in death could man examine it effectively. If one takes the first reliable records of the blue-whale catch in 1909 as the beginning of its commercial life and 1965 as its end, the specific knowledge of age at sexual maturity was attained when its commercial life was 95.2 percent over. In other words, by the time the Japanese scientists confirmed Ruud's findings 95.2 percent of all the blue whales taken in the history of Antarctic whaling had already been killed. The figure is unquestionably low because many unrecorded blue whales were killed in the Antarctic prior to 1909 and also by the Japanese during the early years of World War II. In essence therefore, the blue whale was on the verge of commercial extinction before man could learn one of the most elemental facts about its life cycle.

The length of the blue whale at physical maturity was determined with little difficulty. Like most mammals it is physically mature when growth in length ceases which occurs when all the cartilaginous growth (*epiphyses*) of the vertebrae have ossified. The last vertebrae to ossify are those in the anterior portion of the chest cavity, and this permits an investigator to determine quite quickly if he is examining the carcass of a mature or an immature whale. Female blue whales have an average length of 87 feet at physical maturity and the males

80 feet. It is characteristic of baleen whales that the female is larger than the male. Only among toothed whales does man's myth of the "weaker sex" have any pertinence.

An average length of 87 feet for females means that many were shorter than that at physical maturity and many were of course longer. Individuals over 90 feet were quite common, but those over 100 feet were somewhat rare. The largest of reliable record were a 106–foot female killed in 1926 near the South Shetland Islands and a 104–foot male shot at the same time and place.[17] A 107–foot female was killed a few years earlier at South Georgia Island.[18] Whalingmen have often spoken of even longer blue whales, but these were neither measured nor shot. Whalers' rulers like those of fishermen are shorter than their imaginations, and their unproved stories should not be taken very seriously. On the other hand, there is no reason to suppose that man killed and measured the largest blue whale, and possibly some did exceed 107 feet.

The weight of a blue whale was of greater significance than was the length because so much of its body was useful to man. Little whales are not worth much, and man usually lets small species live in relative peace. But the blue whale was too big for its own good—it was the prime target. The animal was indeed so big that it was easier to kill than to weigh. How does one weigh an animal whose heart weighs half a ton, whose tongue is bigger than a taxicab, and whose blood supply may exceed 15,000 pints? Several hundred man-hours are required for such a herculean task and no whaling company would willingly waste the labor and money. Shortly after World War II Japan was permitted by the Commander of the Allied Occupation Forces, General Douglas MacArthur, to rebuild her whaling fleets. He wanted to help the American taxpayer by letting Japan develop the ability to feed herself, but he did require that American inspectors accompany the whalers to enforce compliance with existing international regulations. The Japanese resumed their prewar habit of killing a few undersized whales; when they did so the American inspectors made them weigh a normal-sized whale. The Japanese quickly learned to obey the rules, but not before they had added significantly to man's knowledge of the weight of whales. Some of their scientists became interested in the subject and they subsequently, and voluntarily, did valuable research on the weight of many species. Of all the tens of thousands of blue whales killed fewer than 30 were ever weighed, about half of which were done reliably by the Japanese. The results of 4 representative weighings are shown in Table 4.

Table 4

Measurements by weight and percentage of selected body components of 4 blue whales

Item	Whale 79 * 81' male		Whale 831 * 82' female		Whale 1208 † 83' male		Whale 961 † 78' male	
	pounds	percent	pounds	percent	pounds	percent	pounds	percent
Blubber	33,516	19.8	44,761	20.3	61,934	25.5	60,813	34.9
Meat	56,448	33.3	78,057	35.4	97,813	40.4	58,906	33.7
Bones	36,823	21.7	35,721	16.2	30,422	12.6	19,929	11.3
Internal organs	13,891	8.2	20,727	9.4	45,315	18.7	27,205	15.5
Miscellaneous & scraps **	22,711	13.4	33,957	15.4	6,913	2.8	7,901	4.6
Body fluids ††	6,175	3.6	6,615	3.3				
Total	169,564	100.0	219,838	100.0	242,397	100.0	174,754	100.0

* M. Nishiwaki and T. Oye, "Biological Investigation on Blue Whales and Fin Whales Caught by the Japanese Antarctic Whaling Fleets," *Scientific Reports* (Whales Research Institute, Tokyo), v, 134.

† M. Ohno and K. Fugino, "Biological Investigation on the Whales Caught by the Japanese Antarctic Whaling Fleets, Season 1950/51," *Scientific Reports* (Whales Research Institute, Tokyo), VII, 159.

** The first two whales, numbers 79 and 831, were the first the Japanese weighed, during the 1948/49 season. Two years later with more experienced workers, there was a noticeable drop in the proportion of miscellaneous and scraps, although this does not negate the validity of the total weights.

†† During the first weighings an attempt was made to measure body fluids, such as blood and urine, by absorbing them in sawdust. This proved to be unsatisfactory and was not subsequently attempted.

Note: Original weights in kilograms converted to pounds, and percentages calculated by me.

The whales referred to in Table 4 illustrate two important physiological aspects of the species. The first is the animal's enormous bulk. The heaviest of the 4 was a male, No. 1208, whose weight would have surpassed a quarter of a million pounds if it had been possible to weigh his blood, which in blue whales represents about 6.5 percent of total body weight. In addition his other body fluids such as lymph and urine are not included because no accurate method of separating and weighing them was ever devised. Moreover, this male was only 83 feet in length which is by no means a big blue whale. No really big fat blue whale was ever weighed, but because girth increases more rapidly than length a very large one could easily have surpassed 400,000 pounds. An animal of such staggering proportions is far larger than the largest land animal now alive and statistics on length and weight can not evoke a true mental image of its size. Photographic views of 2 large ones in Plates VI and VII may help. But a blue whale must be seen to be believed.

The second important physiological aspect pointed out by the data in Table 4 is the great variation in weight that may be found between individuals of approximately the same length. For example, whale No. 831 weighed 50,000 pounds more than whale No. 79 despite being 1 foot shorter in length. Or, whale No. 961 was 5,000 pounds heavier but 3 feet shorter than No. 79. This variation in total weight was caused by variation in one of the major body components, particularly the oil-rich blubber. It will be noted, for example, that the blubber varied from less than 20 percent to almost 35 percent of total body weight. If more weighings had been performed an even greater range would have been found, especially in females. Substantial variations in weight were also found between the total catch of one year and another, and also between the total catch of one company and another company during the same season. The causes of these variations were never adequately explained, and since they could not be predicted they introduced a significant element of luck or chance into the operations of the whaling companies operating in the Antarctic.

In the early days of Antarctic whaling when whales were plentiful and whalers scarce the only important part of the whale carcass was the blubber. This tissue is notably rich in oil and acts as insulation

Plate VI The model of a 94-foot blue whale, exhibited in the Hall of Ocean Life, American Museum of Natural History, New York City. Made of fiberglass and polyurethane, it weighs 21,000 pounds; if it were a live whale its weight could vary from 250,000 to over 400,000 pounds. N.Y. Daily News Photo.

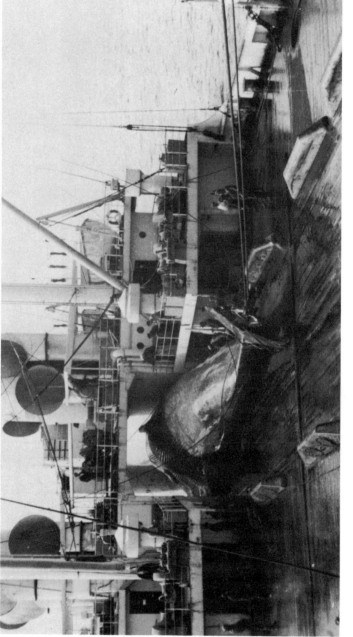

Plate VII Carcass of a blue whale at the top of the stern slipway of a Norwegian factory ship. Compare the "height" of the carcass with the men on the winch deck standing directly above others on the flensing deck. Courtesy of Reidar Brussell, Sandefjord, Norway.

and food supply for the whales. The dorsal blubber is particularly thick with a fat content of about 80 percent. The thinner flank blubber may have only 34 percent fat, and the average for blubber as a unit is about 60 percent.[19] Many laymen think that such a fatty tissue must be soft and mushy, something like Camembert cheese. Blubber is soft, but it is deceptively tough and a very sharp knife is required to cut it, as with a piece of tough bacon. Two views of blubber being removed from blue whales may be seen in Plates VIII and IX. The sheath of blubber within which a whale lives produces a strange phenomenon. When a whale dies its body temperature starts to rise, not fall. The heat and gasses generated by decomposition cannot escape through the insulating blubber and so accumulate within the body. After twenty hours the meat begins to bake and after thirty-three the oil is unusable.[20] If a carcass remains unbutchered for more than two days the accumulated gases can cause it to explode and spray decomposed entrails over a wide area.

The bones of blue whales and other rorquals became the second most important source of oil when whales began to be scarce and whalers numerous. Most of the bones were so long that no steam kettle in the world could contain them and so special steam-driven saws were developed to cut them into manageable-sized chunks. Plate X shows part of this laborious process that was worth the effort because bones were 30 percent oil by weight.[21]

The least valuable and last major body component of the blue whale to be used was the meat, or muscle, a tissue notably low in fat content. For many years it was considered so useless that it was dumped overboard, and few cetologists bothered to study it. Fortunately one Norwegian did examine it in detail and part of his findings are summarized in Table 5. The average fat content of the dorsal meat was 4.65 percent, and this section represented over half the meat total of a blue whale. In a few other places on the carcass the fat content was somewhat higher and therefore 5 percent is the generally accepted figure for blue whale meat as a whole.

The role of the blue whale as a species in the Antarctic whaling industry is treated in Chapter V. It is interesting to point out here the monetary value of a single blue whale, a value directly related to its enormous bulk. The preceding discussion of the oil content of

Plate VIII   Ventral blubber being removed from a female blue whale. This
dangerous method of outboard flensing was used prior to the invention in
1925 of the stern slipway for factory ships. Note that the ventral pleats ex-
tend to within a few feet of the vulva, flanked by the mammary glands.
Courtesy of E. Bryn, Tønsberg, Norway.

Table 5

*The percentage composition of blue-whale
dorsal meat*

	Water	Dry Material	Fat
Thin male, 78'	75.50	23.22	1.38
Average female, 90' lactating	73.90	22.90	3.20
Fat female, 80' pregnant	69.10	24.95	5.95
Very fat female, 87' pregnant	70.80	21.11	8.09

Source: E. F. Heyerdahl, "Hvalkøttets utnyttelse til olje-fremstilling," *Norsk Hvalfangst Tidende* (August, 1929), pp. 229–33.

the major body components is the basis of the following calculation
to determine the oil content of the 4 whales listed in Table 4.

lbs. blubber	201,024 × .60 =	120,614 lbs. oil (53.8 tons)
lbs. bones	122,895 × .30 =	36,869 lbs. oil (16.5 tons)
lbs. meat	291,224 × .05 =	14,561 lbs. oil (6.5 tons)
	Total =	172,044 lbs. oil (76.8 tons)

During the period from 1950 to 1963 the average price per ton
of whale oil in Europe was £67 17s 5d ($191.37).[22] The oil content
of those 4 whales was worth an average of £5,211 16s ($14,697.22).

The utilization of whales for oil only was the usual procedure of
Norwegian and other European whalers. The Japanese had a quite
different procedure. They used the blubber and bones to produce
oil for sale on the European market, and they used the meat for
human consumption on the Japanese home market. From the 4
whales, referred to in Table 4, the Japanese could obtain 132 metric
tons of meat by sacrificing 6.5 long tons of oil. During the years 1950
to 1963 the average price per ton of whale meat in Japan was ¥86,066
($239.05).[23] These 4 whales by the Japanese method of production
had an average product value of £4,771 2s ($13,453.31) for the blub-
ber and bone oil, plus ¥11,366,737 ($31,571.33) for the meat, making

Plate IX
Two blue whales on the flensing deck. The whale on the right has been flensed. The white membrane is connective tissue between the blubber and the underlying meat, patches of which are visible along the ventral line. For scale, note the head of a flenser just above the fold of the blubber strip being removed from the whale on the left. The tail flukes of both animals were trimmed off to facilitate towing to the factory ship. Courtesy of the National Institute of Oceanography.

Plate X   Chunk of blue-whale skull bone being dragged to opening to bone cookers below deck. A bone saw may be seen to the right of center, extending upward at a 45° angle; another is visible to the extreme left. One of the lemmers is beginning to separate the ribs of a blue-whale rib cage, part of which may be seen suspended to the left of center.

Courtesy of Reidar Brussell, Sandefjord, Norway.

a total of $45,024.64. These whales, then, were worth about $3,675 a piece to European whalers and $11,250 to the Japanese. The comparative advantage to Japanese whalers was so great that from the meat alone they got more than twice as much revenue as Europeans got from the entire whale. This price advantage to Japanese whalers was to have tragic consequences for the blue whale.

If one male and one female of any species are all that remain alive the species can theoretically survive. This may be true, but before they can reproduce they have to find each other. For whales that is not always easy, especially for blue whales. The solution to the problem depends solely on the animal's range of communication. The blue whale, like all whales, has no vocal chords. It should therefore be dumb, and for decades man believed that it was. Whalers have known since their first contact with blue whales that they do communicate somehow. Following World War II the rapid development of efficient recording devices made possible significant advances in man's knowledge of cetacean sounds, but not those of the blue whale. No blue whale "voice" has ever been recorded. Presumably, it must make some sound, since it does communicate, but how remains a mystery. Perhaps it makes sound by controlling air flow through the larynx or by expelling air through the blowhole while submerged. Man's only knowledge of the subject comes from analogy. There is a tendency for the wave lengths of cetacean sounds to decrease with increased size of the species, and the lower the frequency, the greater the distance the sound can travel underwater. Some 20-cycle impulses have been picked up at distances up to 35 miles, and it is almost certain that those impulses were produced by fin whales.[24] If the 20-cycle sounds were made by fin whales and if the blue whale can produce sounds of lower frequency, it might be able to communicate at distances greater than 35 miles. This, however, is sheer conjecture, but nothing more is possible. Man's ignorance of the ability of the blue whale to communicate is complete. He knows nothing about it.

When the decline in the blue-whale population became alarming during the late 1950s and early '60s, a few individuals speculated, not in writing, that the animal was not really few in numbers. They claimed that the animal was so intelligent that it had learned to stay far away from the humans who were killing it. In other words, there still were blue whales, but man could no longer find them.

Plate XI   Brain of an 81-foot blue whale. The protective tissue has been removed from the right lobe of this brain that weighed 11 pounds 8 ounces. The large convoluted cortex is typical of an intelligent mammal. The pan containing the brain measures 12 inches × 14 inches. Courtesy of the National Institute of Oceanography.

There can be no doubt about the high order of blue whale intelligence. (Plate XI shows a blue-whale brain.) The size and convolutions of its brain and a high ratio of brain weight to brain stem, all attest to it. Also, the observed intelligence of several cetacean species that man can keep in captivity suggests that all members of the cetacean order are quite intelligent. But even if the intelligence of the blue whale were exceeded only by that of man himself, it would not be of much help. The animal must eat, and its food supply is concentrated in the Antarctic during the summer months. The whalers knew this and their fleets of catcher boats moved through the area in broad sweeps. Their spotter aircraft, their radar, their radio communications, and their asdic for tracking submerged whales combined to render blue-whale intelligence a futile aid to survival. An individual blue whale might survive today, but the odds against it were too great. Tomorrow it would die. Tomorrow came often.

If tomorrow had not come, how long would a blue whale live? The life span of the blue whale is a physiological factor of importance, because it has a direct bearing on the reproductive capacity

Plate XII   Kidney of a blue whale. The plainly visible abscess on the left side of the kidney is an abnormal condition. Courtesy of the National Institute of Oceanography.

of the species. Unfortunately, man knows very little about the subject. The baleen-plate method of age determination can rarely be used much above the age of six. Counting *corpora albicantia* offered some insight into absolute age, but because more than one *corpus albicans* could be produced with each ovulation, the method was not precise. Moreover, this method was not applicable to males.

The most promising method of determining the age of rorquals was based on the structure of an elongated horny plug found in the outer auditory passages. That plug, when opened longitudinally, showed a series of laminations similar to the rings in a tree. It was certain that these laminations accumulated with age, but the exact rate of accumulation was never determined. The structure of these plugs was not discovered until 1955, by which time the blue-whale population was so reduced that the fin whale was the mainstay of the industry. Research based on these horny plugs was limited to the fin whale and nothing was learned about the absolute age of the blue whales.[25] This was particularly regrettable because it appeared that the horny-plug method was more applicable to blue whales than to other rorquals. Man's knowledge of the life span of the blue whale is not much greater today than it was when he began hunting the animal. All that can be said of it is that it is probably over twenty and less than forty years.

Whatever the span of years allotted to the blue whale, it, like all animals except man, had to adapt its life cycle to conditions prevailing in its environment. The process of adaptation, although successfully carried out, was not an easy one in regard to food supply. The food of the blue whale consisted of small crustaceans resembling shrimp that are about 1.5 inches to 2 inches long when mature. There are several species of these large planktonic animals in Antarctic waters but one, *Euphasia superba,* was all but the exclusive food of the blue whale. *Euphasia superba* and related species, referred to by the whalers as krill, are herbaceous animals that depend for their food on microscopic diatoms that thrive in cold water. Warm water can not contain much dissolved oxygen, and therefore krill is abundant only south of the Antarctic Convergence, the place where northward-moving cold Antarctic water meets southward-moving warm water from middle latitudes. The Antarctic Convergence is usually found between 48° and 62° South, and is shown in Figure 1. Krill is not evenly distributed throughout Antarctic waters, but is found in concentrations ranging in size from half an acre to a square mile. The most important general area for concentrations of krill is a band of water some 600 miles wide, between the pack ice and the 2° C. isotherm (35.6° F.). This is a region of prevailing easterly winds that produce a surface current to the west. When this current meets the Palmer Peninsula, it is deflected to the North and East, forming the Weddell Current that passes South Georgia. Here the band of krill concentration is of double thickness, so to speak, covering a region of 1 million square miles. It is so rich in krill that it once supported the world's largest population of whales of many species. Whaling-men aptly called it the "whales' larder," in part because the Pacific Sector of the Antarctic was relatively poor in krill for reasons unknown.[26]

The krill upon which the blue whale depended for its existence was concentrated in time as well as space. Plankton requires sunlight

Figure 1

Pelagic whaling areas of the Antarctic

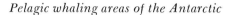

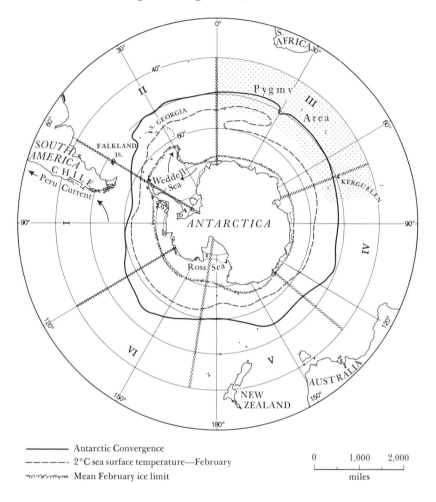

——————— Antarctic Convergence
– – – – – 2 °C sea surface temperature—February
ᴍᴍᴍ Mean February ice limit

0   1,000   2,000

miles

to grow, and in the high latitudes of the circumpolar Antarctic seas there is a very great seasonal variation in the number of daylight hours. Long summer days that stimulate planktonic growth also cause a melting back of the pack ice that exposes a larger area of water to sunlight. The result is a greatly increased quantity of food for krill, and krill for whales during January, February, and March—the Southern Hemisphere summer. The whales were aware of this long before man figured it out, and they duly arrived each year in November and December to be on hand when the feast began. Many baleen species depended on this seasonal sustenance, and the result was a massive influx of whales. When they had gorged themselves, the exodus four months later was equally impressive. This seasonal change in total cetacean population was so great, and so important to man, that it was the object of intensive study; the major results are shown in Figure 2. A glance at Figure 2 will suffice to explain why the whalers always wished to be south of the Antarctic Convergence by early January. In the early days of Antarctic whaling there were so many whales that it was worthwhile to begin hunting in early December or even late November. There was usually a good supply of whales available in April, but the beginning of autumn near Antarctica inevitably brought stormy weather. This made it

Figure 2

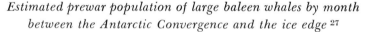

Estimated prewar population of large baleen whales by month between the Antarctic Convergence and the ice edge [27]

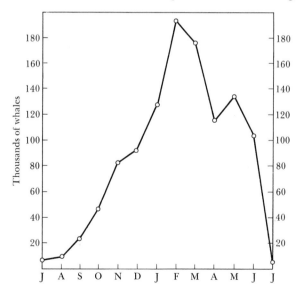

more difficult to see the whales' spouts and more costly to tow carcasses to factory ships, and whalers usually quit and went home when
this weather change occurred.

While blue whales were in the Antarctic waters during the four
summer months they obviously spent a great deal of time just eating.
Their intestines, upon examination, were always full, and 70 percent
of them had "much" krill in their stomachs. Only 10 percent had
empty stomachs, and this was probably due to the violence of their
death struggles with explosive harpoons.[28] Outside the Antarctic
blue whales almost always had empty stomachs, a condition hardly
surprising in view of the lack of concentrated food supplies in warm
waters. Thus it appears that blue whales ate for four months and had
to go hungry for the next eight. The very appearance of the whales
and their eating habits confirmed this. When blue whales arrived
in the Antarctic in November they were dreadfully thin, and when
they left it they were fat. The joy of eating must have been great
for when actually feeding in a patch of krill they were often so ob-
livious to all else that catcher boats could approach and kill them
with ease. Simply to eat, therefore, presented the blue whale with a
cruel dilemma it probably could not understand. To go to the Antarctic for food brought risk of violent death; to stay away guaranteed
peaceful death from starvation.

Why did blue whales leave the Antarctic if there is some food there
in winter and virtually none elsewhere at any season? The most
logical explanation is that newborn calves without protective blubber
probably could not survive the freezing temperatures.[29] The fact that
pregnant females always left the Antarctic in winter supports this
hypothesis. The male blue whale never abandons its mate whatever
the circumstances, and this habit can further explain the seasonal
exodus to warmer waters.

The concentration of blue whales in the Antarctic during a few
short months gave man his first knowledge of the cyclical nature of
the animal's life. Fetuses from the carcasses of slain females provided
the second. If mating took place throughout the year, average fetal
length would be about the same at any season, but it was not. Every
year the fetuses were longer month by month during the whaling
season, as shown in Table 6. The existence of a mating season was

obvious. It was a relatively simple matter to determine the approximate fetal growth rate, and this in turn was used to determine the mating period. The date of death of a pregnant female and the length of her fetus were used with fetus-growth rate to calculate the approximate date of conception. It was found that nearly 90 percent of conceptions took place between June 20 and August 20.[30] Fortunately for the blue whale man was never able to determine where the conceptions took place.

What gestation period is required to produce a 3-ton 25-foot calf? A precise answer to this question was never obtained. If the gestation period were much longer than a year some large, nearly term fetuses would have been found early in the whaling season, but none ever were. On the other hand, a gestation period of only eight or nine months would seem insufficient to produce a blue-whale calf. Even an elephant requires nearly two years to produce its tiny baby. We

Table 6

*Average blue-whale fetal length
by month*

Month	Length (in feet and inches)
September	1' 10"
October	2' 8"
November	4' 4"
December	5' 11"
January	7' 11"
February	11' 6"
March	15' 0"
April	16' 6"

Source: *International Whaling Statistics,* ed. The Committee for Whaling Statistics, Det Norske Hvalråds Statistiske Publikasjoner (Oslo), XVI (1942), 50.
Note: The data here listed were collected in the period 1925 to 1930. Any year would show similar progression, but with the later reduction in season length, figures for early months became unavailable.

can only assume that the blue-whale gestation period is over ten- and less than twelve-months' duration.

A gestation period of about a year followed by a nursing period of about seven months made it impossible for a female blue whale to have more than one calf every two years. To produce an offspring every eighteen months would have required breaking the feeding cycle, since a calf probably could not survive birth in the Antarctic waters and the mother surely could not survive a year and a half without food. Also, there is no evidence of any blue whale mating in cold Antarctic waters.

Could a female produce one calf a year? That, too, would seem impossible. To do so would require that a female conceive shortly after giving birth, but pregnant and lactating females were not found. To have done so would have required strength beyond even that of a blue whale. When a pregnant female leaves the Antarctic she must migrate thousands of miles to warm tropical waters, give birth, nurse her calf while it grows from 3 to 23 tons, and migrate thousands of miles back to the Antarctic—all with no food! To do that and support a growing fetus at the same time would probably be fatal. One offspring every two years was unquestionably the maximum possible.

A fertility rate of one calf every two years does not mean that female blue whales reproduced at that rate. There was evidence that females would occasionally skip a year and give birth every three years. The task of reproducing was undoubtedly strenuous and a sexually mature female neither pregnant nor lactating was referred to as "resting." The matter was studied intensively because it concerned the recruitment rate of the species and how many would be available to the whalers. Unfortunately it was not possible to determine the net reproduction rate because representative samples of the female population could not be obtained. It was forbidden to kill a female accompanied by a calf, and this tended to increase the proportion of pregnant females in the catch. There is no doubt, however, that the rate of reproduction did fluctuate from time to time. During the 1930s when the blue whales were hunted intensely and their numbers began to decline, more females produced a calf every two years rather than three.[31] The luxury of a year of rest apparently could not be enjoyed when the species was in danger. When whaling was resumed after World War II, the rate of reproduction had dropped back to the level prevailing in the late 1920s, but with increased whaling it soon increased again to the level of the late 1930s. The problem remained under study for many years, but by the mid-1950s there were so few blue whales left that no meaningful samples of the female population were available.[32] The exact rate of reproduction was never learned.

The biotic potential of the blue whale was so low that it could not keep up with the death rate imposed on it by man. The average female by age ten could produce, at most, only two offspring, an exceptionally low figure even for an aquatic mammal. The reproductive capacity of the blue whale was the lowest of all baleen species. This, combined with its great bulk that made it the most valuable, was to have tragic consequences.

If pregnant females and their mates always left the Antarctic at the approach of winter, where did they go? When they arrived at the beginning of summer they were always thin. Had they been somewhere where there was no food? The apparent answers to these questions would indicate that the blue whale migrated annually to warm tropical or subtropical waters, but there is no proof of it. The only direct evidence was the discovery in the nineteenth century of fragments of American bomb lances in the bodies of blue whales killed off the coast of northern Norway. Since the Americans had been hunting only in the western Atlantic south of Newfoundland the whales must have migrated several thousand miles.[33] That discovery led to the idea of marking whales in order to study their movements, but it contributed little insight into the movements of the once-large population of Southern Hemisphere blue whales.

Some natural evidence for migration comes from the parasitic crustacean known as *penella*. This animal, which looks like a piece of wire 4 inches long, roots itself in the whale's blubber just under the skin. It is a warm-water species that is never found on whales in the Antarctic, but scars left by its presence are rather good evidence that the whales have been in warm tropical waters.

An additional indicator of latitudinal migration is a comparison of the time of maximum number of whales at different latitudes shown by the catch at permanent land stations. Table 7 shows such

Table 7

The monthly catch of blue whales
at selected middle- and high-latitude land stations

	Durban,* South Africa 30° S. 31° E.	Saldanha Bay,† South Africa 33° S. 18° E.	South Georgia ** 54° S. 37° W.
April, 1930	3	1	—
May	22	33	—
June	81	72	—
July	104	76	—
August	45	70	—
September	10	57	16
October	0	26	235
November	—	13	297
December	—	—	292
January, 1931	—	—	173
February	—	—	57
March	—	—	13

* "Fangstatistisk, Natalkysten," *Norsk Hvalfangst Tidende* (February, 1931), pp. 53–56; and (May, 1931), p. 135. (Data cover results of two whaling companies.)
† "Fangstatistisk, Cape Colony," *NHT* (May, 1931), pp. 135 and 137. (Data cover results of two whaling companies.
** "Fangstatistisk, Syd Georgia," *NHT* (May, 1931), p. 137; and (June, 1931), pp. 145–46, 147–49, 151, and 163. (Data cover results of five whaling companies.)

a juxtaposition in time. It is evident that when the number of available whales is decreasing along the coast of South Africa it is increasing at South Georgia in the Antarctic. Conversely, when it is decreasing in the Antarctic, it is increasing in South Africa. There is no evidence that the blue whales that passed South Africa were the same ones that passed South Georgia to the Southwest. The land stations were chosen because there are none along a common meridian of longitude, that is, directly north and south of each other. The figures do, however, point to a substantial latitudinal migration, the exact routes of which remain a mystery. All that is known of those routes is that they must have been well out to sea because blue whales taken by land-station whalers were very few compared to the thousands taken pelagically on the high seas.

How close to the Equator did the blue whales go in winter? No

one knows. On rare occasions a lone individual would be reported off
Ecuador, for example. Along the coast of the former French-Congo,
land-station and floating-factory whalers between 1912 and 1935 killed
a total of 10,261 whales of many species, but only two of them were
blue whales.[34] It seems safe to conclude that blue whales generally
did not migrate as far as the Equator. There is no evidence that one
ever crossed it, either, and there would be no reason to do so.

Because there were a few blue whales that remained in the Antarctic even in winter, one authority concluded that the blue whale
population in winter was widely scattered between the ice edge of
Antarctica and the tropics,[35] an area covering more than one-third
the surface of the entire earth. This conclusion is supported by the
absence of any known concentration of blue whales in tropical or
subtropical waters, and it is hard to imagine that any such concentration could remain undiscovered in the twentieth century. Furthermore, the conclusion is supported by the social habits of the blue
whale. Of all cetacean species, the blue whale is the loner. It never
congregates in large herds and even its pods are small. The animal
is most often found alone or accompanied by a mate. Three adults
together is a rare sight indeed.

If man never learned the whereabouts of the blue whales in winter, he did learn a great deal about their specific distribution in
summer. That estival distribution is of profound significance in the
animal's struggle to survive, and ignorance of it has led many writers
to misjudge the chances of survival.

With the development of pelagic whaling after 1925, hunting
quickly spread around the entire Antarctic continent. New stocks
of whales were exploited for the first time, and it soon became apparent that the whales were not evenly distributed around the continent. Factory-ship records disclosed the existence of distinct areas
of relative concentration. Norwegian scientists suggested that the
Antarctic be divided into 6 areas for purposes of statistical research.[36] The boundaries of these areas enclosed the cetacean concentrations and are shown in Figure 1. It became almost immediately
apparent that the blue whales in one area constituted a distinct stock
that did not wander at random throughout Antarctic seas. When the
whales in one area began to decline in numbers, those in a neighbor-

ing area did not. Measurement of the stock in various ways pointed
this out. For example, the percentage of sexually immature whales in
an area correlated positively with the length of time the area had
been hunted.[37]

Several scientific organizations from nations engaged in pelagic
whaling participated in whale-marking programs in order to learn
more about whale migrations and movements. The marks usually
consisted of a numbered stainless-steel shaft, about the size of a large
cigar, coated with antiseptic ointment. It was fired into the whale's
blubber with a shotgun, and the time and place recorded. If a mark
were subsequently recovered when the whale was butchered, much
would be learned about its movements. This procedure confirmed
rather than added to man's knowledge of blue-whale dispersion. The
reason for the limited success of whale marking was simply the small
number of marks recovered. From 1924 to 1964, over 900 blue whales
were marked, but only 80 marks were ever recovered. The rate of
recovery was so low that not a single blue-whale mark was ever found
outside the Antarctic. Concerning the mingling of whales of one area
with those of another, no blue-whale mark from Area I was ever
recovered in Area II. No mark from Area II was ever recorded in
Area III, and not until the mid-1950s did a recovered mark show
the movement of a whale from Area III to Area II.[38] The blue whale
was not the only species to show a strange aversion to crossing the
Prime Meridian.

Another interesting way of proving that blue whales did not wander at random throughout the circumpolar Antarctic seas was by
measuring the iodine content of their oil. It was found that the iodine
content of oil produced from whales in Area II was higher than that
in oil produced from whales in Area III. The further east the source
of oil, the lower the iodine content, and the amount in each area fell
within a specific range.[39] If the whales wandered around the Antarctic they would all have had the same iodine content resulting
from a common food source.

There is very little evidence for the mixing of the stock of blue
whales of one area with those of another. Rare indeed was one peri-
patetic individual that swam from Area II to Area VI through 170
degrees of longitude in forty-seven days. That fellow traveled a min-

imum of 1,900 miles, and far more if he went the "long way around" and made a few side trips en route. Such erratic behavior was not typical of the species. Obviously, most blue whales stayed home in their own area, and minded their own krill. The result was that in summer the blue whales feeding in Antarctic waters were divided into 6 distinct stock units. There may have been some limited mingling of the stock of one area with that of another, but it was never significant. It could not replenish a depleted stock in one area from a less depleted stock in an adjacent area. Consequently, it is more nearly correct to consider the population of Southern Hemisphere blue whales as consisting of 6 subpopulations, or stocks, each of which is limited to its area in summer and to the tropical waters north of it in winter.

The most important details about the physiology and ecology of blue whales have been presented in preceding pages. Less important items have been omitted. For readers interested in such subjects, for example, as the endocrinology of the blue whale, an extensive bibliography has been appended. That bibliography is probably smaller than what one would expect for an animal as large and as important as the blue whale. The reason is simply that what man does not know about the animal exceeds what he does know about it. A partial list of the unknown would include the following: Where are blue whales born? How does the birth of the blue whale compare with that of small whales observed in captivity? Do they have an infant mortality rate of 40–50 percent like some marine mammals? How does a blue-whale calf with overlapping jaws get milk from its mother's nipples without taking in quantities of sea water? Is a female capable of raising triplets? (One female carcass yielded 7 fetuses.) How deep can blue whales dive? Why do they dive at all when their food is on the surface? Is it to use pressure as a substitute for scratching? They sometimes have barnacles and lice that must cause an itch. But how does a whale scratch in an ocean without doorjambs, trees, or fenceposts? How do blue whales navigate across thousands of miles of ocean to feed every year in the same place in the Antarctic? Why do they return to the same place? Do they travel at night? (Recent studies indicate that the California gray whale probably interrupts its migration at night.) How do they find patches of krill? Can they possibly hear the subsonic sounds made by those tiny creatures? Do blue whales sleep at the end of the feeding season? That is the only time in a year when they can float; at other times their specific gravity is heavier than that of water. Do they ever fall asleep and drown at other seasons? What diseases can kill a blue whale? How long do they live? How big can they grow? How do they communicate? If they never cross the Equator, how did they come to be found in both hemispheres? How intelligent are they? The list could be greatly expanded and the answers, if available, would fill a large volume. But many of these questions will probably never be answered. The answers might require the death of more blue whales and too many have already died. Part of the beauty of life is its mystery. Perhaps some of the awesome mystery still left to the blue whale can yet inspire men to want to save it. Is there still time?

Our days on the earth are as a shadow and there is none abiding.

1 CHRONICLES 29:15

III

DECIMATION

THE SLAUGHTER OF TENS OF THOUSANDS of blue whales in the 1930s inevitably raised concern for the safety of the species, and a few international attempts were made to reduce the level of killing. These efforts were ineffective largely because two pelagic whaling nations, Germany and Japan, refused to cooperate. The military defeat of Germany and Japan in 1945 raised the hope in other whaling nations, notably England and Norway, that international cooperation could now produce a system of conservation regulations to protect all species of whales from over-exploitation. That hope seemed justified with the creation of the International Whaling Commission that began to function in 1949.

The formulation of a conservation policy for any wild animal being hunted in its native habitat can be successful only if it is based on reasonably accurate information about the effects of hunting on the population in question. The acquisition of such information usually presents many difficulties, not the least of which is determining the accuracy of the information obtained. In the case of the blue whale the primary question facing the International Whaling Commission was, "Are the stocks of the blue whales decreasing?" Most of the scientific advisers to that organization answered the question affirmatively. They were then faced with a much more difficult question, "How much are they declining?" Even if a precise answer could have been given to this question little if any benefit would have accrued to the blue whale. The decision to give it more protection resided with the national delegates to the International Whaling

Commission, and most of them for a long time refused to believe, or minimized the importance of, the scientists' answer to the first question. Before passing judgment on those delegates it is necessary to examine the evidence presented to them for the decline of the blue whale. The examination of that evidence will also make it possible to see how close to extinction the animal has been driven. Before proceeding several explanatory comments are necessary. In the first instance, the data on the catch of blue whales that reflected its decline were presented to the International Whaling Commission in the form of statistical tables. They are presented here in the form of graphs in most cases.

A reference to any one Antarctic whaling season must mention two successive years. The whales began to congregate there in November and December and could usually be hunted through March. Thus, for example, the first postwar season was 1945/46. Moreover, during the 1950s there were eight seasons when hunting began legally in January, but reference is still to two years because the whaling fleets had to sail in October from their home ports. On occasion it is simpler to refer to a season by a single year, and in such a case it is customary to use the second half of the binomial. For example, the 1932 season would refer to the season that began in December, 1931, and ended in April, 1932.

The examination of the various measures of population decline will have in most cases the 1962/63 season as the terminal date. That was the last season during which it was legal to hunt blue whales throughout the entire Antarctic region. It would be possible to begin the evidence of population decline with data collected prior to the 1930/31 season, but it would be somewhat impractical. Before that, pelagic whaling was in its developmental stage and in that season it reached its maximum growth in terms of total number of factory ships. That was also the season with the largest single catch of blue whales, 29,410. Thus, the 1930/31 whaling season was a turning point in the history of the blue whale. Since that time all aspects of the study of the animal indicate that its population was moving inexorably downward.

Finally, the study of the population decline of the blue whale must be modified slightly as a result of events during World War II. Most

factory ships of the world participated in the 1939/40 whaling season,
although many of them never returned home. That season can usually
be included in the study but several of the following can not because
nearly all factory ships were either sunk or converted to military uses.
At the end of the war a great effort was made to send out several
expeditions to relieve the shortage of edible oils in Europe, but a lack
of construction materials restricted the total for 1945/46 to a mere 9.
The first postwar year to approximate normal peace-time activity was
1946/47. Therefore, no references are made to the seasons 1940/41
through 1945/46.

The least valid measure of decline of the blue whale population
is the total number of animals killed each season. This does not take
into account factors such as changes in the length of the season, catching effort, or changes in the minimum length requirement. Nevertheless it does furnish valuable background knowledge for other more
useful measures, and it is therefore shown in Figure 3. At first glance

Figure 3

Annual catch of blue whales in the Antarctic,
seasons 1930/31 through 1962/63 (war years omitted) [1]

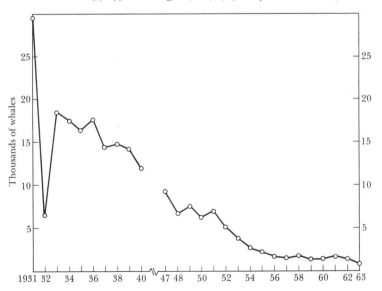

Figure 3 would seem to indicate an erratic decline but this was due
to the whalers rather than the whales. The drastic decline in the 1932
catch was caused by overproduction in 1931 and a resultant drop in
the price of whale oil. As a consequence all Norwegian and half of
the British factory expeditions stayed home during the 1932 season.
This cutback in production caused the price of whale oil to rise and
normal whaling activities were resumed in the 1933 season. The more
minor fluctuations in the catch shown in Figure 3 were the result of
shifts in the locale of maximum whaling effort from one area to
another, that is, from an area of relative blue whale depletion to an
area of relative abundance. Despite these fluctuations it is plainly
evident that during the three decades in question the catch of blue
whales underwent a steady decline. In 1931 nearly 30,000 died; in 1963
some 900 died. How could anyone believe the blue whale population
was not declining? It is a puzzle.

An animal population with an increasing percentage of individuals
in younger age groups often indicates a population increasing in
total numbers. Such could not be the case with the blue whale, and
the reason relates to its rate of reproduction. The number of calves
produced depends, of course, on the size of the sexually mature population, but a female can produce at most one offspring every two
years. Thus, if from any one year to the next the number of sexually mature adults decreased there could not have been any increase
in the population since the surviving adults could not produce in
that year more offspring than the larger population in the preceding
year. It was not possible to measure the changes in the number of
adult blue whales from year to year but it was possible to determine
the percentage of the catch that was sexually mature or immature.
To the extent that the catch was a representative sample of the adult
population, and there is no reason to suppose that it was not, any
change in the percentage of immature animals would indicate a relative change in the number of adults in the population. Figure 4
shows the changes in the percentage of sexually immature whales in
the catch. It is apparent that the annual increase in the percentage
of immature whales since 1950 was abrupt and, with minor exceptions, continual. During that time the blue-whale population could
not have been increasing.

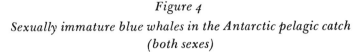

Figure 4

Sexually immature blue whales in the Antarctic pelagic catch
(both sexes)

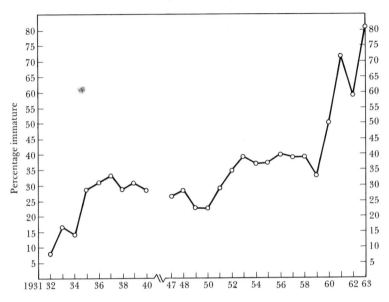

The apparent decrease in the percentage of immature blue whales from 1937 through 1950 is misleading. In 1937 most of the whaling nations of the world agreed to institute for the first time minimum-length requirements for all species. Seventy feet was the required minimum adopted for the blue whale. In years prior to that when there were no length requirements many very small young blues were taken. This naturally tended to increase the immature rate. In the 1937/38 season there was of course a significant decrease in the immature rate. The cessation of whaling after 1940 allowed many young blue whales to reach sexual maturity before they were hunted again. After 1950 the beneficial effects of the wartime rest were canceled out by increasing whaling, and the immature rate resumed its upward trend.

The percentage of sexually immature blue whales actually gave an erroneously favorable impression of the reproductive capacity of the species. Many delegates to the International Whaling Commission undoubtedly felt that as long as over half the population was sexually mature the species was in no great danger. They did not realize that something more than the attainment of sexual maturity was required for a female to produce a calf. That something was time beyond the age of sexual maturity required to produce an independently viable calf. Thus, as we know, a typical female reaching sexual maturity at age five and a length of 77 feet would require almost two more years in which to mate, gestate, give birth, and nurse her calf until it could survive by itself. At this time the female would be almost seven years old and have attained a length of just over 82 feet. Therefore, 77 feet as a measure of sexual maturity was misleading. I propose the term *effective sexual maturity* as a more valid substitute for which the criterion should be 82 feet for females.

If the catch of blue whales over the thirty years in question is viewed from the point of view of effectual sexual maturity a much more serious situation is apparent. The average length of female blue whales killed in the Antarctic has been plotted in Figure 5. (Because

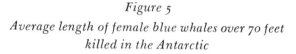

Figure 5

*Average length of female blue whales over 70 feet
killed in the Antarctic*

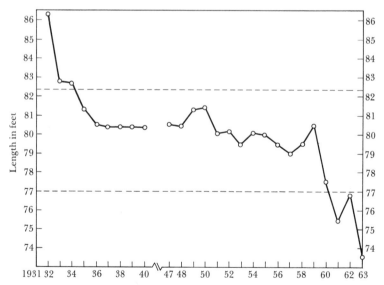

of the 70-foot minimum adopted in 1937 the graph has been adjusted to eliminate individuals shorter than that in years prior to 1937.) The usual downward slope is evident. It will be noted that in 1960 the average length of females declined to 77 feet, sexual maturity, giving an immature rate of 50 percent. However, the year in which the average length fell below that of effective sexual maturity was 1935. This means that since that date more than half of all female blue whales did not live long enough to produce even one calf. In order to have a stable population of any species females must produce an average not 1 but 2 offspring in order to replace the parents. In order to have an increasing population females must produce an average 3 offspring, 2 to replace the parents and 1 to constitute the increase. In either case infant mortality losses must, of course, be made up by additional births. Thus, because over half the female blue whales died before reaching effective sexual maturity the population of the species must have been declining, war years excluded, since 1935.

Because of the blue whale's habit of not wandering at random throughout the Antarctic it is instructive to examine the results of whaling on the species in one or two specific locales.

The longest continuous period of whaling in any one place in the Antarctic was on the island of South Georgia. During the decade of the 1920s the annual average catch of blue whales there was 2,215. During the 1930s it declined to 464. In the 1950s it was down to 14. The last blue whale shot at South Georgia was during the 1961 season. None has been seen there since.

It is theoretically possible that blue whales simply learned to stay away from South Georgia and the deadly cannon based there. If they did learn to avoid it and moved elsewhere in the waters of Area II their fate was the same. Man is just as good a pelagic as land-based whaler. The decline in the catch of blue whales in Area II is shown in Figure 6. The decline is so inexorable and final that no comment is necessary—except perhaps Amen.

At this juncture it may seem ridiculous or superfluous to present additional evidence to show that the blue-whale population was declining. It should seem ridiculous and superfluous, but this same evidence in unabbreviated form and additional evidence as well all

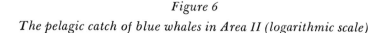

Figure 6

The pelagic catch of blue whales in Area II (logarithmic scale)

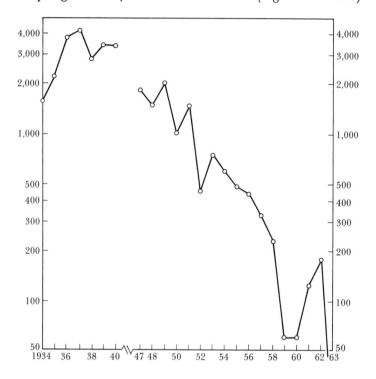

failed to convince the Whaling Commission that the blue-whale population was seriously declining. Even in the late 1950s some delegates
to that organization would admit only that the blue whale seemed
less abundant than it did in the 1930s. Two additional barometers
of decline will complete the evidence that the Whaling Commission
looked at but failed to see.

A particularly valuable indicator of the decline of the blue whale
is based on its relative rather than absolute numbers, the relativity
being expressed as the blue-whale percentage of all whales killed in
the Antarctic. Three other species of baleen whale available there
were the fin whale, the humpback, and the sei (*Balaenoptera borealis*),
that were, respectively, about one-half, four-tenths, and one-sixth the
weight of a blue whale. The time and effort required to kill any

one of them were about the same, and therefore whalers preferred to kill a blue whale whenever possible. Therefore any decline in the blue-whale percentage of the total catch would mean either that the blue whale was declining in numbers or the others were increasing. The other species had a reproduction rate about as low as that of the blue whale, and large population increases for them are impossible on a short-term basis. Therefore, a decline in the blue-whale percentage of the catch could only mean that the species was declining in absolute numbers. Figure 7 shows the changes in the blue-whale portion of the catch. The steep and continuous decline in the slope of this graph can lead only to the conclusion that the blue whale was fast disappearing.

The delegates to the International Whaling Commission did not like to face such conclusive evidence, and they looked for a way to discount its validity. They found it. Prior to World War II whaling began usually in late November. After the war it began, by interna-

Figure 7

*Blue whales as a percentage of all whales
killed in Antarctic pelagic whaling*

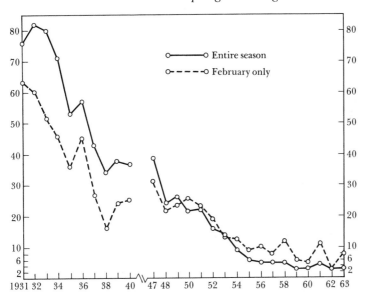

tional agreement, in late December and sometimes early January. This was done to allow the whales time to get fat. Since the blue whale was usually the first of the several species to arrive in the Antarctic and was most abundant in December the elimination of those early months from the whaling season had the effect of reducing the blue-whale portion of the catch in later years. This was a logical argument, but human logic can backfire. The earliest month that was always open for whaling throughout the years was February. The blue-whale percentage of the February catch is included in Figure 7 for purposes of comparison. The decline for that month so closely parallels that for the entire whaling season that there is no room for doubt that the blue-whale population was declining rapidly both relatively and absolutely. How did the delegates to the International Whaling Commission react to this evidence? They ignored it.

The best measure of any change in an animal population under-going commercial exploitation is the yield per unit of effort. The validity of this method of population analysis is based on the assumption that any change in the productivity of a unit of catching effort must reflect a like change in the animal population being exploited. The term used to describe whaling effort is a *catcher-day's-work*, with the production per unit of effort measured in number of whales. In the case of the blue whale any change in the number killed per catcher-day's-work would indicate a corresponding change in the species' population. Changes in the catch of blue whales per catcher-day's-work are shown in Figure 8. It will be noted for example that in the 1931 and 1932 seasons a hundred catcher-day's-work produced 105 and 132 blue whales respectively; in 1961 and 1962 a hundred catcher-day's-work could produce only 6 and 7 blue whales. As with other measures of decline only one conclusion seems possible: since 1934 the blue-whale population was steadily declining.

The catch of blue whales per catcher-day's-work as an indicator of population decline was an unpleasant one for the delegates to the International Whaling Commission. The more they examined it the more it seemed to underestimate the decline of the blue whale. The problem was that a catcher-day's-work in 1930 was by no means the equivalent of a catcher-day's-work of 1960. In 1930, for example, catchers averaged 219 gross tons with 729 horsepower. Increased com-

Figure 8

The Antarctic pelagic catch of blue whales per catcher-day's-work

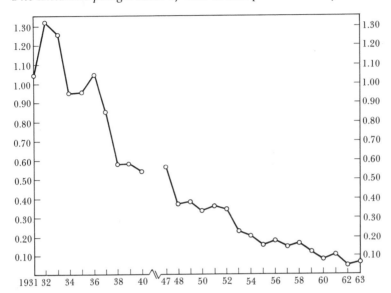

petition for decreased numbers of whales made necessary more efficient catchers, and by 1963 catchers averaged 703 tons with 2,957
horsepower. In theory any increase in catcher efficiency resulting from
any cause, such as increased horsepower, should result in an increase
in the yield per day's work. That the opposite took place can only
mean that the blue-whale population declined even more rapidly than
originally indicated. Moreover, the increase in catcher efficiency was
even greater than that brought about by increased tonnage and horsepower. For example, after World War II catchers were modified by
such technical improvements as radar, asdic for tracking whales
underwater, and variable pitch propellors for greater maneuverabil-
ity. The scope of these changes was such that no formula has yet been
devised that can produce an accurate comparison of the efficiency of
a catcher in 1930 with a catcher in 1960.[2] If such a formula could be
devised and applied to the catch of blue whales the decline in its
population would be shown to have been much more precipitous
than originally indicated—perhaps the first cetacean fall without a
decline.

All the preceding measures of decline of the stocks of blue whales were presented annually in cumulative and detailed form to the national delegates, the commissioners, to the International Whaling Commission. They did not give protection to the blue whales, or to any other species, because they claimed there was no conclusive proof that the blue-whale population was declining. One wonders by what mental tergiversations they could support such a claim. Man's ingenuity works wonders even in perversity.

Delegates were often able to point to an apparent increase in the stocks of blue whales in almost any year by taking a short-term microview of the catch statistics. For example, in Area III in the 1949/50 season the blue-whale catch per catcher-day's-work was 0.32. In the following year it rose to 0.35 and in 1951/52 it rose again to 0.37. Such trivial details were seized upon and repeatedly used as justification to wait a year and observe the results of another whaling season before taking any action to protect the species. This procedure went on for so many years that ingenious tergiversation became fatal procrastination.

By 1960 it was clear that the International Whaling Commission would never act on the recommendations, or accept the findings, of its scientific advisers on the conditions of the stocks of whales of all species. In that year the Commission managed to agree to engage a small group of experts in the field of population dynamics to study the whole problem of the Antarctic whale stocks. These experts were from nonwhaling countries and had no connection with the whaling industry. Their specific tasks were: to assess the stocks of every baleen species, to estimate the sustainable yield of each species, and, to recommend what the catch of each should be. These population experts became known as the Committee of Three and their specific recommendations are dealt with in Chapter VII on the International Whaling Commission. At this point their findings on the size of the blue-whale population make it possible to obtain a clear idea of how close the species is to biological extinction.

In order to arrive at a reasonably precise estimate of the blue-whale population, and of other species as well, the Committee of Three had to handle a voluminous amount of data. They had to determine the rate of whaling mortality for each age group and the changes in the catch per unit of effort. Frequency of sightings of blue whales were tabulated for an extensive period, and vast amounts of data were collected from whaling companies on every whale caught for the previous ten years. All data were transferred to punch cards for computer processing, and a preliminary report was ready by 1963. Research continued since that date, and a final revised estimate was obtained: the blue-whale population of the Southern Hemisphere in 1963 was about 600.[3]

The estimate was for blue whales exclusive of "pygmy" blue whales that were considered to be a distinct stock for purposes of assessment. A separate study was made for the so-called pygmy blues, and their population as of 1960 was estimated to be less than 2,000 individuals.[4]

The estimates of the Committee of Three are the most important single factor in any attempt to foresee the outcome of the blue whale's struggle for survival. It is therefore pertinent to question the competence of that group. The performance of the Committee of Three has been so satisfactory that it has been permanently retained in an advisory capacity by the Whaling Commission, which is indeed a compliment in view of its harsh recommendations to the Commission, mentioned later. The Committee of Three also received cooporation and financial assistance from the Food and Agricultural Organization of the United Nations. When the Committee of Three had completed its final report the Scientific Committee of the Whaling Commission met with it jointly to review the findings. In a subsequent speech about that joint meeting to a plenary session of the Commission the chairman of the Scientific Committee stated quite bluntly that he and his colleagues questioned the three experts in an attempt to find flaws in their calculations and methods, but to no avail. He stated in conclusion, "We feel convinced that these calculations are the best that can be done at the present time."[5] The speaker was Dr. N. A. Mackintosh, one of the world's leading cetologists. On a few occasions, when asked, the three population experts were able to predict almost to a whale how many of a given species would be killed in the next Antarctic season. They knew how many whales were there; all they needed to know then was how many catcher boats the whalers were going to use. It seems safe to conclude, therefore, that the Committee of Three was composed of qualified experts whose findings are reasonably accurate.

How many blue whales are alive today? The experts estimated that in 1963 there were about 600 regular blue whales, but since that time man has killed at least 741. Moreover, very few blue whales could have been added to the population because in 1963 over 84 percent of the females were sexually immature. Those that had attained effective sexual maturity must have constituted less than 5 percent of the population, or fewer than 30 whales. These unfortunately would be the biggest and most of them were probably among the 741 killed since 1963. Today the blue-whale population probably numbers something between 0 and 200 individuals. What a monument to man's power of destruction of God's creation!

The pygmy blue whale was estimated to have numbered about 2,000 individuals in 1961.[6] During the next four years man killed 2,361 of them, and it would seem therefore that their population must be about 0. In 1965 the whaling nations agreed to stop killing them. This action supports the estimation of a 0 population because whaling nations have never given any species complete protection until it was of no commercial value and virtually extinct. It is quite likely also that during the last four years of its existence no additions at all were made to its population. Evidence is presented later that indicates that the pygmy blue whale was probably nothing but another name for very young, sexually immature blue whales.

What are the chances for survival of the species if its population is between 0 and 200? Obviously much depends on just where in that range the population is. But in order to better understand the factors effecting those chances let us assume for the moment that the population is 200. Further, let us assume that they are equally divided sexually, that 10 percent of each sex have attained effective sexual maturity, and that they have found each other. That means that there will be 10 pairs of blue whales producing offspring. Assuming a maximum rate of reproduction there will be at most 5 blue-whale calves born in each year, assuming no infant mortality. These calves will have a staggering problem just finding each other, finding a mate, in their own approximate age group. During the feeding season the whales are "concentrated" between the Antarctic Convergence and the ice edge, an area of some 9 million square miles. This means that the 5 hypothetical calves born each year will have a density distribution of 1 per every 1.8 million square miles, an area 36 times the area of the state of New York. Even if the blue whale does have the longest cetacean communication range, the calves will have a difficult, if not impossible, task of finding each other in such vast spaces. The problem would be less difficult if all the calves were born in the same area. But the problem might be beyond solution if only 1 calf were born each year in each of the 6 Antarctic areas. The problem might also be beyond solution if 2 male calves were born in Area I, 2 females in Area II, and 1 of either sex in Area IV. In any case man's ignorance of the blue whale's range of communication makes it impossible to know for certain if the problem of finding a mate will be less difficult or more difficult than the preceding hypothetical example suggests.

It is certain, however, that any hope for the survival of the blue whale grows dimmer upon examination of the assumptions made in the preceding hypothetical example. The assumption that there are 200 blue whales alive rather than, say, 10 in all the Southern Hemisphere is not a very safe one. Nor is it safe to assume that 10 percent of those still alive have reached effective sexual maturity, although most young blue whales alive will in time reach that age, unless they are shot in the interim. Several years may already have elapsed with no blue whale births at all. Furthermore it is wrong to assume no infant mortality. The first year of life is a dangerous one for all mammals. Nothing is known of the infant mortality rate of the blue whale except that it surely is above 0; it could be 40 percent, 50 percent, or 6 percent. Whatever it is the population of the species is so low that the death of 1 blue-whale calf could lead to the ultimate disaster.

If the reader is deeply attached to the wildlife of the earth, you are by now probably reading on in hope of a miracle—much as a man at the bedside of a dying loved one seeks a miracle. It is my unpleasant task to have to present yet three more fateful problems that further decrease the survival chances of the great blue whale.

Considering the man-made plight of the blue whale it would seem merciful to call off the hunt. Mercy can not often diminish the desire for corporate profits and so the killing of blue whales has not yet ceased. Peru agreed in 1966 to stop killing them, but only for two years. Chile agreed in 1968 to stop killing them, but only for one year. (Apparent mercy may be greed if the objective is to allow the whales time to grow.) The cold Peru, or Humboldt, Current that flows northward along the west coast of South America seems to be a migration route for blue whales and a very few are still using it. The shooting of one more blue whale by either of these countries could be the death knell of the species. How can it be stopped?

Japan could stop it because it is her whalers who use Peruvian and Chilean bases, and who import the production into Japan. The reasons for Japanese unwillingness to stop this killing are explained in Chapter VI.

Has the killing of blue whales stopped in the Antarctic? Yes, maybe. The Soviet Union and Japan are the only nations now engaged in pelagic whaling, and they agreed in 1965 to give the species complete protection there. However, illegal whaling has always been a problem and the Soviet Union has never allowed international inspectors on her ships to verify compliance with the regulations. Japan's record of compliance with whaling regulations is anything but good. Will the gunners of the whaling fleets of these nations let a blue whale live if they see one?

Apart from man, the only animal capable of killing a blue whale is the killer whale (*Orcinus orca*), a toothed whale of legendary ferocity. The killer whale inhabits all the world's oceans, and its favorite food seems to be porpoises, dolphins, and seals. It is a fearless animal that has been known to attack the largest whales, including the blue, that are many times larger than itself. Its preference is for the young of all species.[7] The magnitude of blue-whale mortality due to the killer whale is unknown, but it is surely above 0. Whatever it is, man has made it worse. The killer whale has almost no commercial value. Its blubber is thin and the oil inedible. The males are about 30 feet in length and the females only 15. Consequently man has killed relatively very few of them, and there is no evidence that their numbers have decreased. Now that there are so few blue whales left alive it is likely that its mortality rate caused by the killer whale will increase reactive to its total population. Any such increase, no matter how slight, could be fatal to the species.

The most fateful of all the factors working against the survival chances of the blue whale may be one the animal has not faced before. Whenever an animal population is reduced to a very small stock of individuals there is a risk that it will tend to extinction. This risk is not diminished if hunting ceases, and it increases the longer the population remains at a very low level. The specific cause of this tendency to extinction is a reduction in the reproduction rate itself. Nothing is known about the stock size for any cetacean species when this drop in the reproduction rate occurs, but one of the experts hired by the Whaling Commission stated in 1963 that the blue whale was even then possibly beyond recovery.[8] Hundreds of blue whales have been killed since then, and the killing goes on. How much longer can the species survive? Has it survived may soon be a more pertinent question.

Before drawing a final conclusion about the chances for survival of the blue whale it may be wise to examine an analagous case from the past, that is, another cetacean species that was hunted to the point of extinction. It is, after all, difficult to render extinct any marine animal and if it did not happen to other large whales perhaps it will not happen to the blue whale.

The species that was most intensively hunted with a population decline resembling that of the blue whale was the Biscayan or North Atlantic Right whale. The Right whale became so scarce a century ago that it could not support a whaling industry, and the killing of Right whales all but ceased. Practically none was taken in the twentieth century, and none at all since 1929 when it was given complete protection by international agreement. A few are still alive today. If the Right whale has been able to avert biological extinction is it not logical to assume that the blue whale can do the same? No, unfortunately it is not. There are several reasons for this. The Arctic Ocean where the Right whale feeds in summer is much smaller than the Antarctic, and this would make it easier for individual Right whales to find each other. Also, the Right whale logically has a higher rate of reproduction because the blue whale has the lowest of any baleen whale about which the facts are known. And there is also some evidence that the Right whale has a longer life span than that of the blue whale, making possible a larger number of offspring per female. These potential advantages could all help to raise the survival chances of the Right whale above those of the blue whale.

The most important factor that must be examined in using the analogous case of the Right whale to judge the survival chances of the blue whale is the size of the population when whaling ceased. Here, too, the Right whale had an advantage. When whaling ceased and the animal began the struggle for survival its population was certainly much larger than that of the blue whale today. The reason for this concerns the number of different species being hunted in each case. The whalers who exploited the Right whale had only that one species to hunt. When the number of whales was reduced to a low level all whaling had to cease because it did not pay to seek out the widely scattered individuals. There were still quite a few Right whales left but not enough to support the industry. The whalers could not turn to another species, and so they ceased operations. When that occurred the Right whale was commercially extinct. That happened to the Right whale in several oceans and to other species as well during the course of whaling history. The rich Antarctic whaling grounds in this century provided an alternative when one species was no longer capable of supporting the industry.

The Antarctic supported large numbers of whales of several species. As the blue whale became progressively unable to support the whaling industry the whalers came to rely to a commensurate degree on the next most valuable species, the fin whale. They continued to kill the blue whales even when their reliance on the fin whale became almost exclusive. Thus they continued to hunt the blue whale long after it alone could have supported an industry. This process was carried yet one more step. When the stocks of fin whales began to give out the whalers shifted their efforts to the sei whale, but continued to kill not only fin whales but also the last remnants of the blue-whale stocks as well. Thus the blue whale was hunted to the point of commercial extinction, but unlike other whales in history its point of commercial extinction was almost synonymous with biological extinction because the few remaining individuals had significant commercial value.

Figure 9

The Antarctic catch of blue, fin, and sei whales

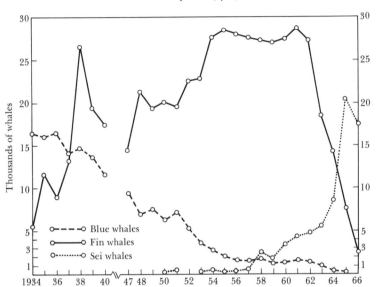

The changing reliance of the industry from a larger, more valuable species to a smaller, less valuable one as the former declined in numbers is shown graphically in Figure 9. Quite clearly the decline in the blue-whale catch is accompanied by an increase in the catch of fin whales. When the latter begin to decline the catch of sei whales begins to increase. It is significant that in the year when the sei-whale catch reached its peak the last catch of blue whales, 20, was made.

When would the killing of blue whales have ceased if there had not been available other less valuable species to sustain the industry? During the 1950s the floating-factory expeditions averaged a catch of all species equivalent to 828 blue whales. (2 fin whales, 2.5 humpbacks, and 6 sei whales were considered the raw material equivalent of 1 blue whale.) They operated with an average of 12 catcher boats each. Assuming a whaling season lasting from December 1 to March 31, the total catcher-day's-work would be 1,452. In the 1949/50 season the blue-whale population was such that the catch per catcher-day's-work was 0.35. In that year, therefore, an average expedition would have been able to catch only 1,452 × 0.35, or 508 blue whales, clearly not enough to sustain commercial exploitation. A total catch of 828 blue whales would require a catch per catcher-day's-work of 0.57 whales. Such a catch was not possible after the 1946/47 season. Obviously, the most efficient expedition might have continued hunting somewhat longer. Nevertheless, the conclusion is inescapable that due to the existence of other species the blue whale was hunted to a population level far below that of any other species in the long history of whaling.

The Right whale, then, had a larger population than the blue whale when whaling based on it came to an end. Individual Right whales probably have less difficulty finding each other, have a higher rate of reproduction, and a longer life span. None has been killed in almost half a century and yet the species is still on the verge of biological extinction. What, then, are the chances for the survival of the blue whale? None. Isn't there a single positive factor that can counterbalance to some small degree those now tipping the scales so heavily against the blue whale in its struggle for survival? Yes, there is one— the will to live.

Few and evil have the days of the years of my life been. . . . GENESIS 47:9

IV

ANTARCTIC
PELAGIC WHALING

THE PELAGIC WHALING INDUSTRY that knowingly and apparently willingly, drove the blue whale to the brink of biological extinction resembles little the old-style industry that preceded it. Actually, it resembles in many ways the highly complex industries that typify the twentieth century. Yet the techniques and the equipment that it developed through the years remain largely unknown to nonwhalers.

In order to process the carcasses of hundreds of large whales while operating on the high seas, a complete factory is necessary. The factory, of course, must be installed in a ship capable of remaining at sea for about seven consecutive months. Such a ship must carry with it not only a crew of regular seamen but also a full complement of factory workers. As a result a floating factory whaleship is an extraordinarily compact and complex vessel.

The design of a factory ship is largely governed by the procedure whereby a whale carcass once drawn up on deck via the stern ramp is dragged forward at each step in the process of dismemberment. Because of this procedure the normal placement of the smokestack must be modified; two smaller ones are used, each being placed midway between the midship line and the sides of the hull. (See Plate XIII.) The first step in the dismemberment process takes place on the flensing deck, at the top of the stern slipway, where the blubber is removed in long strips. These strips are dropped into large openings in the deck that lead down to cutting machines that dice the blubber into small pieces. The diced blubber is then fed down into high-pressure steam cookers which extract the oil. The oil, moving further down in

Plate XIII Factory ship Thorshøvdi in dry dock. The largest floating drydock in Scandinavia (671 feet long), belonging to Framnæs Mek. Værksted, is required to handle this 23,250 d.w. ton ship. The stern slipway may be seen leading up between the twin stacks to the flensing deck. Courtesy of A/S Framnæs Mek. Værksted, Sandefjord, Norway.

the ship, is purified, all water removed, and finally stored in large tanks in the hold. The whale carcass with blubber removed is dragged forward several yards and the meat is removed; it is again dragged forward, and the bones are removed and sawed up. The meat and bones are each put through a descending series of apparatuses that remove and purify the oil prior to storage in the hold.

The living quarters for the crew and factory workers, numbering together about 400 men, are located fore and aft. Here too are located such necessary facilities as dining rooms, theater, hospital, and laboratories. Elsewhere throughout the ship are vast stores of food, fuel, and other supplies sufficient for many months. A factory ship must also serve as a supply ship for its fleet of catcher boats. Because the catchers must be fast and small they can not carry enough food and fuel for an entire voyage, and they must periodically take on fresh supplies from the factory ship.[1] Factory ships, therefore, must be large vessels, and since their early development they have been constructed on an ever-increasing scale. By 1963 the size of factory ships varied from a minimum of 16,920 d.w. tons for the *Kyokuyo Maru* 2 to a maximum of 46,000 d.w. tons for the *Sovietskaya Ukraina* and the *Sovietskaya Rossia*.[2]

The catcher boats that accompanied each floating factory had a limited assignment: locate, kill, and, time permitting, tow the dead whales to the factory ship. Consequently, catcher boats were small, from 350 to 700 gross tons, and fast, top speed being about 20 knots or slightly more. A 90 millimeter cannon mounted high in the bow was the weapon used to kill the whales. (Plate XIV shows a whale gunner in action.) It fired a 200–pound steel harpoon containing an explosive charge timed to go off a few seconds after it penetrated a whale's body. Usually one shot was enough to kill a blue whale in ten or fifteen minutes, but on occasion several harpoons and an hour or more were required. The catchers that performed this unpleasant task were as seaworthy as they were efficient. They had to operate in and south of the Roaring Forties which are among the stormiest waters of the world, and before arriving there they had to travel many thousands of miles from their home ports in high latitudes of the Northern Hemisphere.

The construction costs of a complete pelagic whaling fleet were con-

Plate XIV   Whale gunner in action harpooning a blue whale. A harpoon in flight tends to bobble at the tip, and this shot was a hit despite the momentary appearance of the projectile. The gunner's bridge extending from the captain's bridge to the bow may be seen in the lower left. Courtesy of Captain G. Anker Carlsen (shown firing), Sandefjord, Norway.

siderable. Immediately following World War II the cost of a factory ship was about $6 million.[3] The cost of factory ships became progressively greater with increased costs of labor and material in the postwar years. In 1955 the *Willem Barendsz* was built in Amsterdam at a cost of $10,520,000 (40 million guilders).[4] Two floating factories produced in 1963 in West Germany for the Soviet Union cost $16 million each.[5]

The high initial construction costs of a factory ship often induced whaling companies to lengthen and modernize older ships rather than purchase new ones. For example, in 1951 the Norwegian factory ship *Kosmos IV* was lengthened by about 13 meters, new cookers were installed, and the electrical system was renewed at the insistence of insurance underwriters. The cost of this work, done in Kiel, West Germany, was $1,831,000 (N.kr.13 million).[6]

The cost of new catcher boats was rarely published. The prestige of these smaller vessels was slight compared to that of a floating factory, and the construction of a new one had a negligible impact on the industry as a whole. The Dutch company that acquired the *Willem Barendsz* planned in 1951 to purchase 7 new catchers and reconstruct an old one for an estimated total cost of $3,808,000 (13.6 million guilders). Assuming the cost of reconstruction to be about half the cost of a new one the Dutch catchers would have cost about $477,000 each.[7] Acquisition of these catchers was delayed until 1955 during which time the original estimated cost of the *Willem Barendsz* increased by 21 percent. Assuming a commensurate increase in the cost of catcher construction their ultimate cost was about $577,200 each. A factory ship required the services of about a dozen catcher boats and therefore the minimum initial construction costs of a single floating-factory fleet were about $12 million. Many fleets constructed in the middle or late 1950s must have cost almost twice as much.

The heavy capital investment in a whaling fleet made it imperative that the vessels be used productively as much as possible. The length of the whaling season in the Antarctic and the time required to travel there and back totaled about seven months; five months of every year were available for nonwhaling purposes. Storms, gales, and the rigors of whaling required that every ship, factory and catcher alike, be dry-docked, its hull inspected and painted at the end of each whaling season. (Plate XV gives an impression of the wear and tear on whaling vessels.) This reduced the idle time but there were still over four unused months. The factory ships had large oil-carrying capacity, but they were not built for speed. Several Norwegian companies used their floating factories as oil tankers in summer between Venezuela or the Persian Gulf and Europe, but only two or three round trips were possible. The Globus Whaling Company (Globus Hvalfangersels-kapet) of Larvik, Norway, for example, used its factory ship *Norhval,* as a tanker during the summers of 1951, 1952, and 1953. This tanker trade netted an annual average supplemental income of only $61,000 (N.kr.431,000), and the practice was soon discontinued.[8] No other remunerative nonwhaling use for a factory ship was ever devised. Catcher boats were even less useful for nonwhaling purposes. They had no storage capacity and could not there be used as fishing vessels.

Plate XV   Two successive views of the catcher Thorørn *in heavy seas in the Antarctic. This vessel is in a tight spot in such weather with a man in the crow's nest, a man on the gunner's bridge, and the cannon loaded.* Courtesy of A/S Framnæs Mek. Værksted, Sandefjord, Norway.

By construction and design they could serve as naval patrol vessels, but such a need did not exist during postwar years. In essence then, the productive capacity of the whaling fleets was limited strictly to whaling. The whaling companies felt therefore that it was better to go whaling even if little or no profit could be expected. To remain home during a whaling season would entail a net loss resulting from such fixed costs as insurance, watchmen, and ship and machinery maintenance. The fleets had to be used for whaling each year or be scrapped. The heavy capital investments in the fleets and the heavy fixed costs made the directors of the whaling companies anxious to maximize their production, regardless of the effects on the stocks of whales. To any decrease in the number of whales or to any decrease in the price of whale oil, there was one inflexible corporate reaction— maximize production, kill more whales.

The inflexible nature of the whaling industry was characteristic of all pelagic fleets regardless of nationality, and this was to have serious consequences for the industry as a whole and for the stocks of whales in the Antarctic. With the passage of postwar years the demand for whale oil declined in Europe as supplies of less expensive, competing oils became available. The number and size of European whaling fleets did not decrease to a commensurate degree for reasons just explained. Even a simultaneously decreasing number of whales did not

force European whalers to decrease their activities. During these same postwar years Japan began to experience a period of prosperity that brought with it an increased demand for whale meat—a Japanese substitute for beef. Thus, when European whalers should have been, but were not, decreasing in size and number of their fleets Japanese whalers were encountering a stimulus to increase theirs. For the whales this meant disaster. Even in the 1947/48 season the 17 pelagic expeditions then operating had more than enough capacity to catch the number of whales allotted by international agreement. As years went by the number of whales allotted was decreased because there were fewer whales. But the number of whaling expeditions continued to increase. The changing number, size, and nationality of the factory ships is shown in Figure 10.

Industrial inflexibility in a capitalistic sense was not alone in causing an increase in the catching capacity of the world's fleets at a time when it should have been decreasing. In the late 1950s when the stocks of whales of many species were showing tragic evidence of decline the Soviet Union adopted a long-range plan to construct en-

Figure 10

Factory ships operating in the Antarctic, 1946/47 through 1964/65

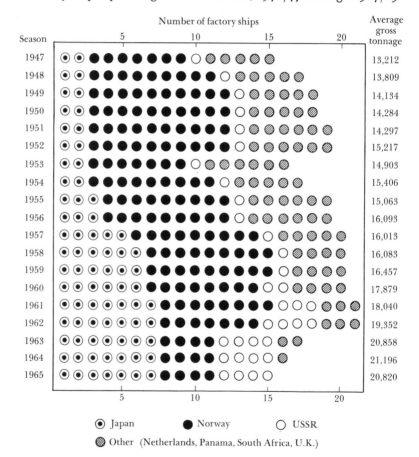

Season	Number of factory ships	Average gross tonnage
1947		13,212
1948		13,809
1949		14,134
1950		14,284
1951		14,297
1952		15,217
1953		14,903
1954		15,406
1955		15,063
1956		16,093
1957		16,013
1958		16,083
1959		16,457
1960		17,879
1961		18,040
1962		19,352
1963		20,858
1964		21,196
1965		20,820

◉ Japan   ● Norway   ○ USSR

◎ Other (Netherlands, Panama, South Africa, U.K.)

tirely new and very modern whaling fleets. Between 1959 and 1962 her Antarctic fleets increased from 1 to 4, including the 2 largest factory ships ever built. This action by the Soviet Union caused consternation among the whaling companies of other nations. It was evident to everyone related to the whaling industry that a shortage of whales of crisis proportions was in the immediate offing. Why the Soviet Union chose that time to expand her fleets has never been explained. The scientific advisers to the International Whaling Commission were in all but unanimous agreement that there were not enough whales to support the catching capacity of the industry before the Soviet expansion. Those who criticized the Soviet expansion as untimely (scientists often use very diplomatic language) were soon vindicated. Four years later, in 1966, the Soviet Union was forced for lack of whales to begin decreasing her fleets. Whatever the explanation for the Soviet expansion one point is clear. The blue whale like other cetacean species of the high seas had to undergo relentless exploitation as a result not only of inflexible capacity of European and Japanese whaling industries, but also for reasons known only to a few state planners in Moscow.

The pelagic fleets spent most of their time in Areas II, III, and IV which had the largest stocks of whales. In the middle and late 1950s other areas came to be hunted more frequently due to a general scarcity of whales. But wherever the fleets operated the ideal condition was to have a steady supply of whale carcasses delivered to the factory ship for processing. (A few hour's supply of whales is shown in Plate XVI). Too few carcasses meant idle factory workers. Too many carcasses waiting to be butchered meant poor quality oil. Three types of factor brought about by nature, man, and the whales, often prevented ideal conditions from being normal conditions.

One troublesome problem that had a serious effect on whaling was wind. Very little of a whale's body is ever visible above water, and the only practical way of sighting one is to watch for its spout, or blow, which is simply condensed water vapor formed when a whale exhales. Wind can dissipate a spout rather quickly and a high wind can cause it to disappear almost instantly. Heavy seas and storms render harpooning and towing of whale carcasses laborious and slow, and even dangerous or impossible in severe storms. In addition, a

Plate XVI Dead whales moored astern the British factory ship Southern Harvester. These 4 blue whales and 1 fin whale (light color) would normally sink at death. Their body cavities have been inflated with compressed air to keep them afloat, hence their somewhat distended appearance. Courtesy of Dr. Harry R. Lillie, London, England.

factory ship in a storm rolls like any large ship, and it would be unwise to attempt to dismember a large whale at such a time; a round, 75-ton carcass on a pitching and rolling deck posed serious problems. In stormy weather, therefore, whaling had to stop.

Man himself rendered whaling more difficult in ways other than by reducing the number of whales. If a fleet had the misfortune of hunting in an area recently vacated by another fleet the former would find either few whales or whales so skittish as to be difficult to approach. Another problem created by man was the increased necessity over the years of whaling farther and farther north. The blue whale, more than other species, seemed to have a preference for colder waters close to the ice edge and among the bergs. As the blue whale became scarcer whalers were forced to spend more time farther north in the region of prevailing westerly winds and more frequent cyclonic storms. This caused longer periods of interrupted whaling. It also meant whaling in latitudes where days were shorter and nights longer, and whaling always ceased at night.

The whales too injected an element of uncertainty into whaling operations. A given locale might be rich in whales one year and not the next, or at different times within a given year. As a fleet moved through the Antarctic it might encounter regions populated with blue whales or fin whales or sei whales or no whales. In addition, whales of whatever species found might be mature and fat or mature and thin or immature and below minimum-length requirements.

It is evident that a given whaling fleet in any season might have many days of highly remunerative whaling or many days of futile searching in empty seas. The success of any whaling fleet in any season often depended on chance. This element of chance, or luck, had an important effect on the attitude of the whaling companies toward conservation matters that are dealt with in Chapter VII. Two examples here will point out the importance of the element of chance on the fortunes of the whaling companies.

The Kosmos Company of Sandefjord, Norway, operated with two factory ships from 1947/48 through 1960/61. These ships the *Kosmos III* and the *Kosmos IV*, were almost the same size, and they operated with the same number of catcher boats in every season but two. It is reasonable to assume that any difference in their performance on the

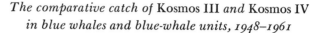

Figure 11

The comparative catch of Kosmos III *and* Kosmos IV
in blue whales and blue-whale units, 1948–1961

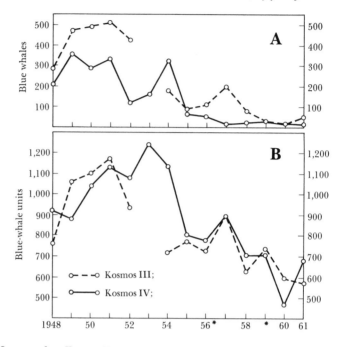

* Seasons when Kosmos III operated with one more catcher than Kosmos IV.

whaling grounds was a function of chance. Figure 11A shows the
catch of blue whales for each of the two ships for thirteen seasons. In
almost every season *Kosmos III* caught more blue whales that *Kosmos
IV,* and in some years the disparity was very great. For example, in
1952 *Kosmos III* caught more than three times as many blue whales
as did *Kosmos IV,* but in 1954 only about half as many as her sister
ship. (During the 1953 season a collision at sea kept one of the Kosmos ships out of operation.)

More important than the catch of any one species was the total
catch of all whales, or the cetacean raw material input. The most
common measure of baleen-whale raw material was the *blue-whale
unit.* One blue-whale unit was the equivalent of 1 blue whale, 2 fin

whales, 2.5 humpbacks, or 6 sei whales. This was the supposed oil-producing ratio of one species to another.[9] Using this measure Figure 11B shows that in four out of thirteen seasons there was a difference of over 100 blue-whale units between the 2 *Kosmos* ships. A difference of that magnitude was significant because 1 blue-whale unit was sufficient to produce about 120 barrels of oil and a few dozen tons of meat. In one year, 1953/54, the difference between the two ships was very great; *Kosmos III* got 704 and *Kosmos IV* got 1,122 blue-whale units. It is interesting to note that over the thirteen-year period *Kosmos III* and *Kosmos IV* got a grand total of 10,715 and 11,187 blue-whale units respectively, a difference of only 4 percent. These nearly equal long-term catch totals might indicate that any one company could expect to get its proportionate share of whales in the long run even if it encountered extreme fluctuations in the short run.

The second example of the role of chance in the Antarctic whaling operations concerns the variation in the average length of whales killed by the various companies. Just as a given company might encounter many blue whales or sei whales so might it encounter large or small whales, fat ones or thin ones. Any year chosen at random would illustrate this, but 1953/54, the year with the greatest disparity between *Kosmos III* and *Kosmos IV,* has been selected to show how variation in whale length might accentuate or diminish variation in numbers. Table 8 shows the variation in the average length of blue and fin whales by sex taken by the 17 factory ships operating in 1953/54. The female blue whales taken by company No. 1 averaged 7.2 feet longer than those taken by company No. 16. An average difference of 7 feet may not seem significant, but it represents a difference of over 25 tons of whale, of valuable raw material. An 82.6-foot blue whale averages 97.9 tons, and a 75.4-foot blue whale averages 72.7 tons. (The formula used to derive these weights may be found in the sources to Table 10.)

If company No. 1 and company No. 16 each caught their proportionate share of female blue whales that year (one-seventeenth of 1,447, or 85 whales) then company No. 1 would have received 2,142 tons of raw material more than its less fortunate rival. Company No. 1 also had better luck with respect to male blue whales, and male and female fin whales as well. If it was proportionately as lucky with

Table 8

Average length in feet of blue and fin whales
caught in the Antarctic by company 1953/54

Company	Blue whales		Fin whales	
	Females (1,447)	Males (1,220)	Females (11,976)	Males (12,699)
1	82.6	77.0	70.5	66.9
2	82.2	77.7	70.6	66.4
3	80.9	76.7	69.5	65.5
4	80.4	76.5	69.2	65.1
5	81.8	74.1	72.3	65.6
6	80.3	76.4	68.7	66.4
7	80.1	76.5	69.0	66.0
8	80.0	75.3	68.8	65.9
9	79.4	75.7	68.9	65.2
10	79.6	75.8	68.0	66.4
11	79.2	75.3	68.7	65.6
12	78.2	75.6	68.2	65.3
13	78.5	74.9	68.3	65.1
14	77.9	75.5	68.1	65.1
15	76.8	74.2	68.3	65.3
16	75.4	74.0	68.2	65.1
17	76.2	72.4	67.2	64.2
Range	7.2	5.3	5.1	2.7

Source: *International Whaling Statistics,* ed. The Committee For Whaling Statistics, Det Norske Hvalråds
Statistiske Publikasjoner (Oslo), xxxiv (1965), 38–39.

Note: The name and nationality of the companies are
purposely not divulged in regard to average length. It
was generally known where each company operated in
the Antarctic and if the size of whales found there became known a possibly valuable trade secret would be
lost.

numbers of whales as it was with lengths then its total input of cetacean raw material for that season would have far surpassed that of
company No. 16.

The most pervasive of all the adverse problems facing the whaling
fleets was one resulting from a so-called conservation measure. The
whaling nations of the world, and particularly those of Western

Europe, felt that the annual catches in the Antarctic during the 1930s had been much too high, and should be reduced in order to conserve the stocks of whales. As a measure of the catch in terms of raw material the blue-whale unit, originally devised by whaling companies, was adopted in 1946 by the International Convention for the Regulation of Whaling. It was also agreed that, initially, a maximum of 16,000 blue-whale units might be taken per season and that each season would have a specific opening date, usually January 7. The following procedure was devised to ensure that only 16,000 units would be taken. Every factory ship at the end of each week was to report the details of its catch by radio to the Bureau of Whaling Statistics in Sandefjord, Norway. The Bureau would tabulate the reports and, as the limit of 16,000 was approached, would estimate the date when it would probably be reached. The Bureau of Whaling Statistics would then order all whaling to cease on that date. This Antarctic quota system, continued by the International Whaling Commission after 1949, had serious repercussions of a conservation nature that are examined in Chapter VII. At this juncture its impact on the functioning and capital needs of the whaling fleets is of concern.

The Antarctic quota put every floating factory in a race against time with all other expeditions. Every day lost due to storms or lack of whales or with the factory working at less capacity meant an irretrievable loss in production. Financial success could be had only by killing as many whales as possible as quickly as possible before the order to stop whaling came out from Sandefjord. Factory ships and catchers alike worked twenty-four hours a day, seven days a week, weather and whales permitting, until the season was over. Pelagic whaling in the Antarctic was so exhausting and hectic that the whalingmen aptly dubbed it "The Whaling Olympic."

Catcher boats were forced to operate at greater and greater distances from their factory ships as whales became progressively scarcer. This increased the amount of time required to tow the dead whales back to the factory ship; it also decreased the time available for scouting and killing. A few companies tried using helicopters for spotting whales as shown in Plate XVII, but the results did not justify the costs and the practice was not long continued. The only satisfactory solution to this frustrating situation was to use faster and more power-

Plate XVII Blue whale about to die. This picture vividly illustrates the unequal struggle between whale and man. A few minutes before the picture was taken the catcher Globe 14 was moving from left to right, and the traces of its wake may be seen at the top of the picture. The lookout in the crow's nest somehow failed to spot the blue whale at the left. The animal was seen by helicopter, which alerted the catcher by radio. The blue whale fleeing in fright has started to sound. Part of his back is visible and his spout is beginning to dissipate. Death occurred a few minutes later. Courtesy of Captain G. Anker Carlsen, Sandefjord, Norway.

ful catcher boats. When a whaling company acquired better catcher boats it automatically acquired an advantage over its competitors. The competitors in turn had to acquire better catchers in order to overcome the disadvantage. Better catchers lead to fewer whales and fewer whales lead to a need for better catchers. The increase in catcher tonnage and horsepower is shown in Figure 12. The continual increase in catcher size and the continual decrease in the number of whales became a vicious cycle, a cycle in which there were two losers. The companies lost money, and the whales lost their lives.

The increase in size and power of the catchers obviously resulted in increased capital expenditures for the whaling companies, although the exact amounts cannot be determined. Better catchers did not bring increased production or revenue; they brought only the hope that each company would catch its proportionate share of a decreasing number of whales. The cost of acquiring that hope merely added to the already heavy capital investment in the whaling fleets and re-

Figure 12

Average size of catcher boats used in Antarctic pelagic whaling,
by horsepower and tonnage

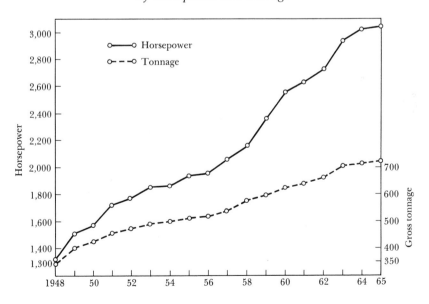

inforced the need to maximize production, or to kill as many whales as possible.

The whaling companies felt compelled to increase the number of catcher boats per factory ship in addition to increasing their tonnage and horsepower. Better catchers alone did not suffice to maintain production from a decreasing number of whales. To increase the number of catchers, however, was much more costly than the periodic replacement of a small old catcher with a new big one. The whaling companies resisted in vain the temptation to acquire more. In 1948 there was an average of 9.5 catchers per factory ship; in 1956 there were 13.5 per factory ship. This increase in the number of catchers required the investment of more capital and added to the fixed costs of the companies. It also exacerbated the "Whaling Olympic." In 1948 a total of one hundred and thirteen days was required to kill the allotted number of whales; in 1956 only fifty-eight days were needed. During these years production per catcher, measured in terms of oil, declined by almost 50 percent. The situation was becoming intolerable. Gunners had to shoot any legal-sized whale. They had no time to seek out the largest ones. On the factory ships the pace was also more hectic. There was so little time to process the whales that efficiency was impaired.

The solution to this vexing problem was to decrease the number of catchers per factory ship and work at a less hectic pace. But all the companies operating in the Antarctic would have to agree to the decrease in the number of catchers. If one company refused to cooperate it would have a distinct advantage over all others, and this would be unacceptable. The Soviet Union, unfortunately, refused to discuss the matter and thus rendered a long-term solution almost impossible. European and Japanese companies did manage to come to a temporary agreement after many months of negotiations, and in 1957 there was a reduction of 2 catchers per factory ship. In the following years additional negotiations were held but no permanent agreement was ever reached.[10] The number of catchers again began to increase, although it never reached the record set in 1956. It may have been just as well, however, that no solution to this was found. If the companies had agreed to a substantial reduction in the number of catchers their profits would undoubtedly have increased. That might have induced other companies to begin whaling, and that would have been an even greater disaster for the whales as well as for the whaling companies.

The blue-whale unit as a measure of the Antarctic quota that produced the "Whaling Olympic" requires further clarification. The blue-whale unit, as previously mentioned, was based on the approximate oil-producing value of the other baleen species compared to the blue whale. The 4 baleen species, as members of the genus *Balaenopteridae,* resembled each other in many of their physical as well as social aspects. For example, the oil of their blubber, bones, and meat was edible and differed only in quantity from species to species. Their internal organs, such as the liver, produced identical products, and no one species produced a product that could not be obtained from the others. They all migrated to the Antarctic in summer to feed and returned to warm waters in winter to mate and give birth. The timing of their migrations did not, however, coincide. The blue whale was usually the first species to arrive in the Antarctic and the first to leave; the sei whale was the last to arrive and presumably the last to leave.

Among the rorquals the difference of greatest significance was size because size alone determined the relative value of the 4 species and the intensity with which each was hunted. The term size is somewhat misleading, because among the rorquals average weight did not correlate with average length. Table 9 shows the average length of the

Table 9

Average length, in feet, of rorquals taken by
Antarctic pelagic whaling,
seasons 1933, 1953 and 1963
(Sexes averaged)

	1933	1953	1963
Blue whales	80.4	77.5	73.1
Fin whales	68.7	67.3	66.2
Humpbacks	39.2	40.9	41.6
Sei whales	—	51.6	49.8

Source: *International Whaling Statistics,* XVI (1942), 41; and LIV (1965), 25.

4 baleen species taken during three Antarctic seasons. Plainly, the blue whale is about 15 percent longer than the fin whale, but its weight and oil producing capacity were about double that of the fin whale. The cause of this phenomenon was that in blue whales the girth, or bulk, increased more rapidly than the length.

A second disparity in the length-weight ratio of the baleen whales was between the humpback and the sei. The data in Table 9 indicate that the humpback was about 10 feet shorter than the sei whale. However, it was a much bulkier animal than the sei and yielded 3 times as much oil. As a consequence the sei was the least valuable of the rorquals and was not hunted until the other species became very scarce.

The sperm whale (*Physeter catodon*) was also hunted in the Antarctic. The species, best known to laymen by its most famous individual, Moby Dick, was not given any blue-whale unit value and was not included in the Antarctic quota. There are two reasons for this. The sperm whale, an *odontocete*, or toothed whale, yields an inedible oil that in actuality is a liquid wax rather than a true oil. It is referred to as *sperm oil* to distinguish it from the edible oil of baleen whales that is called *whale oil*. The Antarctic blue-whale unit quota, it will be recalled, was established after World War II to prevent overexploitation of the stocks of whales during a period of acute shortage of edible fats and oil, a shortage that the sperm whale could not help to relieve. The second reason for excluding the sperm whale from the Antarctic quota was the curious fact that there was no danger of killing too many sperm whales in the Antarctic. The explanation for this is that only male sperm whales were found there. The animal is polygamous, and old bulls ousted from their harems and young ones who never acquired one apparently used the Antarctic as a bachelors' retreat. All the females remained in tropical and subtropical waters where they raised their calves. Pods of sperm whales found there were invariably harems composed of many females and an adult bull. The males that were killed in the Antarctic were in essence a natural sustainable yield of the male of the species that conveniently localized itself. Thus the sperm whale was not included in the Antarctic quota, and it was hunted there without restriction.[11]

The incorrect oil-producing capacity attributed to fin and sei whales under the blue-whale unit system makes that system inadequate to measure the exact contribution of the blue whale itself to total Antarctic production. The exclusion of the sperm whale makes the blue-whale unit less valuable as a measure of total production. Moreover, no measure of the decline of the blue-whale population is adequate to the task of showing the contribution of the animal to total production in a given year because as the average length of blue whales declined so too did their average weight. It is therefore necessary to calculate the total tonnage of cetacean raw material, the biomass, produced each year. Only by calculating that biomass will it be possible to measure with accuracy the contribution of the blue whale to total Antarctic industrial production.

The cetacean biomass for the years 1950 to 1965 has been calculated and is shown in Table 10. The formula used to determine the biomass for each species is given on the page following the table. The role of the blue whale in Antarctic production in terms of raw material is the same as the blue-whale portion of the biomass, and this in percentage terms is listed in parentheses in Table 10. In the following chapter references are made to the blue-whale portion of the biomass when examining industrial dependence on the blue whale. It is sufficient here to note the continual and rapid decline of that portion since 1950. In 1950 the blue whale represented 33 percent of the cetacean raw material produced and only 0.1 percent in 1965.

The most important product derived from the baleen whales of the Antarctic was whale oil. Its value resulted from its being the primary raw material in the production of high quality margarine and cooking oil. As such it had a ready market in the traditional fat-importing nations of Western Europe, particularly Germany and the United Kingdom. Indeed, during the prewar years whale oil formed the basis for the production of 40 percent of the margarine and 30 percent of the lard compound of the United Kingdom [12] and 54 percent of the margarine and lard compound of Germany. During the 1930s European consumption of whale oil was so great that it constituted approximately 10 percent of the total world trade in edible fats and oils. During that decade the price of whale oil fluctuated between £10 and £29 per ton. In 1939, with a threat of war, the desire to stockpile supplies caused the price to rise to £40 per ton.[13]

Table 10

Cetacean biomass, in tons by species,
taken in Antarctic pelagic whaling, 1949/50 to 1964/65

Season	Fin whale	Humpback	Sei whale	Sperm whale	Blue (percent of total)		Total
1949/50	903,050	56,312	2,328	88,665	526,280	(33.4)	1,576,635
1950/51	838,752	44,010	7,938	163,599	571,212	(35.1)	1,625,511
1951/52	1,067,040	40,660	734	184,368	420,168	(24.5)	1,712,970
1952/53	1,059,850	25,853	2,901	75,382	305,414	(20.8)	1,469,400
1953/54	1,224,314	15,503	5,274	77,750	220,088	(14.3)	1,542,929
1954/55	1,242,144	13,558	2,675	182,656	173,040	(10.7)	1,614,073
1955/56	1,213,872	36,659	6,181	213,311	127,269	(8.0)	1,597,292
1956/57	1,259,300	19,012	15,944	134,695	117,390	(7.6)	1,546,341
1957/58	1,210,656	11,128	52,900	182,990	131,352	(8.3)	1,588,026
1958/59	1,266,013	60,134	31,852	154,954	98,853	(6.1)	1,611,806
1959/60	1,255,972	36,260	72,442	120,002	92,976	(5.9)	1,577,652
1960/61	1,315,507	20,104	94,820	131,115	119,683	(7.1)	1,680,229
1961/62	1,251,723	8,652	104,953	128,535	69,563	(4.5)	1,556,019
1962/63	868,674	7,641	118,865	130,248	62,155	(5.2)	1,187,583
1963/64	666,548	51	177,320	168,270	6,270	(0.6)	1,028,459
1964/65	329,667	0	419,341	108,644	1,069	(0.1)	858,721

Sources: Formula for weight of fin whales: $W = 2.17L - 97.7$ (W = weight in long tons; L = length in feet). Source: C. E. Ash, "On the Body Weights of Whales," *NHT*, July 1952, p. 366.

Formula for the weight of humpback whales: $W = 1.70L - 42.8$ (W = weight in long tons; L = length in feet). Source: C. E. Ash, "Weights and Oil Yields of Antarctic Humpback Whales," *NHT* (October, 1957), p. 569.

Formula for weight of sei whales: $W = 0.0016L^{2.43}$ (W = weight in long tons; L = length in feet). Source: C. E. Ash, supplied to the researcher by Dr. H. Omura at request of Mr. Ash. (Omura developed the formula for sei whales in the Northern Hemisphere and Japanese coastal waters as $W = 0.00135 L^{2.43}$. Source: see source of sperm-whale formula below.)

Formula for weight of sperm whales: $W = 0.000137L^{3.18}$ (W = weight in metric tons; L = length in feet). Source: H. Omura, "On the Body Weight of Sperm and Sei Whales Located in the Adjacent Waters of Japan," *Scientific Reports*, Whales Research Institute, Tokyo, IV (1950), 1–13.

Formula for weight of blue whales: $W = 3.51L - 192$. (W = weight in long tons; L = length in feet). Source: C. E. Ash, "On the Body Weights of Whales," *NHT* (July, 1952), p. 366.

Note A: Average lengths and numbers for each species by season used in working out the formulae were obtained from *International Whaling Statistics*, LVIII (1966), 13, 23; and XLIV (1960), 21.

Note B: The cetacean biomass was calculated by Crisp up to the 1958/59 season. (See, D. T. Crisp, "The Tonnages of Whales Taken by Antarctic Pelagic Operations during Twenty Seasons and An Examination of the Blue-Whale Unit," *NHT* (October, 1962), pp. 389–93.) In bringing the calculations up to date I discovered an error in Crisp's calculations on the humpback whale biomass. Therefore, all data in Table 9 on the humpback whale are mine, as well as all other whales since 1959. Blue-whale percentage of total calculated by me.

Note C: The above formulae for weights of whales are not too reliable when applied to an individual whale because of variations in blubber thickness and other body components. They are, however, quite reliable when applied to a large number of whales on a seasonal basis. For a discussion of this problem, see, T. Sparre, "Weights of Whales," *NHT* (January, 1953), pp. 16–17.

The wartime destruction of nearly all the world's whaling fleets and the disruption of international trade deprived Europe of its traditional sources of oleaginous raw materials. A critical shortage of fats and oils developed, and to stimulate production of whale oil the British government fixed the price at £75 per ton. This move undoubtedly did stimulate postwar production, but it may have been superfluous. By 1950 Norwegian-produced whale oil was selling for £120 per ton on the open market in Europe. This was a boon to the whaling companies, but it could not last. Whale oil as a raw material for the production of margarine has many substitutes. Among them are the vegetable oils of cottonseed, soybean, sesame, sunflower, rapeseed, peanut, coconut, palm, and palm kernel.[14] During the 1950s the production and exportation to Europe of many of these oils reached record levels, especially American soybean oil. Peruvian fish oil also entered the European market in record quantities. With the reopening of prewar trade channels these various competing oils caused a long period of slow decline in the price of whale oil. By 1962 the price per ton of whale oil was only £44, a mere £4 above the 1939 price. The price of whale oil has tended to increase slightly since 1962 but not sufficiently to counteract a decrease in total production of oil due to a shortage of whales. With the decline in the price of whale oil the inflexible nature of the whaling industry became a financial burden. The whaling companies had two alternatives: cut back on production to reduce expenses or increase total production to increase revenue. Their capital investments made the former impossible; a shortage of whales made the latter almost impossible. They chose the latter and tried to increase production. The killing of blue whales had to continue.

The second most important product obtained from the blue and other baleen whales of the Antarctic was meat for human consumption. The production and sale of whale meat was almost exclusively Japanese because only in that nation did the culinary habits of the people create a substantial market for it. This was a distinct economic advantage to the Japanese whaling companies because, as has been pointed out, a significant portion by weight of a blue or other baleen whale consisted of meat that yielded little oil.

The importance to the Japanese whaling companies of their production of whale meat was so great that it can hardly be overemphasized. During the 1950s their production of whale meat at domestic land-based whaling stations alone exceeded that of all non-Japanese companies operating pelagically in the Antarctic. By 1960 total Japanese production of whale meat exceeded 155,000 tons and was greater than her domestic production of beef from cattle. The peak of production came in 1964/65 when Antarctic operations alone produced 147,721 tons. Most of this production was frozen and sold as a competitor and substitute for beef, but at one-third the price. Tail flukes, for example, were considered a delicacy and eaten raw, and sold for about 3 times the price of ordinary whale meat. Thin belly blubber was sold as "whale bacon" since it so closely resembled pork bacon. Even jaw cartilage was pickled and found a ready market.[15] To anyone with culinary courage all this is not surprising because whale meat closely resembles beef both in color and texture. (A close-up of blue-whale meat is shown in Plate XVIII.) From a nutritional point

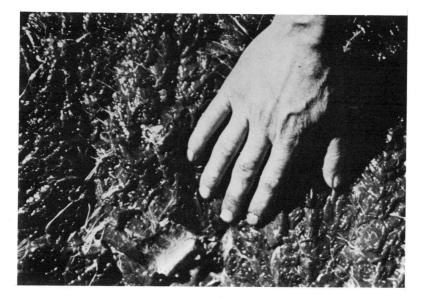

Plate XVIII   Blue-whale meat pre rigor mortis. Courtesy of Crowell Collier and Macmillan, Inc.

of view whale-meat consumption is also sound because it is the equal of beef and pork with a protein content varying from 18.5 to 24.7 percent.[16]

Japanese whalers, it will be recalled, received an average of $239.05 per ton of whale meat. European whalers rendered the meat from their whales, and each ton yielded about 100 pounds of oil worth $9.50. Why did the Europeans persist in this futile practice? They had no choice. Their meat could not be sold in Japan because foreign exchange was often not available. Moreover, it is not likely that Japan would have allowed the importation of much European-produced whale meat even if the foreign exchange had been available. Every non-Japanese company that could operate at a profit and stay in business meant fewer whales and decreased production for Japan.

European whalers could not sell whale meat in their home markets simply because people would not eat it. Several promotional campaigns were apparently made to stimulate the sale of whale meat in several European countries, but without success. The Norwegian company Kosmos A/S did succeed in developing in 1961 an outlet for whale meat as pet food in the United Kingdom. Although the Kosmos company did in its annual report divulge the name of the English purchaser, Petfoods, Ltd., they would not tell me the price they received. The reason for this is not known since the price of all other important products was divulged. It may have been kept secret for fear that knowledge of substantial profit based on pet food at the risk of exterminating the blue whale might arouse moral condemnation of the company. I was, however, able to learn the price received by Kosmos for the whale meat it sold for pet food. The information came from an employee of the company who was morally disgusted by this and other practices of his employer. In 1961 the price per ton was £75 ($210), and by 1967 it had risen to £100 ($280). The Kosmos company enjoyed a great advantage in this market for its whale meat, and in some of its annual reports it admitted as much. It did not admit, naturally, that profits were being maintained at the risk of biological extinction of the blue whale that was being killed to feed cats and dogs in England.

Three other Norwegian companies beginning in 1961 were able to sell whale meat directly to Japanese ships in the Antarctic during the whaling season. The quantity involved was small, about 6,000 tons per year per company, at prices ranging from £25 to £36.5 per ton ($70–102).[17] The late development of this market supports rather than contradicts the previous statement that Europeans could not sell whale meat on the Japanese market. It came at a time when whales were becoming very scarce and when the Soviets were expanding their capacity, both of which made further expansion of Japanese fleets quite impractical. Also, the price paid by the Japanese was so low that they probably made a small profit on the resale in Japan. Finally, the total amount of meat involved was so small, about 15 percent of Japanese production, that it did not seriously compete with Japanese production.

The aversion of Europeans to whale meat is rather perplexing in view of their willingness to eat such items as snails, squid, periwinkles, and the like. I have eaten whale meat (not from blue whales!) many times in Norway, where small quantities are sold. It was not only palatable but also tastier than the beef served there. Moreover, it was always the least expensive entree on the menu with the exception of hash and hotdogs. It is possible that the quality of that meat was better than that produced in the Antarctic because the whale meat sold in Norway is produced at domestic coastal whaling stations where facilities for rapid butchering and freezing are superior to those on a pelagic factory ship. Whatever the explanation for the European aversion to whale meat one final illustration will emphasize the extent of the difference in the market for whale meat available to European and Japanese whalers. European whalers always considered sperm-whale meat unfit for human consumption under any circumstances. Its foul odor and taste are repulsive. As a result of this attitude the international regulations adopted for the utilization of sperm-whale carcasses stipulated that the meat might be dumped overboard.[18] What European whalers thought about sperm-whale blubber after the oil had been boiled out is better left unsaid. Japanese on the other hand not only consider sperm-whale meat edible but even use dried sperm-whale blubber as an additive in stews and soups.[19]

The third product of significance produced by Antarctic whalers was sperm oil which can be produced only from sperm whales. This oil is not edible under any circumstances, and its uses are therefore radically different from the oil from baleen whales. Sperm oil was once famous as an illuminating fuel, but electric light put an end to that market. Today its uses stem from 4 of its unique qualities: it reacts only slightly to changes in temperature; it does not film over or turn rancid; it is noncorrosive; and it will not oxidize unless ignited.[20] It is used, therefore, as a lubricant for specialized machinery, for the manufacture of soap, detergents, and higher alcohols used in the refining and softening of textiles.[21] As a result of these industrial uses and the absence of increasing supplies of numerous competing substitutes, the price of sperm oil has tended to increase during the last twenty years. Moreover its price fluctuations seem to be directly related to the general level of industrial activity. For example, the price of sperm oil nearly doubled during the Korean War and returned to the prewar price when the conflict was over. During the period from 1950 to 1965 the average price received by Norwegian whaling companies for sperm oil was £66.1 ($186.40) per ton. It had no single national market but was sold to industrial users in Japan, Western Europe, and North America.

The whales of the Antarctic made possible the production of many other items among which were: ambergris, baleen, blubber for leather, bone fertilizer, bone meal, liver oil, liver meal, meat meal, sperm whale teeth, and whale meat extract. All these items combined, however, were of lesser importance than any one of the three previously discussed products, namely, whale oil, meat, and sperm oil. No one whaling company ever produced all of them, and even those items produced by a company one year might not be produced at all the following year. There were some companies that produced none of them in commercial quantities. Also, sales of these products were invariably in such small quantities that the price and place of sale were in most cases never recorded. It has been impossible to obtain significant market details concerning them, and fortunately such details are not necessary to attain the objectives of this book. Knowledge of the details of the market for meat and oil make it clear that the blue whale was too valuable a source of wealth to live.

But he that maketh haste to be rich shall not be innocent. PROVERBS 28:20

V

INDUSTRIAL ECONOMICS
AND EXTERMINATION

THE UNDERLYING REASON for the failure of the International Whaling Commission to give protection from overexploitation to the blue whale was pressure against such a move exerted by the whaling industry. That industry, regardless of nationality, claimed that because of rising labor costs and declining prices of whale products serious economic hardship and possibly failure would result from any decrease in the size of the catch, especially of the larger species. The claim of economic hardship should have been investigated by the Whaling Commission before acting on it because the Commission was formed for the expressed purpose of preventing the overexploitation of the whales of the world. The Whaling Commission made no attempt to study the economic position of the whaling industry until after the blue whale was virtually extinct. The industrial representatives on the Whaling Commission cried economic hardship so loudly and long that their claims were believed. But were those claims justified? Would the industry have faced economic hardship or possibly ruin if it had ceased to kill blue whales before they were threatened with extinction?

Before proceeding to analyze the data that can answer that question, another one must be asked in order to establish a proper frame of reference. When should the killing of blue whales have been stopped in order to avert the danger of extinction? The question cannot, of course, be answered with absolute certainty. The year 1963 was obviously too late. In that year its population was an estimated

600, and the consequences of that have already been examined. The first attempts to give the species some protection began in the early 1950s when it was becoming clear that its population was being drastically reduced. By 1956 the annual catch of blue whales fell below 2,000 for the first time in the history of pelagic whaling, a figure far below the 31,000 killed in 1931. Moreover, the catch per unit-of-effort by 1956 was down to 0.2 blue whales per catcher-day's-work, indicating a very low population level. For purposes of this inquiry into the validity of the claims of the whaling industry it is assumed that by 1956 the blue whale should have received very great if not complete protection. In any case, there can be no doubt that with each passing year after 1956 the blue whale was in progressively greater need of complete protection.

The pelagic whaling companies that operated in the Antarctic were from several nations, but only those from Norway and Japan will be studied to evaluate their claim of a need to kill blue whales. The whaling companies of Norway and Japan together represented about three-fourths of the total world industry. The omission of other national industries from the inquiry is not as serious as it would appear. After 1957 there were only 3 other countries represented: the Netherlands, the United Kingdom, and the Soviet Union. The Netherlands had only one fleet owned by a company that received substantial grants from its government. Indeed, this company had its dividends guaranteed by the Dutch government and could have survived quite well without recourse to blue whales.

The whaling companies of the United Kingdom will be omitted from the economic inquiry for two reasons. First, the British pelagic fleets were few in number compared to those of Norway, and their impact on Antarctic whaling was therefore of much less importance. The second, and main, reason for omitting the British companies is to avoid useless repetition of conditions prevailing among the Norwegian companies. The British whaling industry had a cost-price structure all but identical to the Norwegian. The companies of both nations usually sold their whale oil in the United Kingdom, and nearly always at identical prices. The whalingmen who worked the ships of both nations belonged to the same unions and earned identical wages. Whatever need the Norwegians had for the blue whale

Figure 13

Average price of whale oil received by Norwegian whaling companies,
1950–1963 [1]

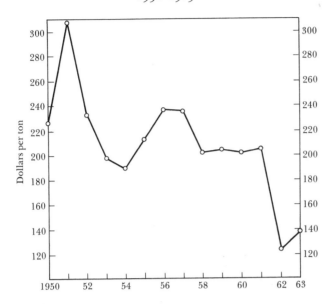

was shared by the British, and there is no need to conduct the same inquiry twice.

The omission of the Soviet Union from the economic inquiry is the result of necessity. The Soviets publish no information about the details of the operation of their whaling fleets. Not even rudimentary cost and price data are available about them, and all my letters of inquiry to Soviet whaling officials remain unanswered.

Would the whaling industry have faced economic hardship or possibly ruin if it had ceased to kill blue whales before they were threatened with extinction? Was the blue whale slaughtered almost to the last individual for reasons of economic necessity? Or, was it for a little more profit that could safely be labeled economic necessity because no one bothered to question the claim? Let us look first at the economic position of the Norwegian whaling companies.

A preliminary study of costs and prices affecting the Norwegian whaling industry indicates a deteriorating situation during the postwar years and during the final decline of the blue whale. This is readily seen by an examination of prices, labor costs, and output per factory ship.

The Norwegian dependence on whale oil as the principal product of the industry would not have been a disadvantage if whale oil had not had so many competing substitutes. Whale oil played a decreasing role in the market for edible fats and oils in Western Europe as a result of factors mentioned in the preceding chapter, and its price tended to decline commensurately. Figure 13 shows the decline for the years 1950 through 1963. This weakening of the price of whale oil created poor long-term profit prospects for the Norwegian whaling industry.

A second factor that seriously diminished long-term profit prospects for the industry was rising labor costs. The men who worked the whaling ships, from cabin boys and gunners to chief engineers were unionized, and they negotiated new wage contracts biannually with the Whaling Employers Association.[2] As might be expected wage rates increased steadily for all categories of employees during the period in question, and the annual average wages paid to the men of the whaling fleets are shown in Figure 14. The somewhat erratic fluctuations in the amount of wages paid are the result of annual changes in the length of the whaling season that produced great variations in the amount of overtime work. The upward trend in wage costs is nevertheless plainly evident. This was distinctly unfavorable for the long-term profit prospects of the whaling industry and combined with the trend of lower prices of oil it gave the impression that the industry was indeed in dire economic straits.

A third factor to which Norwegian whalers could point as a source of present and future troubles was the declining stocks of whales. This of course meant decreased production per unit-of-effort, and there was no possibility that this trend could be reversed. The decrease in the production of oil per unit-of-effort, which in a corporate sense is a floating factory-day's-work, is shown in Figure 15. The decline in productivity after 1956 was both sharp and steady. Total production did not begin to decline abruptly until 1963 and was maintained in the interim only by killing larger numbers of whales of small species. But for purposes of operating profitably it was the

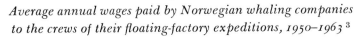

Figure 14

*Average annual wages paid by Norwegian whaling companies
to the crews of their floating-factory expeditions, 1950–1963* [3]

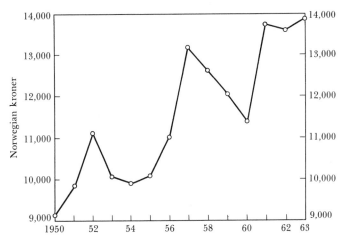

production per unit-of-effort that mattered, and that production was declining. The outlook for the Norwegian whaling industry indeed seemed bleak during these years.

It is hardly surprising that the claims of economic hardship were not questioned. The pelagic whaling industry of Norway could indeed point to declining prices for whale oil, decreasing productivity because of a shortage of whales and rising costs of labor. The whaling companies had virtually no control over the price of oil and very little over the labor costs, and it was therefore logical for them to resist any limitation on the number of whales they might catch. This was particularly the case with the larger whales, especially the blue, the killing of which in large numbers was one sure way to increase productivity and revenue.

A close look at the financial position of the Norwegian whaling industry brings to light a situation rather different from what one would expect in view of the adverse price and cost factors just mentioned. The average annual net income for the industry as a whole did not show a tendency to decline for a ten-year period beginning with the 1952 season. Indeed, apart from a very good year in 1951

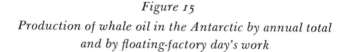

Figure 15

*Production of whale oil in the Antarctic by annual total
and by floating-factory day's work*

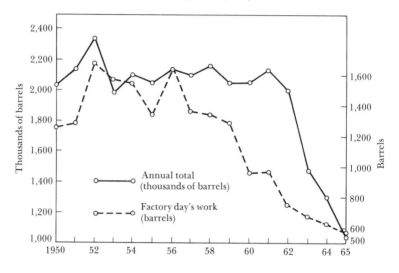

and a very bad one in 1962 the fourteen seasons from 1950 through 1963 showed a surprisingly stable level of net income. This is shown graphically in Figure 16 and is based on income data published in the annual reports of the Norwegian whaling companies. As a measure of industrial earnings the term *average annual net income* may be open to some criticism. It has been used here because the great variation in the catch of whales from season to season by the individual companies tended to obscure the fact of stable income for the industry as a whole. The actual earnings for the individual companies are shown in Figure 17.

Spokesmen for the Norwegian whaling industry never mentioned that their net profits were remaining fairly level. That would have eliminated any logical support for their objections to decreasing the catch of whales. They also avoided calling attention to any factor that might suggest that their net profits were not declining. The maintenance of their profit level must have been the result of a general increase in operating efficiency. Indeed, there are 3 substantial

Figure 16

*Average net-operating income of seven Norwegian factory ships
in the Antarctic* [4]

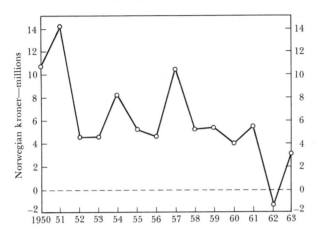

pieces of evidence that point to increases in efficiency that may have
brought about substantial decreases in operating costs.

1) Several factory ships were lengthened to increase their carrying
capacity. This decreased their dependence on the services of a supply
ship and a tanker to carry whale oil back to Europe.

2) The agreements reached in 1956 to limit the number of catchers
permitted the factory ships to accomplish the same amount of work
with 2 catcher boats less. This was a substantial saving because it cost
about N.kr. 1 million ($145,000) to operate a catcher for one season.
A decrease in the amount of catchers presumably made it possible to
eliminate some of the less efficient gunners and other crewmen.

3) In 1960 the whaling nations agreed on a division of the Antarctic quota whereby each nation received a percentage share of the total
blue-whale units. In turn the companies of each nation agreed on a
division of their national quota. This meant an end to the "Whaling
Olympic" because henceforth a factory expedition could operate almost at leisure until it reached its quota. This permitted a reduction
in overtime work and an increase in catcher and factory efficiency.

A stable profit level enjoyed by the Norwegian pelagic industry

Figure 17

Net-operating income of seven Norwegian
factory ships in the Antarctic

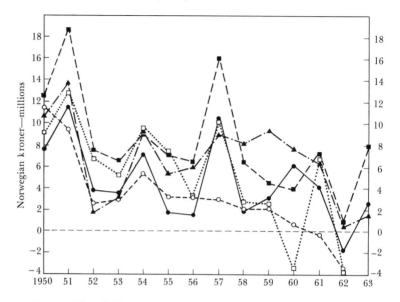

■ *Kosmos III* and *Kosmos IV*, owned and operated by Aksjeselskapet Kosmos. Profit from each ship was not listed separately, and the above figure therefore is one-half the total for the corporation. (*Kosmos III* was out of operation in 1953, and withdrawn from whaling after the 1961 season.)

● *Sir James Clark Ross*, operated by Hvalfangeraktieselskapet Rosshavet.

▲ *Thorshavet* and *Thorshøvdi*, owned and operated jointly by Aktieselskaper Ørnen and Odd. (Total profits shared.) (*Thorshøvdi* out of operation 1953.)

□ *Norhval*, jointly owned and operated by Aktieselskaper Polaris and Globus. (Last season, 1962.)

○ *Pelagos*, owned and operated by Hvalfangerselskapet Pelagos. (Last season, 1962.)

during the last years of the decline of the blue whale casts doubt on the claims of economic hardship. It does not, however, disprove the industrial claim that economic hardship or even failure would have been the result of giving complete protection to the blue whale. In order to investigate this claim further two methods of inquiry must be adopted, methods governed by the two ways in which the International Whaling Commission could have given complete protection to the blue whale. First, the Whaling Commission could have banned the killing of blue whales and at the same time forbidden the killing of more fin whales to make up for the loss in blue-whale raw material. Second, the Whaling Commission could have banned the killing of blue whales and allowed additional fin whales to be killed. The first method of inquiry, Method *A*, examines the impact on the Norwegian industry of an elimination of the blue-whale raw material input, that is, a ban on blue whales accompanied by a ban on killing additional fin whales. This method is concerned therefore with a simple reduction in revenue. The second method of inquiry, Method *B*, examines the impact on the industry of the cost of catching additional fin whales to make up for the loss of raw material of a ban on the killing of blue whales. This method is concerned with a simple increase in catching costs because raw material input and gross revenue would remain unchanged.

— METHOD *A* —

If the Norwegian whaling industry had ceased killing blue whales and not killed more fin whales to make up for the loss in raw material the total raw material input would have decreased by the blue-whale portion of the biomass. At the same time the gross revenue of the industry would have decreased by approximately the same proportionate amount because production and revenue were directly proportionate to the weight of whales processed. The calculation of these decreases is shown in Table 11. Column A lists the gross income from whaling that the companies actually received. Column B lists the blue-whale percentage of the cetacean biomass taken in the Antarctic, and Column C lists the same in terms of blue-whale portion of total income (Column A × Column B = Column C). Column D shows what the gross income of the industry would have been without any blue whales (Column A minus Column C). Column E lists the actual expenses of the industry, and this subtracted from Column D shows in Column F the net income the industry would have received if blue whales had been excluded from the catch. Column G shows the net income the industry actually received, that is, with blue whales being a part of the catch.

It is most interesting to compare what the industry earned with what it would have earned if blue whale had been given complete protection (Columns F and G). The reduction in net earnings resulting from a ban on the killing of blue whales would have been less than 50 percent in every year but 1956. A reduction of even 30 percent would, of course, have been substantial, and the industry would have understandably objected. However, the industry could have survived, and it is important to note that economic disaster in the form of a net loss would not have occurred before it actually did. The industry operated at a net loss for the first time in 1962, precisely the year a net loss would first have occurred if the killing of blue whales had stopped in 1956.

The pelagic whaling industry of Norway was composed of corporations that had been founded as whaling companies during the first quarter of this century. All these companies eventually branched

Table 11

Calculation of the effect of a ban on the killing of blue whales on Norwegian net whaling income, 1956–1963

	A	B	C	D	E	F	G
	Gross whaling income (in millions N. kr.)	Blue-whale portion of cetacean biomass (in percent)	Blue-whale portion of whaling income (in millons N. kr.)	Gross whaling income minus blue whale (in millions N. kr.)	Actual operating expenses (in millions N. kr.)	Income minus blue whale (in millions N. kr.)	Actual net income (in millions N. kr.)
1956	245	8.0	20	225	210	15	35
1957	298	7.6	23	275	224	51	74
1958	212	8.3	18	194	175	19	37
1959	218	6.1	13	205	181	24	37
1960	193	5.9	11	182	165	17	28
1961	206	7.1	15	191	172	19	34
1962	118	4.5	5	113	125	−12	−7
1963	70	5.2	4	66	55	11	15

Sources: Columns A, E, and G, *Statistisk Årbok,* Norges Statistisk Sentralbyrå, 1965, p. 110; Column B, Table 10 above; and Columns C, D, and F, calculated by me.

out into shipping and related industries. By about 1955 the continued expansion of their shipping activities had reached such proportions that they were no longer whaling companies with shipping interests. They had become shipping companies with whaling interests. If the decrease in net income that the whaling companies would have encountered with a total ban on blue whales is measured against their total corporate income a totally different economic situation is found.

The net income from all sources of the Norwegian whaling companies and the blue-whale portion of it is shown in Table 12. Column D lists the total net income from all sources, that is, shipping and others that are itemized in Columns A, B, and C. The loss in revenue from a ban on blue whale is shown in Column E, and Column F shows this loss as a percentage of total net income. The loss in revenue resulting from a ban on the killing of blue whales assumes much less importance when measured against the total income of the whaling companies. To be sure, the loss in 1956 would have been rather high, nearly 18 percent, but after 1958 it fell below 10 percent and continued to decline thereafter. The blue whale, therefore was of some importance to the whaling industry, but it was of small significance to the companies engaged in whaling. It is certain beyond all doubt that these companies as a whole would not have faced anything approaching economic hardship, let alone disaster, if they had ceased killing blue whales after 1956. Their claims were false. Only they knew this, and so the killing continued.

The blue-whale percentage of total net income of the Norwegian companies was actually much lower than the percentage figures shown below. It is regrettable that these figures are exaggerated because they make it difficult to demonstrate how truly insignificant was the value of the blue whale to the whaling companies. There are 3 reasons why the percentage figures are exaggerated.

1) If the whaling companies had ceased killing blue whales there would have been a concomitant decrease in operating costs. This would have resulted from the use of fewer harpoons, less line, decreased towing time and fuel consumption, and a reduction in labor costs of catching and processing. It is impossible to estimate with any accuracy the magnitude of these cost reductions, but in total they would probably have been substantial.

Table 12

Net income from all sources of Norwegian whaling companies,
and blue-whale portion of total, 1956–1963
(in millions of Norwegian kroner)

	A Net income from whaling	B Net income from shipping	C Net income from other sources	D Total net income all sources	E Income from blue whale	F Blue-whale income as percentage of total
1956	35	71	6	112	20	17.8
1957	74	77	8	159	23	14.4
1958	37	83	16	136	18	13.2
1959	37	77	20	134	13	9.7
1960	28	73	22	123	11	8.9
1961	34	99	97	230	15	6.5
1962	−7	103	39	135	5	3.7
1963	15	99	48	162	4	2.5

Sources: Column A, *Statistisk Årbok*, Norges Statistisk Sentralbyrå, Oslo, 1965, p. 110; Columns B, C, and D, *Beretning og Regnskap* of the whaling companies listed in Figure 17; Column E, from Table 11, Column C; Column F, calculated by me.

2) Data on the total net income from all sources of the Norwegian whaling companies, against which the value of the blue whale was measured, are incomplete. There were 2 companies that furnished data about their whaling income but not their income from other sources. They were members of the Federation of Norwegian Whaling Companies (Det Norske Hvalfangstforbund) that submitted annual income data for the industry as a whole to the Norwegian Central Bureau of Statistics (Norges Statistisk Sentralbyrå). These 2 companies were privately owned, and because they did not publish annual reports for stockholders their income from shipping and other nonwhaling sources is unknown. The exact names of these two companies are unknown, but one operated the factory ship *Suderøy* and the other factory ship *Thorshavet*, which ceased whaling operations in 1959 and 1962 respectively. Therefore, the figures on the impor-

tance of the blue whale to the industry for the years 1956 through 1962 are exaggerated because of incomplete data on total income of the companies engaged in pelagic whaling.

3) The Norwegians never killed their proportionate share of blue whales. This may well be the most important reason why the figures on the importance of the blue whale to the Norwegian companies are exaggerated. It will be recalled that the blue-whale portion of the gross income of the industry, in percentage terms, was assumed to be the same as the blue-whale percentage of the cetacean biomass. That assumption implied that the Norwegians caught their proportionate share of the blue whales. They did not. In 1956, for example, the Norwegians should have taken 43 percent of the blue whales because they had 43 percent of the catchers in use in the Antarctic. They actually caught only 35 percent of them, a negative deviation of 19 percent of their proportionate share. The Norwegian proportionate share for each year and what the Norwegians actually did catch each year are listed in Table 13. Column E of Table 13 lists the amount by which the actual catch deviated from the expected share. With the exception of only one season, 1957, the Norwegian industry failed by a substantial margin to obtain its proportionate share of blue whales. This of course means that the blue whale was of even less importance to the Norwegian whaling industry than previously measured.

The failure of the Norwegian industry to kill its proportionate share of blue whales can be explained in part by the ever-present element of luck. It can also be explained by the smaller size of Norwegian catchers relative to those of other nationalities. Bad luck and smaller catchers together cannot account for the almost spectacular failure of the Norwegian industry to get its share of blue whales beginning with the 1960 season. From 1956 through 1959 the Norwegian blue-whale catch varied from minus 2 to minus 19 percent of its proportionate share. This deviation was of about the same order of magnitude as the Norwegian performance on whales of all species during these same years, as shown in Column E of Table 15, on page 122. Suddenly, in 1960, the Norwegians killed 72 percent fewer blue whales than their share, and this apparent failure continued for four seasons. In 1963 the Norwegians killed 97 percent fewer blue whales than could be expected. During the four-year period the Norwegian

Table 13

The deviation of the Norwegian catch from its proportionate share of blue whales in Antarctic pelagic whaling

	A	B		C	D		E
	Total catcher boats	Norwegian catcher boats		Total blue-whale catch	Norwegian blue-whale catch		Deviation of Norwegian blue-whale catch from proportionate share (in percent)
		number	total (in percent)		number	total (in percent)	
1956	257	110	43	1,611	567	35	−19
1957	225	94	42	1,505	623	41	− 2
1958	237	94	40	1,684	578	34	−15
1959	235	93	40	1,191	391	33	−18
1960	220	70	32	1,230	115	9	−72
1961	252	81	32	1,740	138	8	−75
1962	261	71	27	1,118	132	12	−56
1963	201	32	16	947	4	0.5	−97

Sources: Columns A, B, C, and D compiled from annual articles in *Norsk Hvalfangst Tidende*, or *International Whaling Statistics*.

industry killed, on the average, 75 percent fewer blue whales than its proportionate share, but only 3.8 percent fewer of other species. There is only one possible explanation for this far below average catch: Norwegian whalers simply did not bother to try to kill blue whales but concentrated their efforts in areas known to be richer in other species. They were obviously content to take only those blue whales they happened to find while hunting other species. This means that the Norwegian industry knew in advance that it had little need of, and would take very few, blue whales during those years. It is therefore permissable to measure the importance of the blue whale to the industry from the point of view of hindsight, that is, how important was their actual catch of blue whales from 1960 through 1963 rather than their expected proportionate share. The answer is shown in the last two columns of Table 14 where the pertinent calculations have been made.

The actual catch of blue whales did have some significance in terms of whaling income in the 1960 and 1961 seasons as shown in Column E_1 of Table 14. In 1962 when the industry first operated at a net loss the income from the blue whale was of importance, but in 1963 this income represented a mere 0.6 percent. When the actual income from the blue whale is measured against total income of the whaling companies it is of minuscule importance. In 1960 it was less than 3 percent and not even one-tenth of 1 percent in 1963. When it is recalled that these measures do not include any reductions in cost and are based on incomplete industrial income it is obvious that the blue whale was of almost no importance to the Norwegian industry after 1959. The killing could have been stopped, the animal could have survived, and the Norwegian whaling industry would hardly have noticed any economic difference.

— METHOD *B* —

When the International Whaling Commission granted some species partial or complete protection it usually did not forbid an increase in the catch of other species. This permitted the whalers to maintain their cetacean raw material input. In practice this was achieved by the Antarctic quota expressed in blue-whale units. For example,

Table 14

Actual income from the blue whale as a percentage of net whaling income, and of total corporate income of the Norwegian whaling industry, 1960–1963

	A_1* Income from whaling	A_2* Income from all sources	B* Income from blue whale	C Blue-whale catch deviation percentage	D* Blue-whale income minus deviation	E_1 Blue-whale income minus deviation as percentage of whaling income	E_2 Blue-whale income minus deviation as percentage of income from all sources
1960	28	123	11	−72	3.1	11	2.52
1961	34	230	15	−75	3.8	11	1.65
1962	−7	135	5	−56	2.2	22	1.63
1963	15	162	4	−97	0.1	0.6	0.06

* In millions of Norwegian kroner.
Source: Columns A, B, and C, from Table 12, above.

if the Whaling Commission in 1957 had banned the killing of blue whales the 1,507 that would have been spared that season could have been replaced by killing 3,014 more fin whales. In this manner the whaling industry could have produced the same amount of whale products. The Antarctic quota for that season was 14,500 blue-whale units, and the killing of the additional fin whales and no blue whales would have kept the total within the prescribed limit. Such a situation is the theoretical framework for the second inquiry (Method B) into the effect on the Norwegian industry of a ban on the killing of blue whales. This inquiry involves a determination of the cost of catching the additional fin whales; there would be no change in gross revenue because the total production of whale products would remain the same.

This method of inquiry should not be interpreted as meaning that a shift to fin whales was a permanent solution to the problem of whale shortage facing the industry. It is undertaken merely to find out if the shift could have been made in order to spare the blue whale the threat of extinction. The fin whale during these years was also heavily hunted but was far from facing extinction. The early years of a shift to fin whales could have been used to cut back on catching capacity that was plainly necessary if the stocks of all species were to be saved.

The first step in this inquiry is to determine how many blue whales the industry could have expected to kill, because that is how the industry had to view at anytime the prospect of a ban on the killing of blue whales. Obviously the whalers could not know in advance exactly how many they could kill in a coming season, but they did know that almost without exception the catch of the species decreased annually. Therefore, the actual total catch of blue whales for any given year will be used as the basis for the inquiry. However, Norwegian whalers well knew that their catcher boats were, on average, inferior in tonnage and horsepower to those of other nations. In 1960, for example, the Norwegian catchers averaged 600 tons; the corresponding figures for other nationalities were: England, 544; Netherlands, 712; Japan, 600; and the Soviet Union, 801. The below-average size of Norwegian catchers resulted in a below-average catch of whales for the Norwegian industry as shown in Table 15.

Table 15   Deviation of the Norwegian catch of all whales from its percentile catcher share, 1950–1963

	A	B Norwegian catcher boats		C	D Norwegian whales killed (all species)		E	F
	Total catcher boats	number	total (in percent)	Total whales killed (all species)	number	total (in percent)	Norwegian catch deviation from percentile catcher share	Norway's expected share —catcher share minus average catch deviation (in percent)
1950	216	119	55	29,017	15,556	53	− 4	52
1951	239	124	52	31,179	15,873	50	− 4	49
1952	268	132	49	32,566	14,763	45	− 8	46
1953	230	95	41	28,325	10,381	37	−10	38
1954	206	100	49	31,215	13,632	44	−10	46
1955	233	101	43	34,388	13,428	39	− 9	40
1956	257	110	43	35,489	13,371	38	−12	40
1957	225	94	42	32,941	14,008	43	+ 2	39
1958	237	94	40	35,997	13,289	36	−10	38
1959	235	93	40	36,261	13,292	37	− 8	38
1960	220	70	32	36,355	10,656	29	− 9	30
1961	252	81	32	38,810	12,490	32	0	30
1962	261	71	27	37,358	9,304	27	0	25
1963	201	32	16	30,159	4,582	15	− 6	15
							Average − 6.2	

Source: Columns A, B, C, and D, *International Whaling Statistics*, LIV (1965), 28.

The Norwegian proportion of the total catcher fleet declined steadily, as shown in Column B of Table 15, from 55 percent in 1950 to 16 percent in 1963. At the same time its share of whales caught declined from 53 percent to 15 percent. It is apparent that the Norwegian catch almost always deviated negatively from its proportionate share of catchers. In other words the Norwegians had *x* percent of the catchers, but they caught less than *x* percent of the whales. In only one season out of fourteen did the Norwegians catch more than their share of whales and then by only 2 percent. In nearly every other year the deviation was negative, and it averaged out to a long-term deviation of minus 6.2 percent. (This means that Norway caught 6.2 percent fewer whales than expected based on the relative numerical size of its fleet.) The relative size of the Norwegian fleet, therefore, reduced by 6.2 percent gives the share of whales that the Norwegian industry could have expected in any season. This has been calculated and is shown in Column F of Table 15. The Norwegian share as calculated was based on its performance on all whales rather than on just the blue whale or any other single species. By using the catch of all species the elements of luck and annual variation have been held to a minimum. Had the expected share been calculated on the basis of performance on one species the results would have been too erratic from the use of too small a sample. There is no logical reason to suppose that the expected share as calculated is not applicable to any single species, and therefore the number of blue whales that the Norwegian industry could have expected to catch is shown in the following calculation.

	Total Blue Whales Killed		Norway's Expected Share (in percent)		Blue Whales Expected
1956	1,611	×	40	=	644
1957	1,505	×	39	=	587
1958	1,684	×	38	=	640
1959	1,191	×	38	=	453
1960	1,230	×	30	=	369
1961	1,740	×	30	=	522
1962	1,118	×	25	=	280
1963	947	×	15	=	142

A ban on the killing of blue whales would have forced the companies to kill more fin whales in order to make up for the loss in raw material. Since the Norwegians were primarily concerned with the production of whale oil the blue/fin oil-producing ratio governs the increased number of fin whales required. Despite the blue-whale unit that classified 2 fin whales as the oil producing equivalent of 1 blue whale the actual ratio was 1.7 fin whales to 1 blue whale (see Chapter IV, n. 9). Therefore, for every 100 blue whales spared 170 fin whales, or 70 additional whales, would be required to maintain the same oil production. The additional number of whales required for the years 1956–63 is shown by the following calculation.

Blue Whales Expected				Additional Whales Needed
1956	644	× 0.7	=	451
1957	587	×	=	411
1958	640	×	=	448
1959	453	×	=	317
1960	369	×	=	258
1961	522	×	=	365
1962	280	×	=	196
1963	142	×	=	99

The increased cost of catching the additional fin whales cannot, unfortunately, be determined with absolute accuracy. No single item of operating costs was ever published by any whaling company. Only the total operating costs of the entire industry were available from the Norwegian Central Bureau of Statistics which obtained them from the Federation of Norwegian Whaling Companies. Nevertheless, an approximation of the cost of catching additional fin whales can be obtained that will permit a reasonably valid comparison of that cost with net whaling and corporate income. The approximation is obtained by estimating the labor catching cost per whale.

The baleen whales taken in Antarctic pelagic whaling were all fast swimmers, about 20 knots when pursued, and the amount of time and effort required to kill one did not differ very much from species to species. This was not true of the slow-swimming sperm whale, but this species constituted a small proportion of the total catch. Therefore, the average catching cost per whale will make possible a calculation of the approximate increased cost of catching additional fin whales. The only cost data available are average wages paid to all employees of the floating-factory expeditions, used in Figure 14, and these are used as the basis for estimating the increased cost of catching additional fin whales. Specifically, estimated catching cost per whale per season is obtained on the basis of total wages paid to the crews of the catcher boats and the total number of whales they killed. This method of estimating catching cost per whale has 3 theoretical shortcomings that must be understood before the validity of the method can be accepted.

1) Disregard of other operating costs. To estimate catching cost per whale solely on the basis of wages paid to catcher-boat crews disregards certain material operating costs of catching. These are, for the most part, costs of harpoons, lines, and fuel consumption for catching and towing carcasses to the factory ship. Because there are no available data or literature on these costs they can not be measured. Total wages paid to catcher-boat crews, however, include payment for the three to three and a half months of noncatching time required to take the boats from Norway to the Antarctic and back home again. Such noncatching time represents about half the total wages paid, and, therefore, it is assumed that these noncatching wages are roughly the equivalent of the equipment operating costs of catching. Fixed costs of operating are not considered because most of them, such as insurance, hull and machinery maintenance, or provisions for the crew, would not be significantly affected by the catching of slightly more or fewer whales.

2) Possible discrepancy between catcher-boat and factory-ship wages. The use of average wages paid to total crews of factory expeditions to determine total wages paid to catcher crews assumes that the average wages paid to each were the same. A lack of data on the precise makeup of the crews of these ships leaves no alternative to the assumption. Several factors seem to indicate, however, that the assumption is a reasonably safe one. First, the crew of a catcher is a miniature version of that of a factory ship, including men in many ratings from mess boy to engineer to captain. Second, basic wage

rates on catcher boats were about 10 percent lower than they were on factory ships, but this was counterbalanced by a small bonus given to all crewmen on the catchers for every whale killed. This would tend to equalize earnings, and these bonuses are included in the available data on average wages. Finally, the number of officer ratings on the catchers was reduced below those on factory ships which would tend to maintain a similar ratio of low to high ratings on the two types of vessel. This is not certain, however, and it may be that on the catchers there was a higher ratio of officers to men, but this cannot be determined. In any case catcher-boat officers had wage rates about 10 percent lower than those of officers of factory ships, but they too earned a small bonus for every whale killed.

3) Estimation of average size of catcher crews. In estimating the catching cost per whale on the basis of total catcher wages and total whales taken by the Norwegian fleets a crucial question arises concerning the number of men employed on the catchers. Strange as it may seem, there is no available data on either the size of the catcher crews or the floating-factory crews. The only available data give total men employed per season per expedition, that is, the grand total for each factory ship and its fleet of catchers. Nevertheless a very close approximation is possible based on the following individual sources.

Ash, the expert already cited on body weight of whales, was for many years chief chemist with the British factory ship *Balaena*. He writes:

> In 1945 the small catchers \had about 12–14 as crew with the British expeditions; and as the catchers were manned exclusively by Norwegians I think you can assume that it was the same for Norwegian expeditions. Later, with larger craft, the figure moved upwards to around 18 for ex-corvettes etc. Diesel engined boats tended to have one or two extra in the engine room.[5]

On the same subject an official of one of the Norwegian companies writes:

> Personally I think the best thing to do is to calculate with a manning of 20 crewmembers on each catcher. This is a fairly good average. Some of the larger vessels had up to 22 men on board and the smaller ones about 18 men. As an example I can mention that our own expedition [*Sir James Clark Ross*] in the season 1962–63 had seven catchers with 137 men aboard, averaging 19.5.[6]

Captain Georg A. Carlsen of the catcher boat *Globe 14*, seen in Plate XIX, stated that the crew of his 613-ton vessel was 22 men.[7]

It is evident that there is a general correlation between catcher size and number of crew, with larger catchers having larger crews. The correlation is not perfect as seen by comparing the average Rosshavet crew with that of Captain Carlsen. The Rosshavet fleet in 1963 averaged 19.5 men on catchers that averaged 622 tons. Captain Carlsen's 613-ton catcher had a crew of 22, which gave it a somewhat higher

Plate XIX   Catcher Globe 14. *The vessel is shown at arrival in its home port, Larvik, Norway, at the end of an Antarctic whaling season. The 22-man crew of this 613-ton catcher consisted of 1 gunner-captain, 2 mates, 1 radio-radar operator, 5 seamen, 1 cook, 1 steward, 2 messboys, 3 engineers, 1 oiler, 2 assistant engineers, and 3 firemen.* Courtesy of Captain G. Anker Carlsen.

man/tonnage ratio. It would seem that catchers of over 600 tons generally had a crew of 20 men and for purposes of this study such is assumed to have been the case. Further, it is assumed that catchers smaller in size than 600 tons had a crew of 19 and those below 550 tons a crew of 18 men. Table 16 lists the average tonnage of the Norwegian fleets and the averages for the fleets of other pelagic whaling nations.

It is now possible to estimate the increased cost of catching the additional number of fin whales required to make up for a total loss of blue-whale raw material. The data pertinent to this calculation are given in Table 17. The calculation is quite simple: number of catchers times average crew per catcher gives total catcher crewmen; total crewmen times their average wages gives total catcher wages; these wages divided by the number of whales killed gives catching cost

Table 16

Average tonnage of catcher fleets,
specifically those attached to the Norwegian factory ships *

	1957	1958	1959	1960	1961	1962	1963
Norway	549	563	564	600	585	592	688
Suderøy	506	506	530	c.w.†			
Sir J. C. Ross	611	531	611	629	611	629	662
Norhval	545	545	545	595	579	567	c.w.
Pelagos	564	564	564	568	568	568	c.w.
Thorshøvdi	579	624	607	639	612	594	704
Thorshavet	513	567	567	595	572	572	712
Thorshammer	528	552	548	603	577	582	c.w.
Kosmos III	567	559	549	578	573	c.w.	
Kosmos IV	522	531	556	594	581	627	673
United Kingdom	555	533	n.a.	544	548	550	654
The Netherlands	666	662	n.a.	712	709	706	701
Japan	535	587	n.a.	600	603	602	609
USSR	375	437	n.a.	801	813	821	823

* Data for the year 1956 not available (n.a.).
† Ceased whaling.
Source: Compiled from annual articles on whaling materiel in *Norsk Hvalfangst Tidende.*

Table 17

Estimated cost of catching additional fin whales

	A Catchers	B Average crew per catcher	C Total crew-men	D Average wages (N. kr.)	E Total catcher wages (N. kr.)	F Total whales killed	G Catching cost per whale (Wages per whale) (N. kr.)	H Additional fin whales needed	J Estimated increased cost of catching fin whales (N. kr.)
1956	110	18	1,980	10,986	21,752,280	13,371	1,626	451	733,326
1957	94	18	1,692	13,288	22,483,296	14,008	1,605	411	659,655
1958	94	19	1,786	12,533	22,383,938	13,289	1,684	448	754,432
1959	93	19	1,767	12,012	21,225,204	13,292	1,596	317	505,932
1960	70	19	1,330	11,419	15,187,270	10,656	1,425	258	367,650
1961	81	19	1,539	13,827	21,279,753	12,490	1,703	365	621,595
1962	71	19	1,349	13,657	18,423,293	9,304	1,980	196	388,080
1963	32	20	640	13,948	8,926,720	4,582	1,948	99	192,852

Source: *International Whaling Statistics*, LIV (1965), 28; and sources cited in other tables and figures.

per whale, in Column G; and, catching cost per whale times the number of additional fin whales needed gives the estimated increased cost of catching them, Column J. This is the increased cost the Norwegian whaling industry would have had to bear if it had been forced to cease killing blue whales and allowed to make up the raw material loss by catching additional fin whales.

It is enlightening indeed to measure this increased cost against the net income from whaling and the net income from all sources of the whaling companies. This is done in Table 18.

In terms of net whaling income the cost of shifting to fin whales would have resulted in a decrease of from 0.89 percent to 2.09 percent, Column c_1, in every year but one. Only in 1962 when the industry operated at a net loss would the cost of catching fin whales have reduced profits by as much as 5 percent.

A spokesman for the Norwegian whaling industry on reading these lines might counter with the argument that it could not know in ad-

Table 18

Estimated cost of catching additional fin whales in terms of net income from whaling, and of total industrial income, 1956–1963

	A *	B *	C *	c_1	c_2
		Net income	Estimated cost of catching additional fin whales		
	Net Income from whaling	from all sources including whaling		as percent of net whaling income	as percent of total industrial income
1956	35,000	112,000	733	2.09	0.65
1957	74,000	159,000	660	0.89	0.41
1958	37,000	136,000	754	2.04	0.55
1959	37,000	134,000	506	1.37	0.38
1960	28,000	123,000	368	1.31	0.30
1961	34,000	230,000	622	1.83	0.27
1962	−7,000	135,000	388	5.54	0.29
1963	15,000	162,000	193	1.29	0.12

* In thousands of Norwegian kroner.
Sources: *International Whaling Statistics; Statistisk Årbok;* and *Beretning og Regnskap.*

vance what price it would receive for its whale oil even if it could accurately estimate the cost of a shift to fin whales. Such an argument would be specious indeed if used as an excuse not to save the blue whale. Not a single Norwegian whaling company kept its fleet at home after World War II because of what appeared to be a low price of whale oil. To have done so would almost certainly have meant an end to its whaling activities because its men would have had to find other work and subsequently would probably have been unavailable for whaling. The argument of unknown whale-oil price as a reason for not wanting to risk some increased cost of catching fin whales in order to spare the blue was of even decreasing validity after 1960. At that time the Norwegian production of meat for pet foods and for sale to Japanese companies on the whaling grounds began to increase substantially. Sales to these markets were carried out on a contract basis with price and quantity stipulated in advance. This of course made it possible for the whaling industry to estimate its future income with more precision than in previous years. The industry knew better than ever that its future in no way depended on the blue whale.

The increased cost of shifting to fin whales compared to the net income of the whaling companies from all sources is shown in Column c_2 of Table 18. The cost of catching the fin whales would have ranged from 0.65 to 0.12 percent of total net income. Such a decrease in net income is so minuscule that no sane person could want to avoid it at the risk of exterminating the blue whale. Yet the Norwegian whaling industry could not have been ignorant of how little importance the blue whale was to its total income. In every year since 1957 the net income of the whaling companies from shipping and other sources was three or more times greater than that from whaling. The shipping was carried out on a lease and charter basis whereby income for any given year was largely known in advance. This permitted the companies to estimate with a high degree of accuracy their future income. They could not have failed to arrive at a very precise estimate of how little it would have cost them to spare the blue whale.

The significant decrease in net revenue that the Norwegian companies would have had if they had spared the blue whale was even less than has been estimated here. It will be recalled that the total net income of the whaling companies is incomplete because two privately owned companies did not publish annual reports and their income from nonwhaling remains unknown. A more important reason why the cost of sparing blue whales would have been even less is due to the failure of the Norwegian companies to obtain their expected share of blue whales from 1960 through 1963. (It was pointed out in Method *A* that the Norwegians avoided areas rich in blue whales beginning in 1960). In calculating the cost of shifting to fin whales, Method *B,* it was shown that in 1963, for example, the Norwegians could have expected a catch of 142 blue whales. They actually caught only 4. The cost of shifting to fin whales in that year would have meant catching only 3 more whales, the cost of which would have been too minute to calculate. The only year when the cost of a shift to fin whales would have had any significant impact on whaling income was 1962 when the net loss would have been increased by 5.5 percent. This was based on an expected blue-whale catch of 380; only 132 were caught. To have substituted fin whales that year would have required 92 additional whales ($132 \times 0.7 = 92.4$). Catching cost per whale that year was N.kr. 1,980, or a total increased catching cost of N.kr. 182,160. This would have increased the net whaling loss of N.kr. 7 million by only 2.6 percent and would have reduced total corporate income of 135 million by 0.13 percent.

No matter what method is used to measure the cost to the Norwegian whaling industry of granting protection to the blue whale the conclusion is the same. The industry would have suffered no economic hardship worthy of mention. Spokesmen for the industry misrepresented facts and told half truths. Their claims were believed, and they were allowed to continue killing blue whales for an insignificant economic convenience.

The roundabout, rather complicated methods used to reach these conclusions are probably as much disliked by you as by me. Simpler and more precise methods could be used to measure the cost of sparing the blue whale, but they would depend on the cooperation of the whaling companies. The latter obviously knew their own catching costs, the exact size of their catcher crews, and their wages but they refused to divulge them to me. Indeed, the whaling companies still operating in 1966 were so opposed to my research that they refused me permission even to enter their offices in Sandefjord, Norway. They stated that only written correspondence would be acceptable, but even letters to them remained unanswered. Their actions are understandable. An accused can hardly be expected to publicize the motive and details of his crime.

The Norwegian whaling companies in association owned and published the *Norsk Hvalfangst Tidende* (The Norwegian Whaling Gazette) the only publication in the world devoted exclusively to commercial whaling. After a fifty-seven-year history the last issue of this journal came out in December, 1968. The editorial announcing that sad fact duly thanked its subscribers, its contributors, and its advertisers for their financial support during the years. What did it say for the whales that had died by the hundreds of thousands to bring vast wealth to companies that made Sandefjord the richest per capita city in Norway? Not a word.

THE JAPANESE WHALING INDUSTRY AND THE BLUE WHALE

The attempt to evaluate the importance of the blue whale to the Japanese industry should ideally follow the methods used for the Norwegian industry. Unfortunately the barely adequate economic and financial data available about Norwegian companies seem almost copious when compared to data on Japanese companies. The paucity of information about the Japanese is so extreme that it merits some comment.

The annual reports of Japanese companies differ drastically from those of Norway. A Japanese investigator, a professor of economic geography at a well-known Japanese university, engaged by me to obtain and translate data about the Japanese whaling companies replied a year after he began work, "These three companies are very big and complex, literally General Foods companies, ranging to the professional baseball team. It is impossible to figure out even the profit of their whaling divisions from the annual reports."

When that and yet another Japanese investigator were unable to obtain basic data, I sought help from the American Fisheries Attaché at the United States Embassy in Tokyo. His efforts were no more successful but he did obtain a partial explanation for the lack of pertinent data. He wrote:

> I have on a number of occasions discussed your request with the officials of the companies but all three were reluctant to provide such information. Finally last week Taiyo [Gyogyo] told me that they regretted but such information was considered by them to be highly confidential and that they could not make it available.[8]

The nearly complete absence of pertinent economic data on the Japanese whaling companies requires a radically different method of estimating the importance to them of the blue whale. Fortunately there are some available data on prices received by the Japanese companies for their major whale products. This will make it possible to judge whether the Japanese pelagic whaling industry was more or less remunerative than the Norwegian, although not in absolute terms.

It was previously shown that the Japanese industry used whale meat as meat for human consumption rather than a poor source of oil. This practice enabled the whalers of Japan to earn more than twice as much for the meat alone as the Norwegians got from an entire whale. By using the blubber and bones as the source of oil the Japanese obtained 3.06 times as much revenue from a whale as did the Norwegians. On this basis a Japanese revenue whale was 3 times greater than a Norwegian whale. If labor costs were the largest item in the total operating costs of the Japanese, as they were with the Norwegian, it is enlightening to compare the revenue-whale-per-man ratio of the 2 industries. This has been calculated, in Table 19, and the results show that the revenue whales-per-man in the Japanese fleets averaged 4.35 compared with 2.91 for the Norwegians. This means that the 1.45 whales caught per man by the Japanese brought 49.5 percent more revenue than the 2.91 whales-per-man caught by the Norwegians. Before assuming that the Japanese industry therefore had a more favorable operating budget, there are several factors that must be considered because of their bearing on the subject.

It will be noted in Table 19 that the number of whales killed by the Japanese per worker was consistently lower than that for the Norwegians. This was largely due to the additional manpower needed by the Japanese companies to work the freezer ships that carried the

Table 19

Whales per man and revenue whales per man taken by Japanese and Norwegian fleets, 1956–1963

	Men employed	Whales killed	Whales per man	Revenue whales-per-man
		JAPAN		
1956	4,071	6,462	1.59 × 3 * = 4.77	
1957	6,486	8,093	1.25	3.75
1958	8,402	11,763	1.40	4.20
1959	7,974	12,558	1.57	4.71
1960	8,100	12,359	1.53	4.59
1961	9,680	13,592	1.40	4.20
1962	9,748	14,351	1.47	4.41
1963	9,676	13,617	1.41	4.23
			1.45 Average	4.35
		NORWAY		
1956	4,952	13,371	2.91 × 1 = 2.91	
1957	4,367	14,008	3.21	3.21
1958	4,396	13,289	3.02	3.02
1959	4,377	13,292	3.04	3.04
1960	3,837	10,656	2.77	2.77
1961	4,094	12,490	3.05	3.05
1962	3,503	9,304	2.66	2.66
1963	1,741	4,582	2.63	2.63
			2.91 Average	2.91

Sources: Men employed tabulated from annual articles in *Norsk Hvalfangst Tidende*. Catch data from *International Whaling Statistics*, LIV (1965), 28.

* The Japanese received 3.06 times as much revenue from a whale as did the Norwegians.

meat back to Japan. It is not safe to assume that the cost of using these extra vessels automatically canceled out the price advantage of the whale meat. These ships were ordinary freighters with a small crew of unskilled workers. None of these ships had to spend the entire whaling season in the Antarctic; they would simply, one at a time, join a factory ship, load up with meat and return home. Unfortunately the cost of these operations is unknown, but it obviously did detract somewhat from the price advantage of Japanese whale meat.

The whale-meat price on which the revenue whales-per-man were based were producer prices. The 3 Japanese pelagic whaling companies that produced and sold this meat were primarily fishing companies, with whaling interests, and they owned and operated retail fish shops in the major Japanese cities. In these shops they sold some of their own whale meat at retail prices. The mark-up must have resulted in increased profit, and it must have increased the Japanese/Norwegian revenue-whales-per-man ratio. Unfortunately there is no way to even guess at the magnitude of this advantage.

The various species of whales caught in the Antarctic had slightly different proportions of major body components, but in one species the quality was noticeably different. The sei whale, the smallest of the large baleen species, is well known for its high quality meat and thin blubber that produces little oil. As the supply of large baleen whales decreased the catch of sei whales increased, and this placed Japanese whalers in a decidedly advantageous position. The meat of the sei whale was of such superior quality that it must have sold at higher prices. Unfortunately there is no specific information available about this, and it would therefore be futile to attempt to measure the market advantage to Japan of an increased catch of this species. It must be concluded, however, that the increasing scarcity of blue whales and fin whales was less of a disadvantage to the Japanese than it was to the Norwegians because of the availability of sei whales.

The calculation of whales-per-man caught by the fleets of Japan and Norway was based on all species of whales including the sperm whale. The Norwegians could not use the meat of sperm whales and simply dumped it overboard. The Japanese derived several remunerative products from this meat, including frozen meat, salted meat, and meat extract. In 1964, for example, the salted meat and meat extract produced by Japanese Antarctic whalers from sperm whales brought identical prices as the same products produced from baleen whales.[9] During this same season of 1964, Japanese pelagic whalers caught 4,598 blue-whale units in baleen whales and 4,706 sperm whales. The sperm whales caught by the Japanese whalers provided them with an extra advantage over their Norwegian competitors. This would indicate that the factor of 3 (rounded from 3.06) used to determine the Japanese revenue whale should have been greater during those years when the catch of large baleen whales was declining and the catch of sperm whales remained nearly constant. Again because of a lack of precise information on the price of meat and meat products by species it is impossible to determine the correct modification of the revenue factor.

The use of the measures *revenue whale* and *revenue whale-per-man* are not *per se* an adequate way of comparing the operating economics of the Japanese and Norwegian whaling industries unless something is known about their respective operating cost structure. Unfortunately the Japanese companies are even more secretive about their costs than about the prices of their products. But in view of the heavily unionized labor market in Norway and the higher prices of operating equipment of Scandinavian and European origin used on Norwegian ships, it would seem impossible for the Japanese whaling industry to have higher operating costs than the Norwegians. If that is correct, and indeed even if their operating costs were the same, then the Japanese revenue whale factor of 3, or the Japanese revenue-whale per-man superiority of 49.5 percent would indicate that the Japanese whaling industry was in a much better economic position than was the Norwegian.

Spokesmen for the Japanese whaling companies often complained that their industry had large unamortized investments in the fleets they developed in the mid-1950s. This claim was widely accepted despite the absence of any financial data to prove its veracity.[10] It was the favorite reason given by the Japanese whalers for not wanting to decrease the catch of whales. If they could not meet those amortization payments economic hardship would result. This claim cannot be accepted until the capital costs of the Japanese fleets are made known as well as the operating profit margin that could be used to amortize those costs. Both of these the Japanese whaling companies have consistently refused to divulge. Perhaps the facts were kept secret because the claim was false. Indeeed there is evidence to suggest that the high capital costs of the Japanese fleets were less burdensome than their owners claimed. The evidence concerns factory ships and catcher boats.

The largest fleet of factory expeditions sent by Japan to the Antarctic was 7. Of these 7 factory ships, 2 were built in Japan in 1951, 1 was built in Japan before World War II, and 4 were second-hand vessels bought from companies when they ceased whaling operations. The companies were: 1 South African, 1 Panamanian, 1 British, and 1 Norwegian. Of the 7 factory ships the amortization costs may have been heaviest for the 4 used vessels because they were used a shorter length of time. However, their purchase prices were kept secret and no other financial details concerning them were ever made known; their amortization costs may or may not have been burdensome. It is certain, in any case, that even if the purchase price of those ships was high it must have been much less than either their original construction cost or the cost the Jananese would have had to bear had they purchased new ships.

A second factor that casts doubt on the validity of the Japanese claim of high amortization costs is the extent to which the Japanese pelagic whaling industry was able to use their Antarctic fleets for North Pacific whaling during the Northern Hemisphere summer. A crucial factor in the cost of any capital investment is the length of time the item remains in productive use. It will be recalled that Norwegian catchers and factory ships had to remain idle for about five months every year. This was not the case with the Japanese fleets, but the Japanese whalers did not explain this advantage they enjoyed. The North Pacific Ocean is much richer in cetacean resources than is the North Atlantic because it is larger and because it was subjected to less intense pelagic whaling during the last century and early decades of the present century. This made it possible for Japanese whaling companies to keep many of their vessels in operation for the entire year. The extent of this full-time utilization of whaling vessels differed somewhat between factory ships and catchers.

Regulations applicable to pelagic whaling nations, members of the International Whaling Commission, forbade the use of a factory ship for the catching of baleen whales elsewhere in the world if it had been used for that purpose in the same year in the Antarctic. There was no regulation against the use of such factory ships for the catching of sperm whales elsewhere, and thus Japan could use a factory ship from the Antarctic to hunt sperm whales in the North Pacific in the summer. This was done on occasion, but not often. There was also no regulation against the use of a factory ship in the Antarctic if it had been used in baleen whaling elsewhere in the same year. This too Japanese whalers did on occasion. North Pacific pelagic whaling was not as important as operations in the Antarctic, and the Japanese normally used 3 factory ships there in the summer. Of the 3, 1 was generally used to hunt sperm whales after its return from a baleen season in the Antarctic. Such a ship was most often operated jointly by the 3 companies that engaged in Antarctic whaling. The other 2 factory ships used in North Pacific whaling were old ships used exclusively for that purpose.[11] The use of 1 factory ship from the Antarctic during the Northern Hemisphere summer may not have been an outstanding advantage to the Japanese, but it was an advantage never enjoyed by the Norwegians.

The use of catchers in North Pacific summer whaling after the close of the Antarctic season was much more important to the Japanese whaling companies than the use of one factory ship in summer whaling. On the Japanese home islands and on the Ryukyu Islands there are about 20 coastal whaling stations that operate during the summer months. There was no regulation forbidding the subsequent use there of catcher boats that had been used in Antarctic whaling and consequently the Japanese companies had the opportunity of keeping many of them in operation on a nearly year-round basis. Table 20 points out the specific use of the catcher boats used in the Antarctic by the 3 Japanese companies from the summer of 1963 to the end of the 1964 summer. It will be noted that of the 82 catchers used by Japan during 1963/64 Antarctic season, 40 were used in the North Pacific in the summer of 1963 and 37 in the summer of 1964. Therefore nearly 50 percent of the 1964 Antarctic catcher fleet was used on a year-round basis. This was a very great advantage enjoyed by the Japanese whaling companies, and although the precise financial advantage cannot be determined it unquestionably increased the return on investment capital and reduced the burden of amortization. Japanese whalers never mentioned this advantage either.

Table 20

Utilization intensity of the Japanese catcher fleet, 1963–1964

	Summer, 1963 North Pacific	1963/64 Antarctic	Summer, 1964 North Pacific	Total catcher voyages	Utilization percentages
Taiyo Gyogyo & Co.—34 catchers	13	34	12	59	174
Kyokuyo Hogei & Co.—22 catchers	11	22	10	43	195
Nippon Suisan & Co.—26 catchers	16	26	15	57	219
Total by season	40	82	37		
Total, 1963–1964				159	193

Source: My tabulations from continuing articles on catching materiel in *Norsk Hvalfangst Tidende* (December, 1964; January, September, and October, 1965).

The use of nearly half the Japanese catcher fleet for year-round whaling may also have resulted in decreased operating costs, specifically labor. Norwegian crewmen were paid on a basis of seven months, but on a scale that had to take into consideration five months of unemployment. Japanese crewmen who worked year round on catcher boats and factory ships could hardly make claim for wages to cover long periods of unemployment. Here again is an advantage enjoyed by Japanese whaling companies about which nothing was said or written.

In concluding the attempt to compare the operating and capital costs of the Japanese and Norwegian whaling companies it seems virtually certain that the Japanese industry must have had higher operating profits as a result of the several advantages derived from whale meat. As to the capital accounts of the two industries, the Japanese had distinct advantage from being able to use many of their vessels for whaling in both the Northern and Southern Hemispheres. In summary, it does not seem likely that the Japanese industry could have been in a worse economic or financial position than the Norwegian, and indeed it was probably better. Thus it appears safe to conclude that the Japanese had no greater need for blue whales during the critical years 1956–63 than did the Norwegians. Japanese whalers, like the Norwegians, did not tell the whole truth about their financial conditions. One suspects that they too were willing to continue killing blue whales for the sake of an insignificant economic convenience.

It will be recalled that the Norwegian whaling companies were also engaged in shipping which by the 1950s greatly surpassed the importance of whaling as a source of profit. In a similar manner the Japanese companies were primarily fishing companies with whaling operations of distinctly minor importance. This is shown in Table 21 where the gross income from whaling and from all other sources are listed. Whaling revenue normally represented less than 20 percent of total revenue and was declining slightly in the 1960s. Furthermore the whaling income included the production from North Pacific and domestic coastal operations that together represented about one-third of the total whaling income. Antarctic pelagic whaling, therefore, represented about 10 to 15 percent of the total income from all sources of

Table 21

Gross income* of the Japanese whaling industry from whale products and all its other sources, 1956–1963

	Gross income from whale products (Including North Pacific and coastal stations)	Gross income from all sources
1956	n.a.	58,162
1957	14,980	72,198
1958	17,672	79,287
1959	19,419	92,143
1960	20,394	111,376
1961	24,676	140,327
1962	21,420	152,502
1963	27,005	171,222

Source: Information supplied to my Japanese investigators by: 1) chief of Accounting Section, Nippon Suisan Inc.; 2) chief of the Fishery Section, Kyokuyo Hogei Inc., and 3) vice chief of the Whaling Department, Taiyo Gyogyo Inc.

* In millions of Yen.

the Japanese whaling companies. This was about the same order of magnitude as the whaling income of the Norwegian companies. Unfortunately it is not possible to compare with precision the role of whaling in the Japanese and Norwegian companies on the basis of gross income of the former and net income of the latter. The two are nonetheless sufficiently analogous as a guide to understanding, and it therefore seems likely that on a total corporate basis the blue whale was of no more significance to the Japanese than it was to the Norwegian companies.

No economic hardship of significance would have been suffered by the Norwegian whaling industry if the killing of blue whales had ceased after 1956. The smaller British industry operated under identical cost and price structures as did the Norwegians. The one Dutch company had government guarantees of minimum profit and dividends. The Japanese whaling industry was in no greater need of blue whales than was the Norwegian. Soviet whaling fleets do not even have to produce any profit at all in the Western sense of the term. Why then did the blue whale have to die?

You delight in laying down laws, Yet you delight more in breaking them.
                                                    KHALIL GIBRAN

VI

NATIONAL WHALING POLICIES

THE ACTION OF WHALERS ON THE SEAS can be controlled only to the extent that their individual governments so decide. The control may be direct, exercised by government-appointed inspectors to enforce national or international regulations. The control may be indirect, resulting from the government's power to influence the formulation of whaling regulations in the International Whaling Commission, or to accept or reject any regulations that the Commission may adopt. My aim here is to elucidate the two extremes of governmental control, that is, the case of a nation willing to exercise very strict control over its whalers and the case of a nation which gave its whalers nearly complete freedom of action. This elucidation is necessary because it was the very existence of such differences in national attitudes toward conservation and control that the International Whaling Commission was unable to protect any species of whale from overexploitation. The efforts to resolve those differences in the Whaling Commission are examined in the following chapter.

The two nations examined here in detail are Norway and Japan. Norway has been chosen to illustrate a nation willing to exercise close control over the actions of its whalers. Norway was the most restrictive in this regard, and it was also the first country in the world to adopt restrictive whaling regulations through legislative action, regulations which ultimately became the model for similar legislation in other countries, especially Great Britain, and in the International Whaling Commission itself. Japan has been chosen to illustrate a nation exercising very weak control over its whalers. This choice was made not only because Japan did not choose to further cetacean conservation by restricting the actions of its whalers but also because there was no better alternative. The Soviet Union, the only other pelagic whaling nation of importance, does not make available to foreigners any information on the subject.

NORWEGIAN WHALING POLICY

The very rapid and extensive development of the pelagic whaling industry that followed the invention of the stern slipway in 1925 raised concern for the future of the world's stock of whales. A meeting of the League of Nations in Paris discussed the problem in 1927 and decided that international regulation of the industry was needed. No international regulation resulted from the meeting, but the Norwegian government did take unilateral action. In June, 1929, the Norwegian Storting (national legislature) passed an Act on the Taking of Baleen Whales. Under the provisions of this act the government was given nearly complete power to control its whaling industry on the high seas. Specific conservation measures were written into the law whereby it was forbidden to kill Right whales, a calf of any species, or a female of any species accompanied by a calf. Minimum lengths were established for all species. The government was empowered to prohibit whaling in tropical and subtropical waters and to prescribe standards for the utilization of whale carcasses. Henceforth all Norwegian whaling ships were required to keep accurate, daily catch journals that were to be inspected by customs authorities when they returned home. Every factory ship was required to have on board a government-appointed inspector whose task was to verify compliance with all regulations; any infractions were to be reported at once to the captain and ultimately to the Minister of Commerce.[1] Later amendments to the act in the mid-1930s required 2 inspectors on factory ships to ensure twenty-four-hour surveillance.

There were also administrative provisions of the Whaling Act of 1929 that were of particular importance to further development of governmental control of the industry and to the future of the industry itself. The Whaling Act established the now famous Hvalråd, or Whaling Council, to advise the government on all matters pertaining to whaling and whaling control, both national and international. The Whaling Council was composed of scientists and members of the Ministries of Industry and Foreign Affairs. A few years later the Whaling Council was expanded to include a representative of the industry. The chairman of the Whaling Council, who by law could not be the industrial representative, usually represented Norway at international whaling conferences and later became the Norwegian commissioner to the International Whaling Commission. In addition the Statens Institutt for Hvalforskning (State Institute for Whale Research) was established to furnish the Whaling Council with scientific advice. It was authorized to carry on research with cooperation from whaling companies and their catch records and with the state inspectors on the factory ships (the director of the Institute was always a member of the Council). Finally, the Whaling Act of 1929 established the Komitéen for Internasjonal Hvalfangststatistiskk to act as a central clearing-house for all statistics pertaining to whaling, pelagic and coastal, from all whaling nations.[2] The major work of this committee is the compilation and annual publication of the *International Whaling Statistics*.

The Whaling Act of 1929 even before any amendments gave the Norwegian government power to regulate its whalers greater than any other whaling nation received to the present day. For example, Japan, the world's most important whaling nation in 1969, still has no independent scientific body to advise it on whaling matters. Nevertheless, the Norwegian legislature passed significant amendments to its Whaling Act of 1929. In 1939 the minimum-length requirement for blue whales was increased from 60 feet to 65 feet. This may seem an ineffectual conservation requirement in view of the length of the species at sexual maturity. At that time, however, the species was so abundant that it was rarely necessary to kill blue whales that small. They were in fact so abundant that the industry offered a bonus to gunners who killed blue whales over 65 feet in length.[3] No other world government at the time had length requirements that strict and most of them had no requirements at all. The British government eventually followed the Norwegian lead but not as effectively; its minimum-length requirement for the blue whale was only 60 feet.[4]

The cetacean resources of the Antarctic were so rich that they induced several nations to begin pelagic whaling in the mid-1930s for reasons related to military expansion. Nazi Germany, for example, began whaling in order to stockpile edible oils. Such nations had no minimum-length requirements or other conservation regulations. They also did not have the whaling skills of the Norwegians who were in great demand by new whaling companies. The Norwegian government, therefore, in 1935 and 1936 passed several new amendments to its Whaling Act. Norwegian citizens were forbidden to work on whaling ships of other nations if those nations did not have whaling laws as strict as those of Norway. Norwegian citizens and corporations were forbidden to lease or sell whaling equipment abroad without prior permission from the Norwegian Department of Commerce. In addition, the government was given the power to regulate the number of catchers used by factory ships and even the production per factory ship if it deemed such actions necessary.[5]

The amendments to the Whaling Act contained unique administrative provisions that have not yet been adopted by other whaling nations. The annual administrative costs of the Whaling Council, the State Institute for Whale Research, and the Committee for Whaling Statistics were substantial. The wage costs of the government inspectors on the factory ships were even greater. To meet these expenses the Whaling Industry's Control Impost Fund (Hvalfangstbedriftens Kontrollavgiftsfond) was created. This fund was supported by an annual levy of 20 øre or more per barrel of whale oil produced by the whaling companies[6] (100 øre equal 1 Norwegian krone which has been worth slightly more than $.14 since World War II). The significance of this fund is that the Norwegian whaling companies were taxed not only to support the Whaling Council that established whaling policy and the Institute that advised on necessary conservation measures but also to pay the inspectors who policed their whaling operations. Thus, the whaling companies paid the administrative costs of all the restraints placed upon them.

A second unique fund was established at the same time. During several whaling seasons in the early 1930s a very low price of oil had forced many companies to keep their fleets at home. This created financial hardships for the whalingmen who were forced to seek part-time work during a period of economic depression. Similar but more severe hardships could result in the future from a shortage of whales in the Antartic that might put thousands of whalingmen permanently out of work. To minimize such hardships the Whaling Industry Security Fund (Hvalfangstbedriftens Sikringsfond) was established. The companies were required to contribute annually to this fund between 40 øre and 120 øre per barrel of oil produced in the Antarctic, the exact rate depending on the financial success of each whaling season. Failure to operate at a profit did not exempt the companies from making an annual payment to the fund. This fund was for the sole benefit of unemployed whalingmen and was administered by the Labor Department. Benefits could take the form of: interest-free loans for the purchase of tools or handicraft equipment, outright grants for the education or retraining of whalingmen for other work, or for public work projects to employ whalingmen.[7] The greatest use of this fund was the granting of emergency loans in 1940 to the families of whalingmen who, as a result of German naval action, were either captured on the high seas or were unable to return to Norway until 1945. Since World War II substantial loans from the Security Fund have not been necessary because of general prosperity and a relative labor shortage. Nevertheless, industrial contributions to the fund continued and by 1965 it had N.kr.23,322,000 in accumulated capital that was earning over N.kr.1 million annually in interest.[8] The significance of this fund was that Norway could advocate effective conservation measures in the Antarctic even if it meant unemployment in the whaling industry. Any unemployment would create no difficulties since ample funds were available to aid any whalingmen who lost their jobs.

All existing whaling legislation was codified into the Whaling Act of 1939. At this time a new provision was added. It was forbidden to sell abroad any whaling vessel of any type even if all refining apparatus or other specialized equipment had been removed. This provision was intended to slow down if possible the rapid development of the pelagic fleets of Nazi Germany and Japan. The refusal of these two nations to cooperate with international efforts at conservation of the stocks of whales is discussed in greater detail momentarily.

The destruction during World War II of nearly all the pelagic fleets of all nations had a direct influence on Norwegian postwar whaling legislation. The Norwegian government assumed that Germany and Japan, militarily defeated and occupied, would not be able to participate in pelagic whaling for several years to come. It seemed, therefore, an opportune time to attempt to prevent the build-up of excessive catching capacity that existed before the war. Thus the Whaling Act was amended in 1945 to limit the export of Norwegian whaling material and skills. One amendment at this time required that henceforth a whaling company must obtain a permit to send out a whaling fleet. As a result of this provision the government on several occasions refused permission to several companies to participate in Antarctic whaling. The government did this because too much catching capacity would have resulted and the stocks of whales would have unduly suffered. On several occasions, too, it refused companies permission to sell old factory ships abroad, thus condemning them to be sold for scrap.[9]

An outstanding provision of the 1945 amendment to the Whaling Act was the famous Article 5a that forbade Norwegians from taking employment in companies of nations that had not engaged in pelagic whaling prior to the war. Article 5a further stipulated that such employment was forbidden even if carried out in compliance with a contractual agreement entered into prior to the enactment of the law itself. The specific aim of this provision was to prevent nations from starting pelagic whaling and thereby keep total catching capacity within reasonable limits in order to protect the stocks of whales in the Antarctic. Other nations could of course build whaling ships but they could not as easily find skilled whalingmen. Norwegians seemed to have a high aptitude for pelagic whaling, and for many years they were the gunners on all British catchers, and many German and Soviet catchers as well. They were always in demand by new whaling companies around the world and to begin whaling without their services was a severe handicap. The laws that sought to limit the export of Norwegian materiel and services achieved some limited successes although little has been written about them. In the late 1940s both Argentina and Italy made plans to begin Antarctic pelagic whaling, and the former contracted for the construction of a factory ship, the *Juan Peron,* that was actually begun in a shipyard in Belfast. Both nations made persistent efforts to induce the Norwegian government to relax its laws on the exportation of whaling equipment and particularly whale gunners. The Norwegian government persistently refused and eventually persuaded both countries that the existent catching capacity was already sufficient to catch the Antarctic quota and that any increase would only end in economic failure.[10] Both nations abandoned their plans for pelagic whaling.

Infracions of various articles of the whaling laws were punishable by severe fines or jail terms or both varying from three months to three years.[11] The law forbidding whalingmen from taking employment in foreign companies, Article 5a, was rigidly enforced. Thus, one Hans Beckman was tried and found guilty of being a gunner for the Dutch company that operated the factory ship *Willem Barendsz.* He was fined N.kr.10,000, and his earnings of N.kr.50,000 were confiscated. He appealed his case to a higher court, lost the appeal, and was fined N.kr.1,500 in court costs.[12]

The Norwegian government, on the advice of the Whaling Council, was equally adamant in its restrictions on the postwar development of Norwegian companies. One of these Kosmos A/S, of Sandefjord, began in 147 the construction of *Kosmos V,* the largest floating factory ship ever built until that time. Before it was completed Norway received in reparations from Germany an old factory ship, the *Walter Rau,* that was allotted to the Kosmos company. The company proposed to use it as a mother ship for fishing since it could not get permission to operate both ships for whaling. After a long series of misunderstandings, disputes, and legal actions the company was forced to use the old German ship for whaling, renamed the *Kosmos IV,* and to convert the large, new *Kosmos V* to an oil tanker. This action kept down the catching capacity of the company, imposed on it extensive conversion costs, and left it with a ship not designed for use as a tanker. The reasoning behind this apparently uncooperative action of the Norwegian government is interesting. Influential members of the government and the Whaling Council felt that the German ship had been awarded by the Allied Reparations Committee to Norway as a whaling nation. They considered that Norway was thus morally obligated to use the German ship only for whaling. Under the circumstances the use of the new *Kosmos V* for whaling would create excessive catching capacity, and it was therefore forbidden.[13]

The Norwegian government imposed severe financial burdens on the whaling companies in addition to the two special fees levied on every barrel of oil they produced. At the end of World War II Norway suffered from a shortage of foodstuffs and was also faced with a threat of inflation. A Price Board (Prisdirektoratet) was established on a temporary basis to regulate the production and prices of essential consumer goods. The Price Board decreed each year that a certain specified quantity of whale oil had to be sold on the Norwegian domestic market rather than to buyers in other European countries. Furthermore the price was set low to avoid inflation. In 1947, for example, the whaling companies were required to sell 35,000 tons of oil in Norway for £40 a ton. The open market price in Europe at that time was £100 a ton. In that year alone the Norwegian whaling companies suffered a reduction in income of N.kr.42 million. By the time price controls were abolished in 1952 the total loss of revenue suffered by the companies was N.kr.244 million.

This was a severe financial burden on the Norwegian companies, especially when it is recalled that during these same years the governments of England, Holland, and Japan were aiding the reconstruction of their companies' fleets by means of price supports, income guarantees, and outright grants. During this period the Norwegian companies were only able to raise N.kr.76 million to invest in the reconstruction of their fleets. This placed them at a severe disadvantage by having to operate with old, rebuilt catchers and factory ships rather than new, efficient vessels. For example, of the 10 Norwegian factory ships in operation in 1952 only 4 were of post-World-War-II construction; 2 had been built in the 1930s, and 4 had been built before World War I. By contrast all 4 British factory ships were of post-World-War-II construction. Thus it is evident that the Norwegian government was quite willing to impose very severe financial restraints on its whaling companies.

The Norwegian government on occasion went so far as to restrict unilaterally the size of the catch of its companies. During the 1960 and 1961 Antarctic seasons Norway and the Netherlands withdrew their membership in the International Whaling Commission. The reasons for their withdrawal are explained in a different context in the following chapter. The whaling companies of these nations were, under the circumstances, theoretically free to carry on whaling without restrictions of any kind. The Norwegian government considered its withdrawal from the Commission to be merely symbolic and on the basis of its own whaling laws required its whalers to abide by the same regulations that applied to nations that remained members of the Commission. The Netherlands government did not follow suit and allowed its whalers to begin whaling whenever they chose and to continue as long as they wanted. This created futile but understandable chagrin among Norwegian whaling companies as expressed, for example, in the annual report of one of them:

> the Norwegian government, to our great regret, has, as last year limited the catching period for baleen whales from December 28 to April 7, while the Dutch can hunt as long as they wish. If the Norwegian expeditions had been allowed to hunt without a time limit they would, in all likelihood, have been able to obtain the Norwegian quota of 5,800 blue-whale units, and the total value production would have been over N.kr. 30 million greater than it was.[14]

One final and noteworthy illustration of the willingness of the Norwegian government to restrict the activities of its whalers concerns the blue whale itself. The Norwegian government proposed at the 1955 meeting of the International Whaling Commission that the blue whale be given complete protection in the North Atlantic Ocean. The proposal was passed, but Denmark and Iceland exercised their right to protest and were thereby not bound by the decision. Norway had the right to protest also, but chose to abide by the decision. For the next six years Norway continued to respect the ban while attempting to induce the two objecting nations to accept it. Thus, for six years Norwegian land-based whalers were denied the right to kill blue whales while Danish and Islandic whalers were free to kill them from their bases in the Faroe Islands, Greenland, and Iceland. Probably a few migrating blue whales spared by the Norwegians were subsequently shot by the others. There is no other recorded case of one nation forbidding its whalers to kill a given species while its neighbors continued to do so. The total number of blue whales involved here was not great, about 10 per year, but they undoubtedly represented a significant portion of the total North Atlantic blue-whale population.

In terminating the examination of the whaling policies of the Norwegian government it is pertinent to quote the words of two officials who summed up the underlying philosophy that guided the formulation and implementation of those policies.

The Norwegian Commissioner to the International Whaling Commission, while trying to convince the Commission of the need to reduce the annual catch in the Antarctic stated:

> The whaling industry is not there to give profit to people; the industry is there to give people work. That must be the leading point for every industry. I wish to state that from the Norwegian point of view.[15]

The Secretary of the Whaling Council was quite specific when describing the attitude of his government toward cetacean resources. He wrote:

> The problems of whaling are of both an economic and of a biological kind. On the one hand the Norwegian State has great economic interest in developing whaling into a national industry, and on the other hand it has become *a national duty to protect this peculiar animal* which furnishes the raw materials for the whaling industry.[16]

The policy of the Norwegian government of attempting to be the protector of the whales of the world was both admirable and naïve. The severe and costly restrictions imposed on its whalers were consistent with that policy, but they were imposed in vain. The blue whale was exterminated despite the persistent efforts of the Norwegian government to prevent it. Opposing policies adopted by other whaling nations were heavy contributors to the tragedy.

JAPANESE WHALING POLICY

Japanese Antarctic pelagic whaling began with the 1934/35 season, and by 1939 operations had expanded to a total of 6 floating-factory expeditions. During those years several international agreements, designed to prevent overexploitation of the stocks of whales, were reached under the aegis of the League of Nations. The agreements included standard prohibitions such as the killing of the nearly extinct Right whales, suckling calves of all species, and females accompanied by a calf. Japan refused to sign or abide by any of the agreements. Moreover, Japan refused to participate in the negotiations leading to the agreements even when for her benefit the North Pacific, her oldest whaling area, was specifically excluded. The reason for the refusal to adopt even rudimentary conservation practices was the urgent demand placed on the Japanese economy by the country's war in Manchuria and China. All the pelagic fleets sent to the Antarctic were owned and operated by the Nippon Suisan Kabushiki Kaisha Company, the main shareholder of which was the Manchurian Heavy Industries Corporation. This corporation was the principal economic and industrial arm of the Japanese army in Manchuria. The objective of the Nippon Suisan Company, as stated in the *1941 Mainichi Yearbook,* was the acquisition of foreign currency and food supplies for the Japanese armed forces.[17] The production of soya and other vegetable oils in Manchuria made it possible for the government to forbid the entry of Japanese-produced whale oil into the country. The oil was sold in Europe, particularly in Great Britain, thereby acquiring for Japan much needed hard currencies for the prosecution of the war effort.[18]

Japan did pass in 1933 the Factory Vessel Law that was amended slightly in 1936 and 1938. This law required that factory ships obtain a license to operate and that they operate well out to sea in order to protect a long-established land-based whaling industry. The law also contained some minimum-length requirements but these were shorter than those in effect for European whalers. For example, it was forbidden to kill blue whales shorter than 65 feet. However, there is no evidence that any of these regulations were ever enforced.[19] The Factory Vessel Law stipulated that Antarctic whaling could not begin before November 1. This was particularly hard on the blue whale because in November other species had not yet migrated to the Antarctic. European whalers could not begin until December 7. The November-1 date was of no conservation value at all and constituted

no restraint on Japanese whalers because there were very few whales
in the Antarctic before that date. Also, November 1 roughly coincided
with the end of stormy winter weather and the beginning of improved
summer weather that permitted pelagic whaling. In sum the Factory
Vessel Law of 1933 was so weak and so poorly enforced that one
wonders why it was enacted at all. Perhaps it was for the sake of ap-
pearances.

It is evident from the preceding facts that the Japanese government
prior to 1940 had no desire to impose restraints on its pelagic whaling
fleets. To have imposed any would have resulted in decreased production at a time when Japanese military agression was placing severe
demands on all sectors of the economy. The pelagic whalers of Japan
were thus free to kill any whale regardless of species or size at any
time.

Naval action during World War II destroyed almost the entire
Japanese whaling fleets. Two hastily repaired factory ships were put
in operation in 1946 with permission from General MacArthur, and
American inspectors were stationed on board to assure compliance
with recently adopted international regulations. Reconstruction of
the fleets proceeded slowly but in 1951, when a treaty of peace with
the Allied Powers restored Japanese sovereignty, the government took
steps to stimulate a more rapid expansion. It founded the Japan Development Bank to finance the reconstruction of the fishing industry
of which whaling was an important subsidiary. The very extensive
loans made by this government bank to the whaling industry are
shown in Table 22. Slightly more than 50 percent of the loans of the
Development Bank went to the whaling industry. These loans greatly
aided the expansion of the pelagic industry, and it is noteworthy that
they began after the Norwegian expansion had been halted by the
Norwegian government in the interest of conserving the stocks of
whales. The Japanese government was anxious to help rather than
hinder the operations of its pelagic whalers. Coming at a time when
the catching capacity of the existing fleets was more than sufficient to
catch the Antarctic quota the action of the Japanese government meant
disaster for the whales: it increased the necessity but eliminated the
possibility of decreasing the size of the annual slaughter.

Postwar Japanese whaling did not develop completely free of legal

Table 22

Loans granted by the Japan Development Bank
to large fishing and whaling companies, 1951–1958*

	1951	1952	1953	1954	1955	1956	1957	1958	Total
Whaling	522	606	480	200	80	200	70	—	2,158
Pelagic tuna fishing	—	301	254	—	—	—	—	—	555
North Pacific fishing	—	100	—	—	200	—	150	150	600
Cold storage and refrigeration	155	303	157		70	105	—	113	903
Total	677	1,310	891	200	350	305	220	263	4,216

* In millions of Yen.

Source: *Japanese Fisheries*, ed. Asia Kyokai (Tokyo, 1960), p. 155.

Note: The loans made by the Japan Development Bank were to the large corporations only. In 1953 the Small Industry Finance Corporation took over the financing of small loans to individual and small fishing companies.

restraints. Law Number 267, of 1949, known as the Fisheries Law, consisted of a wide range of specific regulations that were supposed to govern the relationship between the fishing industry and the national government. The Fisheries Law was an attempt to introduce a measure of governmental control over industry in contrast to the former Zaibatsu system in which a powerful industrial and financial oligarchy had nearly complete freedom of action and on occasion even exercised control over the government itself. The Fisheries Law was concerned with coastal fisheries, inland-water and high-sea fishing operations, including whaling. The law did not establish an effective administrative framework for the formation or execution of sound whaling policies despite the establishment of some apparently strong controls.

Power to enforce the provisions of the Fisheries Law was vested in the Fisheries Agency of the Ministry of Agriculture and Forestry.[20] The law did not, unfortunately, provide the director of the Fisheries Agency with any committee to advise him on whaling matters. There was established a Central Fisheries Adjustment Council, but there were no provisions for representation by cetologists. Moreover, the Adjustment Council's role was designed to be that of arbiter of disputes rather than adviser (Articles 112–14, Section 4, Chapter VI). Cetologists may have been represented there from time to time, but there is no evidence that they exerted any significant influence.

It is not surprising that cetology was a subject neglected by the Fisheries Agency—the Fisheries Law made no provision for the acquisition of data on whales or whaling for use by the government. This shortcoming was evident in two important ways. First, not until the end of 1962 were Japanese fishing and whaling companies operating on the high seas required to compile and submit catch reports.[21] This was a severe handicap to the formulation of sound conservation policies. It often resulted in the companies being much better informed than the government and in government policy being at odds with the facts. Second, the Fisheries Law made no provision for whaling research, and the government was thus forced to rely on the whaling companies for any information it might need. The Whales Research Institute in Tokyo, a few publications of which are cited in an earlier chapter, was established for the sole purpose of cetacean research, but it was founded and supported solely by the Japanese whaling companies for their own needs. While the scientists of the Whales Research Institute are among the world's leading cetologists the aims of the Institute itself may be subject to criticism. For example, in 1965 the Whales Research Institute undertook a study to find a scientific justification to reduce the minimum-length requirements for sperm whales.[22] The whaling companies wanted to propose such a reduction to the International Whaling Commission. That approach to research violates the principle of impartiality imposed by the scientific method, but because the Institute operated at the behest of the whaling companies the violation is not surprising. In any event the Japanese government had no independent, impartial source of cetologic information with which to formulate its whaling policies.

There were provisions in the Fisheries Law that gave the government power to control the whaling companies. Every vessel, for example, was required to obtain a license to operate from the Minister of the Department of Agriculture and Forestry, and a license could be denied to prevent an excessive number of vessels. Futhermore, the minister could withhold a license if there seemed to be any threat to the conservation of natural resources. The minister was also given the power to decide the number and tonnage of all vessels as well as the geographical area and period of operations (Articles 51, 56 and 58, Chapter III, of the Fisheries Law). These specific provisions gave the government legal power to control and regulate the expansion and operations of the Japanese pelagic fleets. To what extent did the Japanese government exercise these extensive powers of control at its disposal?

By the mid-1950s the catching capacity of the world's pelagic fleets was excessive and a reduction in the size of the catch was imperative in order to conserve the stocks of whales. The Japanese government had the power under the Fisheries Law to limit the number of fleets in the interest of conservation By the mid-1950s expansion of the Japanese industry was in full swing and continued until 1966. References to conservation written into the law were obviously ignored.

The number of Japanese pelagic fleets began to decline in 1966 but not because of any sudden concern for conservation. Whales of all species were becoming so scarce that there were not enough to sustain full operation of the fleets. The decline in the number of fleets in the Antarctic resulted in much unused catching capacity. To remedy this the Japanese companies began leasing their catchers to land-based whaling companies all over the world. Some were leased to companies that operated off the coasts of Peru and Chile where the Peru, or Humboldt, Current seems to serve as the one known migration route of baleen whales to and from the Antarctic. Chile and Peru, however, were not members of the International Whaling Commission, and they did not recognize as valid the 1963 decision of the Commission to ban the killing of blue whales in the Antarctic. Nevertheless, the Japanese government, which did recognize the ban, granted licenses to its catchers to operate off Peru and Chile. The ban on the killing of blue whales technically did not apply north of the Antarctic, defined as 40° S. latitude, and so the Japanese government broke only the spirit and not the letter of the law.

In June, 1967, the International Whaling Commisssion agreed, with Japan concurring, to ban the killing of blue whales everywhere south of the Equator. In October, 1967, Japan granted licenses to 2 companies to engage in whaling off the coast of Chile in 1968. It made no stipulation against the killing of blue whales although it had the power to do so under its own Fisheries Law and the legal obligation to do so as a member of the International Whaling Commission. This would have entailed a breach of the letter of the law, and the Japanese government therefore instructed its whalers to establish joint companies with Chilean interests.[23] This they did. Under the Chilean flag they could kill blue whales, ship the whale products to Japan, and remain exempt from any of the regulations of the Whaling Commission. As these words are written Japanese whalers continue to kill blue whales under the Chilean flag with the knowledge and acquiescence of their government.

The Japanese government, as shown by the preceding facts, has not used the power granted to it by the Fisheries Law to limit the operation of its whaling fleets in the interests of conservation. It is either unwilling or unable to enforce its own laws. It is also unwilling or unable to abide by the spirit of the international laws to which it adhered as a member of the International Whaling Commission.[24]

There is on record one incident that illustrates the somewhat odd attitude of the Japanese government toward the problem of proper utilization of the resources of the high seas. In 1963 the Fisheries Agency gave approval to 2 companies to engage in king-crab pot fishing in the Gulf of Alaska. In preparation for that fishing the companies invested about $330,000 each in technical equipment. The United States voiced strong opposition to the venture with the result that Japan forced the companies to cancel their plans. To compensate them for their lost investment the government allowed each company an additional 60 blue-whale units during their North Pacific summer-whaling operations.[25] This, of course, absolved the government of any obligation to make amends by special tax concessions or other equivalent financial methods. But it showed a lack of even rudimentary concern for the stocks of whales because at the time no complete survey had been made of the declining cetacean resources of the North Pacific.

All the evidence presented thus far indicates that whatever action any Japanese official took in regard to whaling was in the interest of the whaling companies. What has not been indicated is the extent to which the actions of the officials were influenced or controlled by the whaling companies themselves. There is no information about this delicate subject from Japanese sources, but what is available elsewhere is most enlightening.

The Japanese commissioner to the International Whaling Commission from 1951, when Japan become a member, through 1965 was not a government official. He was the chairman of the Japan Whaling Association, an organization of whaling companies! That appointment was an astounding deviation from normal practice and one which was to have disastrous consequences for the blue whale. The Whaling Commission had the duty to regulate the whaling industry of the high seas, and since each nation represented there had veto power over any regulation passed the Japanese whaling companies could determine their own policies. There were, to be sure, government representatives in the Japanese delegation to the Commission, but they were merely onlookers. They could not govern the actions of the Japanese commissioner who took orders from his corporate superiors, the heads of the whaling companies.[26] This is a serious charge that must be documented. Such documentation is not abundant because non-Japanese members of the Commission were reluctant to discuss the matter officially. To have done so would have caused only embarrassment and would not have altered the situation in Japan that brought it about. Criticisms of the Japanese became more vocal in the 1960s when the stocks of whales in the Antarctic were in desperate need of protection. In those years information began to trickle out concerning the power and influence of the Japanese whaling companies.

The 1963 meeting of the International Whaling Commission was a critical one in many ways, with strenuous efforts being made by Norway to give complete protection to the blue whale throughout the entire Antarctic. The failure of those efforts was due primarily to Japan and to a lesser extent to the Netherlands. In the words of the American Commissioner the policy of those nations were:

> dictated solely by the short-run economic impact of the proposed actions on the operations of their whaling industry. Conservation received lip service but appeared to have no effect on their positions.

Government representatives of the Netherlands and Japan informally indicated their unhappiness with this state of affairs but apparently were unable to oppose pressures from industry.[27]

A member of the U.S. Department of State who for many years had been an adviser in the American delegation to the Whaling Commission replied to my inquiry about the influence of the Japanese whaling companies:

> It was painfully evident that Japanese industry called the shots and that government spokesmen were embarrassed about the fact. For the last couple of years the latter very seriously wanted their industry to take a more reasonable attitude.[28]

A much more precise illustration of the power and influence of the Japanese whaling companies comes from an English conservationist. Dr. Harry R. Lillie, after service as medical officer on board a British factory ship in the Antarctic, became interested in the problem of conservation of the stocks of whales. He stated that at the 1965 meeting of the International Whaling Commission Japan proposed a blue-whale quota of 4,500 units that was passed. Proposals of other nations were considerably lower, but the proposal of the Japanese was a "try-on" that they never expected to get away with.[29] Prior to the meeting the directors of the 3 Japanese companies had decided on a proposal of 4,000 blue-whale units, but during the meeting the president of one of the companies decided to try the 4,500-unit proposal. This higher proposal was, of course, made by the Japanese commissioner on orders from his corporate superiors. Dr. Lillie's knowledge of this incident was based on personal interviews with the presidents of the 3 Japanese whaling companies, one of whom was willing to explain the incident. Dr. Lillie writes:

> I found in Tokyo that one of the companies, Nippon Suisan Kaisha Ltd., was quite in a class by itself above the others in its realization that the whaling situation had been allowed to become a terrible indictment of all those involved in the industry, the Governments concerned, and the International Whaling Commission.

The ability of the Japanese whaling companies to control government policy would not have had tragic consequences for the whales if it had been accompanied by a concern for their rational conservation.

The lack of any such concern also came to light during Dr. Lillie's interviews, and he writes:

> The President of the largest Japanese whaling company, Mr. K. Nakabe of Taiyo Fishery Co., Ltd., was indeed difficult to deal with, insisting on breaking off all further discussions if I could not agree with him that there were plenty of whales left and that the killing could go on without restriction. The President of the third company, Kyokuyo Hogei Co., Ltd., while not as extreme, was just as determined to go on with the killing until such time as the industry collapsed from the wiping out of the whales.[30]

The ability of the whaling companies to formulate Japanese whaling policies extended beyond the International Whaling Commission which did not attempt to regulate North Pacific operations. In February, 1966, a 4-power whaling conference was held in Honolulu to establish catch limits in that ocean. The participants were Canada, Japan, the United States, and the USSR. Prior to the conference representatives of the Japanese companies met with officials of the Fisheries Agency to decide on the positions to be taken by Japan at the conference. At this meeting the officials of the Fisheries Agency were

> reported to have expressed the view that the great majority of scientists agree that North Pacific whale resources are threatened with depletion, and that . . . Japan should participate in the conference with a positive attitude with respect to establishing regulations from this year, even if it means a reduction in catch quota for Japan.[31]

The whaling company representatives agreed to this in principle. At the conference the Japanese delegation was headed, as usual, by the chairman of their Japan Whaling Association. The results were almost predictable. Japanese whalers suffered no decrease in their blue-whale-unit quota and obtained a 22 percent increase in their sperm-whale quota.[32]

To sum up the inquiry into Japanese whaling policy several points are clear. Prior to World War II the government had no desire to impose restraints of any kind on the pelagic whaling industry because of its contribution to the war effort on the Asian mainland. World War II destroyed the pelagic fleets of Japan, but it did not completely destroy the Zaibatsu system. The postwar government despite the existence of enabling legislation was unable to exert its authority. The pelagic whaling companies themselves formulated Japanese policies and decided what restraints, if any, they would accept. The International Whaling Commission in attempting to conserve the stocks of whales according to its mandate found itself torn in two by such widely divergent attitudes as those of Japan and Norway. The fate of the blue whale depended on how the schism was healed.

INFRACTIONS

The International Whaling Commission established several specific regulations such as minimum lengths and protection of whales accompanied by a calf. Inspectors on the factory ships were to report infractions to their respective governments which in turn were to report them to the International Whaling Commission. Each year at the annual meeting of the Whaling Commission a Sub-Committee on Infractions was formed to examine the reports and to make recommendations to the plenary session. An examination of the reports shows that every company of every nation did commit infractions and these ranged from 1 to 20 percent of all whales taken. The average per company was usually about 4 or 5 percent and most of them were excusable. For example, it is all but impossible to estimate within 5 feet the length of a swimming whale, most of which is always under water. Also, it was customary for the inspectors to assume that a lactating whale carcass had been accompanied by a calf and therefore the gunner who killed it had committed an infraction. However, the blow of a baby whale is very difficult to see, and vanishes instantly if there is any wind. Such infractions as these were most common, and the penalty for the gunner and crew involved was the loss of their small bonus.

A study of the reports on infractions could not lead to any precise measure of their importance to the extermination of the blue whale. On the whole they would not seem to be important. However, the validity of the reports on infractions is open to question and it may well be that infractions did contribute heavily to the demise of the blue whale. For example, most blue whales killed were over the prescribed 70 feet in length. Those that were undersized were usually 68 feet but almost never 69 feet in length. That is statistically not possible. Such faulty reports were periodically called to the attention of the plenary session of the Whaling Commission. During the 1963 season, for example, 3,654 sperm whales were killed by the fleets during the voyage to and from the Antarctic. (The minimum-length requirement for sperm whales was 38 feet). Of those whales 20 percent were reported to be 39 feet in length, 48.2 percent were 38 feet, and 1.8 percent were 37 feet or shorter. Concerning that impossibility the committee report on infractions stated:

> The Committee wishes to state emphatically that they cannot accept these figures as a true representation of the size frequencies of the whales caught, and they must reiterate strongly the importance of strict observance of the minimum lengths as a means of conservation, especially with regard to sperm whales.[33]

Part of the reason for the lack of validity of the infractions reports was the variation in the method of operation of inspectors of different nationalities. Norwegian inspectors, for example, were marine officers whose operating procedures were precisely defined and whose reports were closely examined. They usually served for one season only, but never twice on the same factory ship. The reason for this was to preclude the development of friendships with men whose infractions they had to report. On Japanese ships the position of inspectors was associated with such prestige that they themselves did not venture onto the flensing deck to measure or inspect carcasses because it was usually ankle deep in blood and engulfed with the stench of decomposing entrails. The actual measuring of the carcasses was performed by laborers who had no reason to be accurate. To declare a whale undersize or lactating would deny a bonus to their friends on the catcher that had killed it.[34]

There was obviously a need for impartial inspectors on the factory ships who would enforce the regulations in a uniform manner. To this end Norway in 1955 began to advocate a program to place international inspectors on the factory ships of all nations. Many proposals were made in the International Whaling Commission, but they all came to naught. The Japanese eventually accepted the idea, but the Soviet Union consistently rejected it. Often the Soviet Union gave the appearance of approving the idea in principle, but was always able to find some reason to reject the plan. On one occasion, for example, the Soviets rejected a plan because they had not been notified about it sixty days before it was put on the agenda of the Whaling Commission. Norway persistently tried to find a plan acceptable to all because her whalers and officials suspected that serious infractions were committed by others but not reported and that these contributed significantly to the exhaustion of the stocks of whales in the Antarctic. Two instances of severe infractions illustrate the reasons for the Norwegians' suspicions.

For many decades land-based whaling had been carried on along the coasts of New Zealand, particularly in the Cook Straits, and the east coast of Austrialia. The catch was predominantly humpbacks, which had the habit of following coastlines in their migrations. In the early 1960s there was a sudden and drastic reduction in the number of available whales, and an investigation followed. (In the Cook Straits in 1960 a total of 480 humpbacks were sighted; in 1961 and 1962 the number declined to 88 and 12 respectively.) A study of the age distribution of the New Zealand catch from 1955 to 1962 combined with catch per unit-of-effort records for each age group showed the following mean mortality coefficients:

1956	0.58	1960	0.45
1957	0.15	1961	1.61
1958	0.67	1962	1.96
1959	0.18		

A similar study of the Australian catch produced nearly identical results, and presumably the two had a common origin. The problem was that the pelagic catch of humpbacks in the region of the Antarctic poleward of Australia and New Zealand was insufficient to account for the great increase in mortality.

One theoretical explanation for the disappearance of the humpback whales was that they simply changed their migration routes. Independent observers on neighboring South Pacific islands and on ships saw no increase in the number of humpbacks, but rather a decrease. Moreover, of all baleen species the humpback strays least from its habitual areas, summer or winter. A second theoretical explanation was increased natural mortality of epidemic proportions. The humpbacks that were caught, however, were in their usual good health and with normal blubber thickness and oil content. The third possible explanation for the drastic decline in the humpback population was a greatly increased mortality by whalers operating in a region where the humpbacks could be found in large number. The only possible such region was Area V of the Antarctic south of New Zealand. However, in order for the catch there to have caused the population decline it would have had to exceed the reported catch by over 5,000 whales. The Scientific Committee of the International Whaling Commission examined this evidence and concluded that the only satisfactory explanation was a large and unrecorded catch of humpback whales during two successive years in the Antarctic.[35]

It would be difficult if not impossible to refute the conclusion that the vanished humpback whales were killed and not reported. That raises another equally serious problem: an infraction of that magnitude could not have taken place without the knowledge and condonance of a national government and its inspectors. What nation killed the humpbacks? There is a very close relationship between the production of a factory ship and the number of whales it processes. The quantity of oil produced from 5,000 humpback whales added to normal production would have been so disproportionate to the recorded catch that any company committing such an infraction would be detected immediately. All whaling companies examine closely each others' figures on catch, production, and open-market sales of oil in Western Europe. The Bureau of Whaling Statistics also scrutinizes them carefully. The only whalers whose sales go unobserved and whose records can not be examined are those of the Soviet Union. The belief is widely held among European and Japanese whalers that the Soviet Union is responsible for the several thousand vanished humpback whales. Conclusive proof of Soviet culpability is lacking. But 5,000 vanished humpback whales are proof that impartial and trained international inspectors are needed on the factory ships of all nations.

A second example of serious infractions of the regulations that may have contributed significantly to the extermination of the blue whale concerns a whaling fleet of Panamanian registry. The factory ship

Olympic Challenger began Antarctic pelagic whaling in the 1950–51 season. It was owned and operated by the Olympic Whaling Company of Panama; its catchers belonged to a Honduran company. The majority stockholder of both companies was Aristotle S. Onassis, an Argentinian citizen.

From the beginning of its whaling operations the Olympic Whaling Company was a source of both irritation and suspicion to the Norwegian companies. The *Olympic Challenger* used Hamburg, Germany, as its home port and its company agent there, the Erste Deutsche Walfang Gesellschaft, was managed by the former administrator for Nazi Germany of the Norwegian whaling ships that were captured and confiscated during World War II. The manager of the *Olympic Challenger* and its fleet of catchers was a Norwegian citizen, once a member of the Norwegian Nazi party, who had been manager of the German factory ship *Walter Rau*. When the Olympic Whaling Company was being organized its agents went to Norway to recruit skilled labor. The company was informed of the Norwegian law prohibiting this but persisted and hired 15 gunners.[36] The Norwegian government and the Norwegian whaling companies did not forget the incident.

Almost as soon as the *Olympic Challenger* began whaling, rumors began to circulate among British, Japanese, and Norwegian whalingmen that the Panamanian ship was breaking many of the rules. In the vast spaces of the Antarctic it was not easy for whalingmen to observe each other's actions. The necessity of killing as many whales as possible before the season ended left little time for snooping. From time to time the *Olympic Challenger* was observed committing infractions, but none of those occasions were as well documented as the following. On January 13, 1955, the Japanese catcher *Koyo Maru 2,* operating with the floating factory *Tonan Maru,* found and photographed a marked humpback whale carcass at 64° 12′S. 162° 21′W. The *Olympic Challenger* was the only other factory ship in the vicinity at the time. The regulations then in force allowed the killing of humpback whales only between January 20 and 23 inclusive. Five days later the buoy boat *Koyo Maru* (used to retrieve carcasses) saw the *Olympic Challenger* at 65° 47′S. 170° 50′W. When discovered, the Panamanian ship cast adrift 4 humpback carcasses and moved behind a nearby iceberg. The *Koyo Maru* approached to within 100 yards of the dead whales, photographed them, and submitted a report of its findings to the International Whaling Commission.[37]

The International Whaling Commission had no power to enforce its regulations; it could only formulate them and lament infractions. But national governments can enforce laws, and one of them did so with a vengeance. On November 15 and 16, 1954, units of the Peruvian navy and air force bombed and machine-gunned ships of the *Olympic Challenger* expedition for operating within 200 miles of the Peruvian coast. Five of the vessels were taken to port and detained for weeks until a fine of $3 million was paid.[38] The Peruvian action only temporarily halted the operations of the fleet. Shortly thereafter, the *Olympic Challenger* sailed for the Antarctic.

Conclusive proof of the infractions committed by the Panamanian fleet was finally obtained in the winter of 1955–56. Seven German citizens who served a few seasons on the *Olympic Challenger* went to the Norwegian Consulate General in Hamburg and signed notarized affidavits describing the illegal whaling practices they had witnessed. Among the men was the dentist who had also acted as the expedition's assistant medical officer. Their testimony was reinforced by photographs which they had taken of undersized whale carcasses, by diaries of observances of infractions, and by photographs of the ship's logbook that showed false reports of the catch had been submitted to the Bureau of Whaling Statistics in Sandefjord, Norway. The following is a brief summary of the major infractions witnessed by the German whalingmen of the *Olympic Challenger:*

1) During the autumn of 1954 the Panamanian factory ship reported a catch of 2,348 sperm whales off the coast of Peru. The actual catch was 4,648 sperm whales, 285 blue whales, 169 fin whales, 105 humpbacks, and 21 sei whales. Of the blue whales killed, 35 were 59 feet or less in length and 2 were less than 49 feet. It was forbidden to falsify catch reports. Also, it was illegal for factory ships to catch baleen whales between the Antarctic and the Equator.

2) During the 1954/55 season in the Antarctic the *Olympic Challenger* began hunting baleen whales before the season opened on January 7.

3) Whales were killed regardless of size. Baby sperm whales were shot before they even had teeth. Some were only 5 meters long and must have been newly born calves (a sperm whale averages 4 meters at birth). Many young whales were shot, and on occasion 4 at a time were hauled on board by winch. Often a whale was so small that it was only necessary to remove the harpoon and entrails before the carcass was dropped whole into the cookers.

4) Five of the 7 German whalingmen swore they never saw a Panamanian inspector on the flensing deck.

5) False catch reports were submitted to Sandefjord. During the 1954/55 season the *Olympic Challenger* reported catching 170 humpback whales. In reality it caught 1,125. To hide this the ship reported 700 more fin whales than it had killed. The baleen-whale oil produced illegally off Peru was reported as sperm oil. It was also necessary therefore to falsify the sperm-whale catch in the Antarctic.

6) By sending in falsified reports on the size of the catch the *Olympic Challenger* caused the 1954–55 season to be declared closed before the 15,500 blue-whale-unit was actually reached. The *Olympic Challenger* continued whaling after the other expeditions headed home and killed an additional 12 blue whales and 13 fin whales.

7) The *Olympic Challenger* violated the opening and closing dates of the whaling seasons 1950/51 and 1952/53. (Proof of other infractions in these earlier years is lacking.)

The following procedures, while not infractions in themselves, were enforced on the *Olympic Challenger* apparently to prevent disclosure of infractions

1) It was forbidden to photograph baleen plates. The reason is obvious: the color, size, and shape of baleen plates are reliable indicators of the age and species of whales.

2) The entrails of baby whales were processed in cooker No. 8 on the *Olympic Challenger* before being jettisoned.[39] Unprocessed baby entrails would float for some time and be evidence of illegal whaling.

As evidence of serious infractions by the Panamanian factory ship became available, the Norwegian government lodged protests with the Panamanian government. These overtures produced no results. The Federation of Norwegian whaling companies decided to take independent action because by its reckoning the *Olympic Challenger* since 1950 had produced illegally some 217,000 barrels of oil worth about N.kr.60 million. The Norwegian companies, through court action, caused the seizure in Hamburg of 9,000 tons of whale oil belonging to the Olympic Whaling Company. The whale oil, they claimed, was the equivalent in value of the damages they had suffered as a result of illegal whaling by the *Olympic Challenger*.[40] The Norwegian whaling companies, again by court action, had the *Olympic Challenger* and its oil seized in Rotterdam. The charge here was breach of whaling regulations during the 1952–53 season.[41] Onassis countered by going to court and having the Norwegian factory ship *Kosmos III* seized as security for his claim of 10 million guilders against the Norwegians, a sum equal to the Norwegian claims against his company.[42] The corporate legal battle that followed was conducted for the most part in secret. No trials were held. Anders Jahre representing the Norwegian companies and Onassis representing the Olympic Whaling Company reached a private settlement. The Norwegians paid $1 million and the Olympic Whaling Company paid $3 million to a special fund for the Norwegian whaling industry.[43] This special fund was used to construct a luxury hotel with office space for the Association of Norwegian Whaling Companies in Sandefjord, Norway.

The out-of-court settlement of the *Olympic Challenger* affair caused considerable discontent in Norway. Whalingmen were angry because they received no compensation for the loss in wages they had suffered. Public opinion, as expressed in many newspapers, was almost equally critical. Norway, it was reasoned, had developed the pelagic whaling industry and shown the way to others. Norwegian whalers obeyed the rules while others disobeyed them with impunity. During the summer of 1956 the *Olympic Challenger* and its catchers were sold to a Japanese company, and the Olympic Whaling Company ceased all whaling activities. This was interpreted in the Norwegian press as an indicator that Onassis was getting out of the whaling business because of the adverse publicity resulting from the disclosure of so many infractions committed by his company.[44] Onassis's payment of $3 million to the special fund was also seen as an admission of illegal whaling.[45] A more logical explanation for the sale is that Onassis was astute enough to find more remunerative investment opportunities for the funds tied up in his Olympic Whaling Company. There is some indication that after the first few seasons the whaling operation was not regarded by its backers as a booming business venture. During the 1953/54 whaling season the *Olympic Challenger* was used not for whaling but as an oil tanker. Furthermore, statistics show that the Panamanian whaling fleet was not very efficient. While off the coast of Peru the *Olympic Challenger* killed 680 baleen whales (enumerated above) for a total of 415 blue-whale units. Oil production from these was 54 barrels per blue-whale unit. Production by other companies in the Antarctic always averaged over 100 barrels and usually about 118 barrels per blue-whale unit. Production at such a low level of efficiency could hardly have been remunerative.

Legal responsibility for the infractions committed by the *Olympic Challenger* must be placed on the Panamanian government rather than on Onassis or the managers of the Olympic Whaling Company. The principle of the freedom of the seas grants to every nation the right to use the resources of the high seas in any manner it chooses. Any regulations governing the use of those resources must be accepted by a nation before its citizens or corporations are subject to them. The Republic of Panama was a member of the International Whaling Commission in name only. At most meetings of the Commission, Panama by its own choice was not represented; the government did not care to send a delegate. Panama was usually many years in arrears in its annual contributions to the operating budget of the Whaling Commission (annual contributions ranged from £150 to £300). As a member of the commission, Panama did place 2 inspectors on the *Olympic Challenger* to ensure compliance with the regulations adopted by the Commission. The negligent practices of the Panamanian inspectors and the false infraction reports submitted by them showed them to be either incompetent or corrupt (the evidence points to corruption but does not rule out incompetence). The Norwegian Foreign Office sent proof of the infractions to the government of Panama, which replied that the Panamanian inspectors were officials of the government and the government could hardly repudiate itself. Subsequent notes of protest by Norway to Panama went unanswered.[46]

The government of the Republic of Panama obviously was not concerned with enforcing regulations adopted by the International Whaling Commission. Nor was Panama interested in participating in the formulation of those regulations. The actions and attitudes of the government of Panama had destructive consequences on the high seas. Their only virtue was a lack of pretense of concern for the fate of the blue whale and its congeners.

And in much of your talking thinking is half murdered. KHALIL GIBRAN

VII

INTERNATIONAL WHALING CONTROL

THE GREAT EXPANSION of the pelagic whaling industry after 1925 resulted in a cetacean slaughter described in previous chapters. As the slaughter increased so did the fears of scientists that the whales would be annihilated if the whalers were not restrained. The first significant step toward international regulation of the industry was the Convention for the Regulation of Whaling signed in Geneva in 1931. This Convention, patterned on the Norwegian Whaling Act of 1929, was rudimentary by later standards. It did not specify minimum lengths and it did not establish any catch limit. It only gave protection to Right whales, "immature" whales and females accompanied by a calf. The Convention for the Regulation of Whaling came into force only after a specified number of nations had ratified it, in 1935. The inherent weaknesses of the Convention were compounded by the refusal of Germany and Japan to adhere to them. The only pelagic whaling nations that did adhere to the Convention were Great Britain and Norway.[1] The whales received little respite.

During the early 1930s the production of whale oil in the Antarctic was occasionally so great that the price fell below the cost of production. Under such circumstances many companies did not send their whaling fleets to the Antarctic, as for example in the 1931/32 season when not a single Norwegian factory ship left its home port. In an effort to support the price of oil at profitable levels the British and Norwegian whaling companies repeatedly discussed ways of limiting their production and in some years actually succeeded in reaching agreement to do so. The corporate agreements to limit production became progressively more difficult because of the actions of Japan. The Japanese whaling industry, supported by its government, was increasing production in order to support the war effort in Asia. The whale oil produced was sold in Europe to acquire foreign currency, but this had the effect of reducing prices. As Britain and Norway limited production to increase the price Japan was stimulated to increase production and reap the benefits. In 1935 the British and Norwegian governments convened a conference in Oslo to discuss the problem in consultation with their respective whaling companies. It was concluded that any limitation on the number of factory ships would probably stimulate further expansion of foreign whaling industries and was therefore unacceptable. It was agreed that the British and Norwegian companies should continue their efforts to agree on voluntary limits on the amount of oil produced per factory ship.[2] The whaling companies attempted this but were unable to reach complete agreement. The Norwegian government therefore decreed production limits for Norwegian factory ships. The British government did not.[3]

The following year, 1936, British and Norwegian companies were still unable to reach agreement on limiting their production and so their respective governments took over the task and imposed restrictions for the 1936/37 season. The whaling season was to begin on December 8 and each factory ship was permitted a fleet of catchers proportionate to its size. At the request of Norway, no blue or fin whales could be killed between the Equator and 40° S. latitude (this established the whaling boundary of the Antarctic that has been in effect ever since). The Norwegian government suggested that these limitations should apply to all pelagic whaling nations and that an international conference should be convened to formalize them.

In the summer of 1937, representatives of the world's major whaling nations, except Japan, met in London to attempt to regulate pelagic and land-based whaling operations. Scarcely any of the participating nations had domestic enabling legislation to permit them to limit their whalers' activities on the high seas. As a consequence there was no agreement on limiting production or the number of catchers a factory ship might use. An International Agreement for the Regulation of Whaling was, however, signed, and it contained a few rudimentary limitations. Among them the most important were: it was forbidden to kill blue whales less than 70 feet in length; pelagic whaling was permitted only south of 40° S. latitude; and the season was limited from December 8 to March 7.[4]

The International Council for the Exploration of the Sea was concerned about the excessive number of blue whales being killed each year, and at its behest a new conference was convened in 1938. This conference had as its main objective a specific limit on the number of whales killed. Japan refused even to participate in the conference, and Nazi Germany refused to limit the kill of whales. No agreement to limit production could be reached under those circumstances. The conference did succeed in passing 2 significant amendments to the 1937 agreement. It established a Whale Sanctuary where no whaling was permitted, the limits of which were 70° to 160° W. longitude and south of 40° S. latitude. Complete protection was granted to the humpback whale throughout the Antarctic because its numbers were depleted almost to the point of commercial extinction.[5]

The outbreak of World War II temporarily ended international attempts to regulate pelagic whaling. In 1942 the chairman of the Norwegian Whaling Council escaped from Nazi-occupied Norway and made his way to England. Shortly thereafter the British government and the Norwegian government in exile began informal discussions on postwar whaling control. A whaling conference was convened in London in 1944 and was attended by delegates from all the signatory nations of the 1937 agreement, except for Germany of course. A new accord was reached, the Protocol of 1944, that embodied all the provisions of the prewar agreement and an important new provision as well. All participants agreed that the prewar catch of baleen whales had been excessive and that in the future the catch had to be limited if the whales were to survive. It was agreed, therefore, that the total catch in the Antarctic should be limited to 16,000 blue-whale units per season. Each factory ship would report its weekly catch to the Bureau of Whaling Statistics in Sandefjord, Norway, and the Bureau would order all whaling to cease when the 16,000 blue-whale-unit quota had been reached.[6] (This was the beginning of the Whaling Olympic described earlier.) The Protocol of 1944 was a multilateral agreement, like its predecessors of the 1930s, and in the manner of all treaties required ratification by a specified number of signatories. It was not ratified by Eire and therefore never came into force. Fortunately for the whales there were no factory ships in working condition at the time and the agreement was renegotiated and duly ratified a year later.

The calling of a new conference in 1945 to renegotiate the 1944 Protocol was a cumbersome procedure that could not be repeated in the future if international whaling control was to be effective. In that same year Nazi German and Japan, the most uncooperative prewar whaling nations, were militarily defeated and occupied by the Allied Powers. Several European nations were beginning to rebuild their pelagic fleets, and it seemed, therefore, an appropriate time to devise a more effective framework for whaling control. Toward that end most of the world's whaling nations met in conference in Washington, D.C., in the autumn of 1946. Several proposals were made, but the one which was ultimately adopted with only minor modifications was that submitted by the United States.[7] The resultant International Convention for the Regulation of Whaling has been the framework for all international whaling controls from 1946 to the present.

The preamble to the Convention, which established the International Whaling Commission, defined the objectives of the Commission in general terms. The signatory nations desired to establish a new and effective system of regulating the whaling industry in order to insure not only conservation of whales stocks but also their development. These objectives were prompted by the realization that the history of whaling was one of repeated overexploitation of one species and region but that the stocks of whales could increase in number if properly managed. This could be achieved by limiting exploitation to those species that could support it and thereby grant a recovery period to species that needed it. Thus the primary task of the Whaling Commission was to regulate the industry in such a way as to preserve the stocks of undepleted species and permit the increase in numbers of those already depleted.

The International Convention for the Regulation of Whaling was composed of two distinct parts. The first, called the Schedule, contained specific regulations applicable to whaling operations. It prescribed, for example, the minimum-length requirements for each species, the opening and closing dates of the whaling season, forbidden areas, and the Antarctic quota. These regulations could be changed by the Whaling Commission as the need arose. The second and more important part of the Convention contained provisions that were not subject to change by the Commission. Among these, for example, were the duty of the contracting governments to enforce the whaling regulations, the number of ratifications required for the coming into force of the Convention, and the details of the structure and operation of the Whaling Commission.

The International Whaling Commission was composed of 1 commissioner and 1 or more experts and advisers from each signatory nation. The Commission was empowered: to adopt its own rules of procedures; to decide the time, place, and frequency of meetings; and to engage in cetacean research and publish reports of its findings. The most important power granted to the Commission was to amend the provisions of the Schedule when necessary in order to conserve and develop the stocks of whales. Any amendment of the Schedule passed by the Whaling Commission automatically became part of the Convention and binding on all members. This did away with the need to call an annual conference and produce a treaty requiring ratification. In this regard the International Whaling Commission was a significant improvement on the prewar procedure. Once established it could meet annually without formal diplomatic convocation, and its amendments would be binding on all member nations.

The passage of a proposed amendment by the Whaling Commission required an affirmative vote of three-fourths of the commissioners voting. For a period of ninety days thereafter every member nation had the right to submit an objection to the Commission and not be subject to the amendment. When that occured every other member nation had an additional ninety-day period during which it too might lodge an objection and not be bound by the amendment. This procedure amounted to an absolute right of veto over any proposal made in the Commission. In practice this caused an objection by one nation to be followed by objections from all other whaling nations even if they had originally voted for the amendment in question and even if it meant abandoning a conservation measure they were willing to accept. For example, Nation *A* proposes a ban on the killing of blue whales in Antarctic Area II and the measure passes by a three-fourths vote. Nation *B* lodges an objection and is not bound by the amendment. Nation *A* must in turn lodge a similar objection or its whalers will be forbidden to kill blue whales there while the whalers of Nation *B* are free to do so. (You can almost predict the fate of most attempts to reduce the Antarctic catch when it is recalled that the Japanese commissioner to the Whaling Commission was a representative of the Japanese whaling companies.) In actual practice objections were not very numerous. Before a proposed amendment was ready for a vote the commissioners usually knew the opinions of their colleagues. If one nation was adamantly opposed to it, a subsequent objection would render it null and void. Under those conditions the proposal was either retracted or watered down to suit the objecting nation.

The right to lodge an objection, to veto any conservation proposal, was the greatest weakness of the International Whaling Commission. This was foreseen at the Washington Conference when the International Whaling Commission was being proposed, and it was debated at great length. Norway and the United Kingdom opposed the right of objection and wanted all amendments passed by the Commission to be binding on all members. The American delegate, who made the original proposal, defended the veto as a valuable "safety valve." Because of the veto a nation that felt seriously inconvenienced by a proposed amendment did not have to leave the Commission and thereby become free of all controls. Such a nation could veto the objectionable proposal, remain a member of the Commission, and be subject to all the other regulations then in force. The alternative to the right to object, argued the American delegate, would lead to no international controls at all. The conference voted unanimously to retain the veto right of all member nations.[8]

The right to object to any new proposal did achieve the result predicted by the American delegate even though it did preclude success for the International Whaling Commission. Every pelagic whaling nation joined the Commission precisely because it could prevent any serious restraints being placed on its whalers. There were, however, a few nations with a land-based whaling industry that refused to sign the Convention and become members of the International Whaling Commission. The most important of such nations were Chile, Ecuador, and Peru that formed their own regulatory organization known as the Commission for the South Pacific. Those nations refused to join the international effort because they considered the regulations in the original Schedule too restrictive. The right to object pertained only to future amendments to the Schedule, not to the initial provisions written into the Schedule.[9] For many years the International Whaling Commission attempted in vain to induce Chile, Ecuador, and Peru to join it and abandon their own organization. In 1966 they replied that in view of the abysmal failure of the Whaling Commission to preserve the Antarctic whale stocks it would be more appropriate for it to join their Commission for the South Pacific.

Another weakness of the International Whaling Commission was its lack of authority to limit the number of factory ships or to allocate a quota to any of them. Article V of the International Convention for the Regulation of Whaling specifically denied the Commission that authority. Any nation was free to increase the number of its pelagic fleets if warranted by favorable domestic conditions, economic or political. Japan and the Soviet Union did precisely that. Some nations could not decrease the number of their fleets to a commensurate degree because of financial and technical limitations inherent to the industry that are analyzed in Chapter IV. The result was an increasing number of whaling fleets hunting fewer and fewer whales. This situation was foreseen at the Washington Conference, but no serious efforts were made to avert it. To have given the Whaling Commission authority to limit the number of factory ships would have violated the principle of the freedom of the seas that grants to every nation the right to use the resources of the high seas as it decides. Furthermore, the right of veto would have rendered useless any authority to limit the number of factory ships. Had the authority been granted to the Commission and the right of veto denied to the members, few if any nations would have remained members for very long. Any nation so limited would have withdrawn from the Convention and the others would inevitably have done the same. During the short discussion of this crucial matter at the Washington Conference the American delegate presented a unique argument against the granting of such powers of control to the International Whaling Commission: "The United States Government has taken the position that such allocation is not in the interest of free and competitive enterprise and it is not necessary to the conservation of whaling resources." [10] Thus the blue whale and other baleen species inhabiting the high seas were victims of their very habitat. Because of the principles of the freedom of the seas and of national sovereignty no treaty provision could be devised that would grant them protection from overexploitation and eventual annihilation.

The International Whaling Commission has held a formal meeting every year beginning in 1949. The annual meetings were held most often in London, where the permanent Office of the Commission is located. Occasionally a meeting was held in Cape Town, Moscow, Sandefjord, or Tokyo. The meetings were invariably held in June to allow member nations time to assemble data and prepare reports on catch, production, and infractions of the previous season. A June meeting also allowed the whaling industry time to make any technical adjustments for the coming season necessitated by possible amendments to the Schedule. The annual meeting began with a welcoming speech by a governmental official, usually from a department concerned with high-seas fisheries, of the host nation. At the conclusion of the speech all members of the press were asked to leave, and the meeting proceeded in secrecy. This procedural rule of secrecy was adopted by the Whaling Commission, and it effectively prevented the general public from learning that the Commission was not carrying out its assigned tasks. The blue whale was dying unknown to the world. By the time the facts became known an epitaph was more pertinent than a diagnosis.

It was possible for private opinions to be presented to the International Whaling Commission although very few ever were. Letters could be sent to the Office of the Commission and the Secretary would duplicate them for distribution to the commissioners at the first plenary session. At the time of distribution the chairman would open the floor for discussion of them. Invariably there was none. In 1964, for example, 5 letters were distributed from such international societies as the World Wildlife Fund and the Fauna Preservation

Society.[11] These asked the Commission to put additional curbs on whaling, particularly for the threatened blue and humpback whales, and to follow the recommendations of the Commission's scientists. There was no comment from the commissioners. At the same time the Minister of Foreign Affairs of the Republic of Ghana sent a cablegram to the Commission requesting that it expel the delegation from South Africa and refuse to cooperate with that country in the regulation of whaling. The commissioner of the Soviet Union spoke in favor of this request, but he received no support and the matter was dropped from discussion. The Whaling Commission was indeed a closed forum, but the magnitude of this weakness cannot be measured. There is no way of knowing what effect open meetings would have had on the decisions of the Commission. Conceivably they might have helped. The Commission could hardly have been a greater failure than it was.

A customary feature of the opening session of every annual meeting of the Whaling Commission was an address by the director of the Bureau of Whaling Statistics. This was a presentation of statistical data on the most recent Antarctic whaling season and included extensive details on the catch such as average lengths and number of whales killed by species and catch per unit-of-effort by area. Also included were a detailed comparison of the catch of the past season with the preceding season and the trend of the catch over the past five or ten years. This presentation was accompanied by a printed compilation of the statistics, several copies of which were distributed to the various national delegations. Every commissioner, therefore, received the facts about recent trends in the Antarctic catch of all species (these statistics were subsequently published in greater detail as *International Whaling Statistics*). The presentation, however, was in statistical rather than graphic form and only covered trends for the most recent postwar seasons. This tended to give a much less vivid impression of the seriousness of the decline of the blue whale than would have been the case if the long-term trend had been presented graphically. A similar effect may be obtained by comparing the long-term decline of the blue whale in Figure 7, page 65, with the percentage decline of the last five years shown in Table 10, page 98. A graphic presentation might not have induced the commissioners to establish more effective conservation regulations, but in view of their failure to do so it should have been attempted.

At the end of the first plenary session of every annual meeting of the Whaling Commission several permanent committees met and carried out much of the basic work of the Commission. The most important was the Scientific Committee, which studied the latest statistical information provided by the Bureau of Whaling Statistics and several marine institutes such as the National Institute of Oceanography in England, the Whales Research Institute of Tokyo, and the State Institute for Whale Research in Oslo. The Scientific Committee then made specific recommendations to the Commission about the Antarctic quota and other measures deemed necessary for the preservation of the stocks of whales of all species. A second important committee was the Technical Committee, the task of which was to examine the whaling laws and regulations of member nations, reports on infractions, the techniques of whaling, and other subjects referred to it. The Technical Committee also reported its findings and recommendations to the plenary session of the Commission.

The reports submitted by those two committees often included only the majority opinion of their members, and no verbatim records of their meetings were made. The absence of verbatim records of committee meetings is most unfortunate because it was in committee that the various national delegates freely expressed their views on all subjects related to whaling controls and conservation of the whale resources. The commissioners and members of their delegations were members of the committees where they learned the minimum conservation measures acceptable to their colleagues and what proposals could be passed without a negative vote and subsequent veto. As a consequence many committee recommendations were watered down, modifications were made in an effort to ensure passage by the full Commission. As a consequence of that practice research into the attitudes and actions of the various commissioners must rely heavily on their voting record on specific proposals in plenary session debates. Fortunately, proceedings in the plenary sessions were recorded verbatim.

The Schedule of whaling regulations that the International Whaling Commission was empowered to modify included many conservation measures designed to protect the stocks of whales of all species from overexploitation. The most famous of these measures was the Antarctic quota, expressed in blue-whale units, that was designed to prevent a recurrence of the unrestrained catches of the 1930s. The Antarctic quota was a good method for measuring and limiting the total catch in terms of cetacean raw material. As a conservation measure it was useless because it could not prevent whalers from concentrating their efforts on the most valuable species while leaving less valuable ones untouched. They hunted and killed the blue whale as long as possible and then shifted to the fin whale. When the fin whale became scarce they concentrated their harpoons on the sei whale. The negative aspects of the Antarctic quota that brought annihilation to the blue whale was accurately summarized by Ruud, the leading Norwegian cetologist, who wrote:

> Considering the type of regulation that has been chosen to limit the catch, an agreed quota of raw materials expressed in the number of blue-whale units, it must be admitted that it has no foundation in a biological conservation policy since it pays no attention to the fact that the different species of whales may call for different degrees of protection.[12]

If the Antarctic quota was such an ineffective control measure, and indeed even a destructive one, why was it never abolished? When the quota was formally established at the end of World War II, in 1946, there was a severe shortage of edible oils, particularly in Western Europe. The whaling industry could contribute greatly to meeting that need, but obviously it should not do so by endangering the stocks of whales by repeating the great annual slaughter of the 1930s. The problem was thus one of controlling total production, and the Antartic quota seemed to be the best way of solving it. A sound conservation alternative would have been a separate quota for each species based on its sustainable yield with the grand total for all species expressed in barrels, or tons of oil, or even blue-whale units. In 1946, unfortunately, it would have been extremely difficult to determine the sustainable yield of the several species because the effect of the wartime respite on the stocks was unknown. In addition the sei whale had been little hunted, little was known about the species, and no one had studied it to determine its sustainable yield. Also no species was in any danger of extermination in 1946, and so the Antarctic quota system was accepted without serious opposition.

Evidence was presented at the first meeting of the International Whaling Commission in 1949 which showed that the stock of humpback whales had made some recovery since 1938 when it was granted complete protection. The Commission therefore agreed to permit a catch of 1,250 humpbacks per season. Each factory ship was to inform the Bureau of Whaling Statistics by radio of its weekly catch of humpbacks. The Bureau was to estimate the date when the kill of humpbacks would reach 1,250 and order whaling to stop. The system worked poorly and in the 1949/50 season 2,143 humpbacks were killed. The following year only 1,638 humpbacks were killed, but that was still 31 percent more than the prescribed number. In 1952 the Whaling Commission abandoned the idea of a species quota for the humpback and substituted a four-day open season. A four-day season turned out to be insufficient to catch the allotted number of humpback whales, and so the whaling nations attempted to lengthen the season at Commission meetings in 1957 and 1958. Their efforts failed. They were unable to obtain the necessary three-fourths vote because of opposition from nonpelagic whaling nations that wanted to protect the humpback whales. (Among the latter were: Argentina, Australia, Canada, Denmark, France, Iceland, New Zealand, Sweden, and the United States.) The whaling companies of all nations considered the humpback quota and the subsequent four-day season to be grossly unfair because the nonpelagic nations forced them to limit production by a regulation they could no longer veto. The companies developed such a strong aversion to species quotas that the subject has scarcely been raised since that time and no other species quota was ever passed by the Commission. The Antarctic quota is still in use today, and unless species quotas soon replace it only the least important species will survive the deadly consequences.

The refusal of the whaling companies to accept, or even seriously consider, species quotas was not due primarily to their experiences with the humpback quota. It was based on the complications and inconveniences that such quotas would have had on their operations. If there had been species quotas for all 4 baleen species hunted in the Antarctic more frequent and more detailed radio reports would have been necessary to keep the Bureau of Whaling Statistics informed of the progress of whaling operations. If one species had a very small quota almost daily radio reports would have been necessary. More serious than such inconveniences would have been the impact on actual whaling operations. When a factory ship and its fleet of catchers moved through a given region of the Antarctic there was no way of knowing what species would be encountered. If no whales were sighted for four or five days, would it be wise to stop and catch little sei whales if they were the first to be found? or would it be better to pass them by and hope for blue or fin whales? If the quota for the blue or fin whales was about to be reached the question would be even more difficult. And what would a fleet do if by, say, February 10 the quota had been reached for 3 of the 4 species? Would it pay to spend another month and a half roaming the Antarctic looking for the one species still open? The answer to that difficult question would depend on many disparate factors: long-range weather forecasts, recent changes in the price of oil, success of the expedition to date, morale of the crew, number of other fleets electing to remain, and amount of the quota still unfilled. Even with the Antarctic quota system the element of luck was a significant factor in pelagic whaling. Species quotas would obviously have magnified the element of luck and the result would have been extreme fluctuations from year to year in the production of the various companies. The understandable antipathy of whaling company officials to species quotas is summed up by a quotation furnished on one of the rare instances when they were discussed openly in the Commission.

> The Japanese delegation [industry] is of the opinion that, though it is a rational policy to limit the catch of whales by species separately, this method is impractical for the whaling countries and cannot be accepted.[13]

A second conservation measure written into the Schedule by the Washington Conference was the establishment of a Whale Sanctuary in the Antarctic where no whaling of any kind was permitted. The Sanctuary covered the same area as the one established in 1938 that was ineffective because of the lack of cooperation by Nazi Germany and Japan. The biological value of a sanctuary is self-evident provided, of course, that it is inhabited by a significant number of individuals of any species. The Whale Sanctuary was established in an area where there had never been much whaling because no great number of whales of any species had ever been found there. The establishment of the Sanctuary inconvenienced no one precisely because it did not do the whales much good. It did give the impression of concern and support for conservation. Under such circumstances no whaler could seriously object to the Sanctuary, and thus it had little opposition for several years. There were, however, a few whales of many species that inhabited the area in summer, and so the Sanctuary did serve its purpose as long as it remained closed to whaling.

A third type of conservation measure written into the Schedule in 1946 was a minimum-length requirement for every species. For the blue whale the prewar 70-foot requirement was continued even though it was well known that the animal at that length was still sexually immature. If there had been a limit on the number of blue whales killed (a species quota) the inadequate length requirement would have had no serious consequences. There was, of course, no limit placed on the number killed, and thus the 70-foot requirement was useless. Why was the requirement not increased by the delegates to the Washington Conference who were well aware of its inadequacy? A minimum-length requirement of at least 82 feet would have been necessary to give the blue whale any significant protection against annihilation (that length would have allowed the females time to reproduce at least once). An 82-foot requirement, however, would have drastically reduced the number killed, and the whalers would not have allowed it. The whalingmen also had an aversion to all length requirements because of the extreme difficulty of estimating the length of a swimming whale. The most experienced gunners could not estimate within 5 feet the length of a live blue whale. Even the 70-foot requirement posed problems of estimation to most gunners because under their metric system of measurement a 70-foot blue whale was 21.3 meters long. The only logical reason for accepting the 70-foot figure, in 1946 as well as in prewar agreements, was a peculiar change of habit by blue whales when they attained that length. Blue-whale calves were normally very inquisitive and seemed to have little or no fear of boats. They would often approach and examine vessels of all types including catcher-boats. When they grew to about 68 feet or 70 feet in length their curiosity gave way to indifference or fear. Thus the conduct of a blue whale was in part used by gunners in estimating its length, and the 70-foot figure was the least objectionable to both gunners and whaling company officials. Equally inadequate and useless length requirements were adopted by the 1946 Washington Conference for all other species of baleen whales.

A final conservation measure that actually did reduce the rate of decline of the blue-whale population was a postponement of the opening date of the whaling season. The migrations of the baleen whales to the Antarctic were such that the blue was the first to arrive there, followed usually by the fin, humpback, and sei, in that order. The blue was also the first species to leave the Antarctic at the end of its feeding season, and this resulted in a relative concentration of blue whales there during the early months of the Antarctic summer. The following figures illustrate the changing percentage of the blue whale in the catch by month as a season progressed.[14]

1933		1934	
October	92.6	January	56.3
November	90.2	February	45.7
December	84.6	March	50.7

It is evident that any delay in the opening of the season would grant some relative protection to the blue whale because gunners would encounter fewer blue whales and more of other species. Beginning in 1954 an opening date for blue whales one or more weeks after the opening of the baleen-whale season was agreed to by the Whaling Commission. (This is discussed in greater detail momentarily.) In view of the failure of the Whaling Commission to prevent the extermination of the blue whale one may wonder how the Commission was able to grant it that one small measure of relative protection. A week or two shorter open season produced only a small decrease in the number of blue whales killed. The whaling companies did not object to this because it gave the whales they did catch time to become fatter and more valuable. The whales were in the Antarctic for the sole purpose of eating, and they gained weight at an astounding rate. Fin whales gained over one-third of a ton a week during the Antarctic season and blue whales gained about three-fourths of a ton a week. The whalers had no objections to letting their prey become a little fatter—provided they could kill it later in sufficient quantity to maintain production.

THE WHALING COMMISSION
AND THE BLUE WHALE

The first meeting of the International Whaling Commission, in 1949, was devoted largely to organizational problems. It was necessary to establish rules of procedure, determine the number and membership of working committees, and decide on the language of the Commission and on the annual financial contribution of the member nations. The Schedule was in force, the whaling fleets were still relatively few in number, and the Commission could safely postpone for a year its assigned task of protecting the stocks of whales. During the next three years the annual meetings of the Whaling Commission produced no conservation regulations to protect the blue whale.[15] Norway did attempt to reduce the length of the whaling season for the species, but the effort failed. As the years passed the number of factory ships and catcher boats continued to increase, and the blue-whale population continued to decline. The time when the blue whale needed help was at hand.

— 1953 —

Prior to the 1953 meeting of the International Whaling Commission a special Scientific Subcommittee met to examine in detail the most recent catch reports from the Antarctic and to make recommendations to the full Scientific Committee. It noted with alarm the very serious decline in the stocks of blue whales, particularly in Area II. In this area the catch of blue whales per catcher-day's-work had declined from a high of 1.03 in 1934 to 0.11 in 1952 despite a doubling of the tonnage and horsepower of the catchers. The ratio of blue to fin whales during those same years had fallen from 1:2 to 1:15, and the percentage of sexually mature blue whales had fallen commensurately. The Scientific Subcommittee therefore recommended that the killing of blue whales in Area II be prohibited. It also recommended that elsewhere in the Antarctic the blue-whale season begin two weeks after the baleen season, that is, January 16 for blue whales and January 2 for all other species. These restrictions would decrease the total number of blue whales killed, and the Subcommittee therefore also recommended that the Antarctic quota be reduced from 16,000 to 15,000 blue-whale units.[16]

The Scientific Committee accepted these recommendations and then met with the Technical Committee, composed of diplomats and nonscientific advisers, in order to eliminate differences in their respective recommendations. During this joint-committee meeting it was learned that one pelagic whaling nation was violently opposed both to the ban on the killing of blue whales in Area II and to the reduction of the Antarctic quota by 1,000 blue-whale units. The recalcitrant nation was willing to reduce the quota by 500 units and postpone the blue-whale season by two weeks provided Area II was not closed for the killing of blue whales. The blackmail of the threat of a veto induced the Scientific Committee to renounce its original recommendations. It recommended to the Commission that a ban on the killing of blue whales in Area II be postponed for five years but that the opening of the blue-whale season be set back by two weeks. These recommendations passed without a dissenting vote. The blue whale got no reprieve—only time to consume a bigger meal before the killing resumed.

Why did the scientists retreat from a position they knew to be necessary to protect the blue whale? The Commission would have passed their original recommendations but with one objecting nation to cast a veto all whaling nations would follow suit and nothing would be gained. Time to consume a bigger meal was better than nothing at all.

What nation was responsible for this failure of the Whaling Commission in 1953 to protect the blue whale? The Netherlands. The scientific adviser to the Netherlands delegation to the Commission was a famous marine biologist respected for his research on whales (he was the director of the Netherlands Whale Research Group of the Zoological Laboratory of the University of Amsterdam). At the meeting of the Commission's scientists he submitted a memorandum to refute Norwegian claims that the blue-whale population had been so drastically reduced as to require substantial protection. The memorandum was a strange document from so famous a scientist. His arguments contained so many flaws that an untrained laymen could have detected them. He claimed, for example, that the use of the catcher-day's-work as a measure of unit-of-effort to estimate changes in whale population was of dubious worth (that measure is universally used to determine population changes in all aquatic animals). He claimed that the blue-whale population was not drastically declining because the Dutch factory ship *Willem Barendsz* found that they constituted 60 percent of the catch close to the ice edge and only 20 percent farther north in open waters. He did not explain why the Dutch ship did not stay close to the ice where weather conditions also were much better. He claimed also that a decreasing population could not be assumed simply because the percentage of sexually immature individuals was increasing. As evidence he pointed to studies of boars, ducks, and antelopes which showed that an increasing percentage of young individuals indicated an increasing population. That is strange reasoning indeed for a biologist who knows that baleen whales can produce only one offspring every two years whereas boars, ducks, and antelopes can produce several offspring every year.[17] The arguments presented by the Dutch scientist were an enigma, and they remain so to this day. In any event, the Dutch delegation accepted them and acted accordingly to the delight of the Dutch and all other whaling companies. The blue whale would have to wait another year.

— 1954 —

The 1954 meeting of the International Whaling Commission was held in Tokyo rather than in London where its permanent office was located and where most of its meetings were held. The scientific advisers were quite alarmed at the continuous and rapid decline of the blue whale. They felt certain that if the animal was to survive it would need greatly increased protection throughout the entire Antarctic. Their specific recommendations for protection aroused such opposition that most of them were not even presented to the

Commission in the plenary session. Why? Something was rotten in the Netherlands.

The Dutch scientist continued to claim that there were still plenty of blue whales to be found close to the ice edge. He did not explain why the Dutch whalers did not get very many of them. During the 1953/54 season the Dutch fleet caught an average of 18 blue whales per catcher; the South African fleet caught 27 per catcher; 1 British fleet caught an average of 24, and the average for all others was 13. In addition the Dutch claims were shown to be incorrect by a study recently carried out by the British National Institute of Oceanography.[18] Nevertheless Dutch opposition to effective protection for the blue whale was supported by all the whaling nations except Norway and the Soviet Union. The reason for the opposition was not difficult to discern. During the coming whaling season, 1954/55, there would be in operation 19 rather than 17 factory expeditions and if they had to share fewer whales the result would be greatly reduced profits. To that grim prospect there was only one alternative—the killing would have to continue.

— 1955 —

The 1955 meeting of the International Whaling Commission differed in one minor way from its predecessors. It was held in Moscow, and the delegates, at the usual reception in their honor, consumed more vodka and less Scotch. So far as the whales were concerned the results were not much different.

The scientists reviewed the latest statistics on the blue-whale population, and most of them agreed that the species was so far gone that it might be unable to recover. Despite that apprehension and what it implied for the blue whale the Commission merely postponed the opening date of the blue-whale season by ten days, from January 21 to February 1. The inadequacy of the measure was almost ludicrous. The scientists knew it would not arrest the decline of the blue whale, but it was all that the whaling nations would accept.

If the International Whaling Commission was not sufficiently concerned for the welfare of the whales of the world it was indeed concerned for its own reputation. During the 1954 meeting a proposal had been made and passed to ban the killing of blue whales in the North Pacific, and the regulation was entered in the schedule. Japan and the Soviet Union objected to it within the ninety-day grace period, Canada and the United States then followed suit in order that their coastal whalers would not be unduly prejudiced. The result was that the regulation applied to nations that did not carry on whaling in the North Pacific and did not apply to nations that did. The delegates agreed unanimously that the enactment of a regulation that applied to no one made them look a bit ridiculous. They eliminated the regulation from the Schedule.

The 1955 meeting of the Commission was different in one unfortunate manner—it put an end to a sound conservation regulation that had been in force for many years. The scientists recommended and the Commission agreed without a dissenting voice that the Whale Sanctuary be opened for whaling! The objective of the scientists was to relieve the pressure on the hard-pressed whales in other areas by giving the whalers additional space in which to hunt. That praiseworthy aim was supported by the belief that there were few whales in the Sanctuary and therefore not much harm would be done. Unfortunately there were quite a few whales in the Sanctuary. More unfortunately the Whaling Commission, unable to institute new conservation regulations, was equally unable to reinstate those that were temporarily suspended. The Sanctuary remained open despite subsequent efforts to close it, and the blue whales that inhabited it were slaughtered. The Sanctuary is still open today for the killing of the few fin and sei whales that inhabit it.

— 1956 —

When the delegates to the 1956 meeting of the Commission gathered in London they were presented with grim statistics on the catch during the 1955/56 whaling season. The catch of blue whales had declined by 550 animals even with the opening of the Sanctuary. Only 3 blue whales were taken at South Georgia Island, compared with 3,689 three decades earlier. If the species was to survive it would have to be protected—at once.

The delegates and the scientists knew that the number of factory expeditions in the coming season would increase from 19 to 20. That meant that any reduction in the total catch resulting from protection given to any species would have serious financial consequences. They also knew that the Dutch delegation was violently opposed to a reduction of the quota below 14,500 blue-whale units (the scientists a year earlier felt it should then be no higher than 11,000). There was thus little hope of giving added protection to the blue whale.

The whaling companies at this time had agreed to reduce the number of their catcher boats, and they feared that the whaling season might not be long enough to catch the allotted number of whales. They therefore wanted to lengthen the baleen whaling season by advancing its opening date. Now if the opening date of the baleen season were advanced and the blue-whale season remained unchanged there would be a proportionately larger catch of fin whales. The scientists opposed this and recommended that if any help were given to any species it should go to the fin whale and not to the blue whale! They reasoned as follows. Because the blue whale had become so scarce the fin whale had become the mainstay of the industry. Indeed, the fin whale in 1956 constituted some 80 percent of the cetacean raw material taken by the whaling fleets. The average annual kill of fin whales had long since passed 20,000 and was approaching 30,000. So many had been killed that the species was showing unmistakable signs of a serious decline in numbers, although there was no danger of extinction. If the fin whale declined significantly the industry would collapse. The fin whale must therefore be protected to prevent its suffering the fate of the blue whale. The blue whale was no longer of much importance and if necessary it must be sacrificed to help the fin whale.

Such reasoning on the part of the scientists could be criticized as perverse for it seemed to be reverse conservation. Unfortunately they had no alternative. They could not convince the whalers to reduce the number of fleets and to be content with reduced production. They could not convince the Whaling Commission to impose restraints upon the whalers. The scientists could only try to delay the inevitable. For the blue whale the decision of the scientists at the 1956 meeting of the Whaling Commission marked a turning point— a turning point that opened onto the last fateful mile. The year 1956 was possibly the last year when the blue whale could have been saved by giving it complete protection. If the killing continued unabated much longer the coup-de-grâce would surely come.

— 1957 —

The scientists at the 1957 meeting of the International Whaling Commission were concerned exclusively with the fin whale. They made no recommendations for protection of the blue whale. The killing continued.

— 1958 —

The Netherlands refused to accept any longer the Antarctic quota of 14,500 units that had been in force for two years and the quota for the coming season was raised to 15,000 units. This made it certain that more rather than fewer blue whales would be killed. The Scientific Committee in a particularly lengthy report to the plenary session of the Commission made only a passing reference, one sentence, to the plight of the blue whale. No action on behalf of the animal was recommended and none was taken.

The Antarctic whaling industry was rapidly approaching disaster. The Soviet Union had announced plans to expand its catching capacity by 3 new giant factory ships each with a large fleet of new catchers. The catching capacity of the fleets already in operation was excessive and the stocks of whales of all species were declining. Unless these trends were reversed the whaling companies would face economic ruin and the stocks of whales would be obliterated. The solution was either to limit the number of factory ships or to assign a portion of the Antarctic quota to each whaling nation. Unfortunately the International Whaling Commission was specifically forbidden to make such limitations. The founders of the Whaling Commission had agreed that the principle of the freedom of the seas would be violated if the Commission had the power to limit the whaling activities of any country. Under the circumstances representatives of the pelagic whaling nations met privately in London, in November of 1958, in order to seek a solution. They decided that each nation should be allotted a portion of the Antarctic quota that would be valid for seven years. The whaling companies of each nation could decide for themselves their share of their national quota and adjust the number of fleets accordingly. The national quota plan had the advantage of putting an end to the "Whaling Olympic." The disadvantage of the plan was that several nations could not agree on what their share should be. The Soviet Union agreed to accept 20 percent of the quota and not to add more than 3 new fleets. The Netherlands wanted at least 1,200 blue-whale units of a proposed Antarctic quota of 16,500 blue-whale units. The average catch of the Dutch fleet during the four preceding years had been 797 units. Norway was willing to accept 5,200 blue-whale units of a proposed quota of 15,800 units. The Norwegian average catch during the preceding four years had been 5,774. The Netherlands threatened to withdraw its membership in the Whaling Commission if its demands were not met. Norway threatened to do the same if its demands were not met. The Norwegians pointed out that they had made sacrifices in the past by limiting the number of fleets, and they were making sacrifices now by accepting less than their share of the whales.[19] The two positions were irreconcilable.

— 1959 —

When the delegates to the 1959 meeting of the Whaling Commission convened in London the finest of Scotch whisky at their receptions could not dilute their gloom. They knew they were attending what could well be the last meeting of the International Whaling Commission. Two and possibly three of the pelagic whaling nations were on the verge of leaving the organization. If that happened the others would do the same in order to avoid the disadvantage of still being subject to the regulations. The result would be unrestrained whaling in the Antarctic that could lead only to the annihilation of the whales and the destruction of the industry. Under the circumstances the future of the organization rather than the whales received the attention of the delegates. The blue whale was forgotten in the turmoil.

The scientists viewed with habitual alarm the continuing decline of the blue whale. In vain they sought ways to protect the fin whale, the mainstay of the industry. Any recommendation they might make to reduce the catch of either the fin or the blue whale would exacerbate the dispute between the Netherlands and Norway. The dispute already seemed beyond solution. They made no recommendations to reduce the catch of either species.

As the plenary session of the 1959 meeting approached the end of its agenda the demands of the Netherlands had not yet been satisfied. The end of the International Whaling Commission was in sight. In order to avert that disaster the Commission adjourned for five days in order that the delegations might try to resolve their differences in private discussions after consultation with their home governments. Norway, seeking to preserve the Commission, agreed to reduce its demands even further by accepting only 4,850 blue-whale units. The Netherlands was not satisfied and walked out of the Commission. Norway did the same.

When the Netherlands left the Commission it stated that its whalers would not abide by any time limitations to the whaling season and that they would take up to 1,200 blue-whale units. That action placed all other whalers at a disadvantage and so the Whaling Commission advanced the opening date of the season from January 7 to December 28 (the Dutch began whaling in late November). It was not necessary to increase the Antarctic quota because the 15,000 units could now be shared by one less number of factory expeditions. The Norwegian withdrawal from the Commission was symbolic only. The Norwegian delegate promised, to the chagrin of its whalers, that Norway would abide by all the regulations in force as they applied to the nations remaining in the Commission. This action by Norway probably prevented other nations from withdrawing their memberships. Unfortunately, it did not help the whales very much. The quota the Dutch assigned to themselves increased the Antarctic quota and resulted in the death of more whales in the coming season than in any of the preceding eight years. The Dutch quadrupled their catch of blue whales and the number that perished increased despite a declining population. The killing not only continued, it accelerated.

— 1960 —

Shortly after the opening of the 1960 meeting of the Whaling Commission the scientific advisers made a rather startling move—they questioned their own competence in certain fields. They were certain of their conclusions that the stocks of whales were declining, but they were not certain about the amount of the decline. They admitted they could determine neither the exact size of the population nor the sustainable yield of any species. They therefore recommended, and the Commission agreed, to engage the services of three scientists trained in statistical analysis and population dynamics. The three scientists, to be chosen from nonpelagic whaling nations, were to study the whale populations and make recommendations to the Commission on the sustainable yield of each species. The Commission also agreed that the Antarctic catch limits would be brought into line with the final recommendations of the special scientists. Unfortunately, the Whaling Commission had a restricted budget that was inadequate to pay for the services of the special scientists—the Committee of Three. For many years the contribution to the Commission by the member nations was £150 per annum. The sum had recently been raised to £250, and the commissioners did not think they could ask their respective governments for £50 more. A few economy measures were taken, such as reducing funds allotted to the whale-marking program, but the meeting ended without finding a way to balance the budget or pay the Committee of Three.

The continued killing of blue whales was pushing the animal ever closer to the brink of extinction. More than a score of catcher boats operating out of South Georgia were now able to find only about 5 blue whales a year compared with thousands per year in the 1920s and 1930s. The situation was so bad that the Whaling Commission could not ignore it. A motion was made and carried that the opening date of the blue-whale season should be postponed from February 1 to February 14. Japan objected, and the measure became null and void. The Japanese Commissioner explained that the later date would prejudice member nations because nonmember whaling nations (the Netherlands and Norway) would not be subject to the restriction. The explanation was an excuse rather than a reason.

Norwegian absence from the Commission was only symbolic. Norway abided by all the regulations in force, and the Japanese knew it. The number of blue whales that the single Dutch fleet could kill between February 1 and February 14 could not possibly prejudice anyone, and the Japanese knew that too. Japanese intransigence had replaced Dutch intransigence.

The Whaling Commission did make an attempt to induce the Netherlands and Norway to rejoin the organization. They originally left because of a dispute over the Antarctic quota and its division by country. The Commission therefore abolished the quota for two years in the hope of allaying the dispute and restoring the full membership of the Commission. Thus, for the next two years there was no quantitative limit on the Antarctic whalers and the whales paid a severe price for the impotence of the organization designed to protect them. The number of whales that perished in the coming season rose to 41,289, the highest figure since World War II and the second highest figure in the entire history of Antarctic whaling.

— 1961 —

The Netherlands continued in its refusal to rejoin the International Whaling Commission even though Norway had rejoined late in 1960. No proposals were made or passed for the protection of any species. The Commission was still unable to find the money to pay for the work of its population specialists, the Committee of Three. The suspension of the Antarctic quota had one more year to go, and thus no quantitative limits were reimposed on Antarctic whalers. The impotence of the Commission continued and so did the killing.

— 1962 —

The 1962 meeting of the Whaling Commission began under more propitious circumstances. The problem of a division of the Antarctic quota by country had been solved and the Netherlands had rejoined the Commission. Henceforth the quota would be divided as follows: Japan, 33 percent; Netherlands, 6 percent; Norway, 32 percent; United Kingdom, 9 percent; and the USSR, 20 percent. This meant an end to the old Whaling Olympic and permitted increased operating efficiency of the fleets. The subdivision of a national quota of a country having more than one whaling company was decided by the companies themselves. Henceforth a company could hunt at leisure because it was no longer in competition with all the others. Each company could reduce the number of catcher boats, retain the best ones and operate its factory ship with greater concern for the proper utilization of the whale carcasses. Peace had been achieved among the whaling nations but extending it to the whales was another matter.

The scientific advisers to the Commission were now certain that the survival of the blue whale depended on its receiving immediate and complete protection. Its population had fallen so low that during the preceding season for the first time in whaling history not a single blue whale was killed from the bases on South Georgia Island. The scientists' recommendation that the blue whale receive complete protection was a futile cry in a watery wilderness. The Japanese would not even retract their 1960 veto of the postponement of the opening of the blue-whale season from February 1 to February 14.

That action by Japan was surpassed in ignominy by the Commission itself acting in plenary session. A motion was made and passed that no increased protection be given to the blue whale or any other species for another year. The rationale of the delegates for that failure to perform their duty was quite simple. The funds had just been obtained for the work of the Committee of Three, and their findings and recommendations would not be ready for another year. The Commission had bound itself, morally at least, to act on the recommendations of that committee and their nature was not in much doubt. It appeared inevitable that in 1963 the Commission would be faced with the necessity of making drastic reductions in the catch of several species as well as the Antarctic quota. The Commission had just barely survived one storm, and another was clearly discernible. The year 1962 was a moment of calm, and any excuse to preserve it was welcomed by the delegates.

The failure of the Whaling Commission to act in 1962 may have prolonged a moment of internal tranquillity, but it pushed the blue whale beyond the point of no return. In the coming season, 1962/63, almost 1,000 blue whales perished, and they constituted about 60 percent of the total population (the estimated blue-whale population in 1963 was 600). If the limited action taken by the Commission in 1963 to protect the blue whale had been taken in 1962 the animal might have survived. It is both tragic and ironic that the excuse for inactivity by the Commission in 1962 was the absence of a committee report that was not prepared for lack of funds. The cost of the committee's work was £8,000—the market value equivalent of 4 blue whales.

— 1963 —

The 1963 meeting of the International Whaling Commission was as stormy as anticipated. The final report of the Committee of Three was presented, and it recommended that the Antarctic quota be reduced to less than 5,000 blue-whale units. Norway and the United Kingdom agreed that a drastic reduction in the catch was necessary to preserve the stocks of whales and proposed a quota of 4,000 units.[20] Japan refused to accept anything less than 10,000 units, and after much wrangling and heated debate Japanese wishes prevailed. The other nations could have passed a lower figure but a Japanese veto would have negated the measure and the quota would have reverted to the previous 15,000-unit quota. Unfortunately that was not the only instance of Japanese blackmail at the 1963 meeting of the Commission.

For the blue whale the Committee of Three recommended what the scientific advisers to the Commission had long advocated, namely, complete protection for many years to come. The Committee of Three warned the Commission that the blue whale had possibly already been hunted beyond the point of recovery and that continued catching at any level would significantly increase the risk of biological extinction. A motion was therefore made that the killing of blue whales be banned throughout the entire Antarctic. Japan refused to accept this proposal and insisted on the right to continue killing blue whales in one region of the Antarctic that still contained a small blue-whale population. Opinion in the Commission was overwhelmingly in favor of the total ban but a Japanese veto would have nullified it and kept the entire Antarctic open for the killing of blue whales. The Commission had no alternative but to submit a second time to Japanese blackmail. It was agreed unanimously that the killing of blue whales would be banned in the Antarctic except in the areas between 40° and 55° S. latitude from 0° to 80° E. longitude.

The passage of that measure appeared to be the long-delayed grant of effective protection to the blue whale. Unfortunately the appearance was false. During the preceding whaling season over 75 percent of the blue whales killed had been taken in the area kept open for continued hunting. The area, unlike the rest of the Antarctic, apparently still had a small blue-whale population, and the Japanese saw no reason to spare them. The obvious willingness of the Japanese to kill the last blue whale was so blatantly rapacious that even the Japanese themselves felt obligated to proffer an explanation. They were almost equal to the task.

The area kept open for the continued killing of blue whales was not, according to the Japanese, populated with real blue whales but rather the subspecies they called "pygmy blue whales." The Japanese claimed that this subspecies must be considered separately for purposes of biological study, conservation, and whaling. (The records of the Whaling Commission do not indicate the reaction of the delegates to the Japanese use of the term *conservation*.) According to the Japanese the distinguishing characteristics of the pygmy blue whale are: 1) a silvery-gray color rather than the steel blue of regular blue whales; 2) a body length at sexual maturity probably less than 65 feet for both sexes; 3) a shorter tail in proportion to the trunk; 4) shorter baleen plates in proportion to their breadth; and 5) a tendency to congregate in one small area, the area that was kept open for whaling.[21]

There are experts from several countries who seriously question the validity of classifying those smaller blue whales as a subspecies. The characteristics of the pygmy blue whale described by the Japanese are indeed open to question. The Japanese supplied no color photographs to substantiate the claim of a color difference, and some of their own scientists had previously pointed out the great variation in color of regular blue whales. Almost no pygmy blue whales under 70 feet were killed, and it would therefore be impossible to predict that sexual maturity would be attained at 65 feet. The Japanese supplied no photographs to substantiate the claim of a shorter tail:trunk ratio although they did furnish measurements. They neglected to point out that in mammals there are substantial changes in size and length ratios of several body components as an individual matures. There are, in addition, 4 other important considerations that cast very serious doubts on the existence of a pygmy blue whale.

Dr. Remington Kellogg, of the Smithsonian Institution and America's leading cetologist, doubts the existence of a subspecies called the pygmy blue whale. In his opinion the smaller blue whales were either runts, or younger blue whales that podded near Kerguelen Island before migrating to the ice.[22] The runt hypothesis relates to the blue whale 70-foot minimum requirement long in force in the Antarctic. Every species of animal produces some short individuals known as runts, and there is no reason to suppose that blue whales were an exception. The 70-foot minimum would give such runts substantial protection with the result that in time they could have become fairly numerous. The idea that the smaller blue whales were simply young individuals that had not yet migrated to the ice relates to the podding habits of the species. It has long been known that pods of blue whales were very often composed of individuals of the same age group. Moreover, there was also a tendency for pods of blue whales of the same age groups to arrive and depart from the Antarctic almost simultaneously.[23] Either of Dr. Kellogg's hypotheses is supported by more evidence than can be found to substantiate the existence of a pygmy blue whale.

Taxonomists define a subspecies as "a geographically defined aggregate of local populations which differs taxonomically from other such subdivisions of the species." [24] The available evidence does not geographically limit the smaller blue whales to any one area of the Antarctic as outlined by the Japanese. Blue whales referred to as pygmies have been found as far apart as South Africa and Australia. The Japanese articles cited above even point out that certain small whales taken in the 1930s at South Georgia may have been pygmy blue whales. From a taxonomic point of view, therefore, there is serious doubt about the wisdom of assigning subspecific rank to smaller blue whales taken throughout virtually the entire Antarctic Ocean!

The Japanese scientists who did nearly all the writing about the pygmy blue whale were associated with the Whales Research Institute of Tokyo. The work of the institute was devoted exclusively to whales and the findings of its members were published in *Scientific Reports*. It is very strange that not a single word about a pygmy blue whale was ever published in that journal. Japanese writings on the subject appeared only in foreign publications. It would seem that a scholarly journal of cetology would give high editorial priority to the discovery of the second largest whale in existence, especially when its own scientists made the discovery. That omission is hard to comprehend when compared to the inclusion of such minutiae as articles about the deformed jawbone of a sperm whale and a one-eyed whale fetus. Perhaps the scientists of the Whales Research Institute were instructed, as employees of the Japanese whaling companies, to try to convince scientists and officials of other countries of the existence of a subspecies of blue whale. Success in such an endeavor would furnish a good reason, or an excuse, for keeping open an area of the Antarctic still relatively rich in blue whales.

Pelagic whaling had been carried on in the Antarctic for half a century, the pygmy area included. It is inconceivable that an important and numerous subspecies could have remained undiscovered for so long. It seems more than coincidental that the subspecies was "discovered" just when it could supply an excuse for the continued killing of blue whales.

In my opinion the pygmy blue whale was a fraud used as an excuse to continue killing blue whales in a portion of the Antarctic where a few could still be found. The 1963 meeting of the Whaling Commission was as much of a failure as its predecessors despite the apparent progress in granting the blue whale protection throughout much of the Antarctic. The architect of that failure was the Japanese whaling industry.

— 1964 —

The scientific advisers of the Whaling Commission were distressed at the latest reports on the blue whale. During the preceding whaling season the Norwegian fleets reported having seen only 8 blue whales.

The Japanese of course killed blue whales in the pygmy area, but they reported nearly 20 percent of them were regular blue whales. They admitted that it was impossible to recognize a pygmy blue whale until it was dead and hauled up onto the flensing deck of a factory ship. They did not admit that this cast any doubt on the existence of a significant color difference between the two. The scientists, supported by the Committee of Three, agreed that the pygmy area might yield 400 blue whales for three years. They pointed out the consequences of keeping the area open. If 400 blue whales were killed there about 20 percent of them would be regular blue whales, but the animal was so close to extinction that the death of even 1 or 2 should not be permitted. A motion was made and passed that the pygmy area be closed for the killing of blue whales. Japan and the USSR cast the only negative votes. Japan subsequently exercised the right of veto, all others did the same, and the killing continued another year.

— 1965 —

During the 1964/65 season 15 floating-factory expeditions operating with 172 catcher-boats killed 20 blue whales. The supposedly available 400 pygmy blues were not to be found. Had they ever existed? Perhaps Dr. Kellogg was right after all. The pygmies may well have been some young blue whales that podded near Kerguelen Island. In any event Japanese whalers did not kill 1 of the 20 blue whales taken during the preceding season. The Commission appealed to all pelagic nations to withdraw their objections to closing the pygmy area to the killing of blue whales. Japan agreed and so in 1965 the blue whale received complete protection from pelagic whalers throughout the Antarctic.

The killing stopped but only because the animal was no more.

Sic transit gloria maris.

VIII

EPILOGUE OR EPITAPH?

IN 1925 ONE OF MAN's numerous technological achievements allowed him to kill and process the carcasses of large whales on the high seas. The unrestrained slaughter that followed in the southern hemisphere resulted four decades later in the virtual extinction of the biggest animal that ever lived on the face of the earth. The few blue whales surviving there, not yet free from the threat of man's explosive harpoons, cannot perpetuate themselves. In the North Pacific the animal's fate was the same. If by some miracle the blue whale does survive anywhere it will be in the North Atlantic where no pelagic whaling has been carried on for several decades. Even there, however, the chances for survival of the blue whale are almost nil. But as the tragedy of the blue whale draws to a close it simultaneously ushers in a new tragedy for its author—Man.

As man exterminates one species of animal after another and his own multiplies without restraint he moves closer to the tragedy of starvation. The extermination of the blue whale was another irreversible step in that direction. The failure of the International Whaling Commission to protect the blue whale destroyed a large and perpetual source of food. At an optimum population level, of about 60,000 according to the population experts hired by the Whaling Commission, the blue whale could have supplied man in perpetuity with a sustainable yield of some 6,000 individuals annually. Six thousand blue whales with an average length of 80 feet could produce some 580,000 (long) tons of raw material. From that man could produce 105,300 tons of oil, enough to supply 2.5 ounces of margarine or edible oil a day every day for a year to 4,138,000 adult human beings.

In addition 189,000 long tons of meat could be produced, enough for a 6-ounce steak every day for a year for 3,090,000 adult human beings. That supply of food has been destroyed. This book has been limited to the blue whale, but a similar fate has befallen the humpback and the fin whale. If the stocks of fin whales had been managed properly it could have supplied man in perpetuity with an annual sustainable yield of 20,000 whales. Twenty thousand fin whales a year lost to hungry mankind means a loss of over 1 million tons of cetacean raw material, roughly twice as much as the blue whale. Without going into further statistical detail the loss to mankind of the large whales in the Southern Hemisphere is a tragedy involving the destruction of a perpetual source of food for over 12 million human beings. Man may have a higher I.Q. than his cetacean cousins but a superiority in common sense is much in doubt.

The International Whaling Commission did achieve a small measure of success that must not be overlooked. The Antarctic quota did have the effect of keeping the total catch lower than it might otherwise have been. In addition, a shorter season for the killing of blue whales also decreased slightly the number killed each year. The beneficial effects of these actions were investigated by one of the population experts. He calculated the number of blue whales spared each season and their later contribution to the population.[1] He concluded that the restrictions adopted by the Whaling Commission increased the total catch of blue whales by 4,300. The recorded kill of blue whales in the Antarctic from 1909 to 1965 was 328,177.

The tragedy of the passing of the blue whale at the hand of man involves more than a simple decrease in food supply. The blue whale, a close mammalian relative of man, had a nearly identical body temperature, a similar eye, circulatory system, brain, et cetera. Had man studied the animal anatomically as assiduously as he killed him what secrets about himself might he not have discovered? How did the eye of a blue whale survive years of contact with ice water without developing the ills of human eyes? Tens of thousands of blue whales were killed by man but not one suffered from a malignant tumor. Why? Every human being with a loved one suffering from cancer has cause to wonder, agonizingly.

The responsibility for the extermination of the blue whale could be attributed, somewhat simplistically, to human greed. That human failing was understood by the delegates to the Washington Conference in 1946, and they sought to temper it by creating a regulatory body to impose rational restraint on the whaling industry. The International Whaling Commission was a failure for several reasons, some of them obvious. The Whaling Commission chose to hold its meetings in private with access denied specifically to members of the press. World public opinion was thus prevented from exercising any significant influence on its decisions. Furthermore, private meetings undoubtedly kept many people ignorant of what was happening to the whales but knowledge of the existence of the Whaling Commission led them to assume that whalers were subject to effective control. Another cause for the failure of the International Whaling Commission was a perpetual shortage of funds for which it was not directly responsible. Governmental or administrative blindness on the part of the world's great whaling nations is probably responsible for the annual contribution of a paltry £250 to support the work of the Commission. At a crucial moment in the decline of the blue whale, 1962, the report of the Committee of Three Scientists was not ready for the Whaling Commission because no way had been found to pay them. No action was taken to protect the blue whale until their report was ready a year later, during which time about 60 percent of the remaining blue whales were killed, a loss that in all probability deprived the species of its last chance for survival.

The most important and most complex reason for the failure of the International Whaling Commission was the one which denied it the power to impose effective restrictions on its members without their consent. The restrictions should have included a limit to the number of factory ships, a system of international inspection, species quotas, and a limit to the number of whales to be taken by each factory ship or nation. Those restrictions could not be imposed because they would have violated one of man's most sacred political principles— the freedom of the seas. The nation-state system of man is based on the sovereignty of every government with the *de facto* and usually *de jure* legislative and executive power to regulate all activities within its territorial boundaries. By mutual consent of the community of nations oceanic areas beyond their territorial waters, referred to usually as the high seas, are subject to the laws of no nation. Each nation retains the right to utilize the resources of the high seas without restraint in any manner it decides. That was the stumbling block that doomed to failure all prewar efforts to regulate the Antarctic pelagic whaling industry. Nations which did not wish to submit to the restraints written into a treaty on whaling control simply refused to ratify it. Imperial Japan and Nazi Germany under the aegis of the freedom of the seas had the legal right to kill as many whales of any size or species when or wherever they chose. The International Whaling Commission established after the war faced the same basic problem and could not solve it. Some nations did not like the conservation restrictions adopted at the inception of the Whaling Commission and refused to join. Most nations joined because they had a right to veto any proposed restraints on their whaling activities. All members had the right to withdraw from the Whaling Commission and make their own rules or none at all. The concept of the freedom of the seas remains unchanged. The International Whaling Commission is as impotent as ever. The remaining whales of the world have no more protection against the threat of extinction than did the blue whale.

In all the vast reaches of the high seas of the Southern Hemisphere the Right whale is no more. The humpback is no more. The blue whale is no more. The fin whale is nearing commercial extinction. The little sei whale will be next. How many more irreversible tragedies will man inflict on his cetacean cousins? How many more sacrifices will be laid on the high altar of the freedom of the seas? Will the process continue until the altar itself has lost all meaning? It need not. Man has learned that his individual freedoms are not destroyed when limited by a modicum of consideration for the rights of others. Libel laws are less an infringement of free speech than a protection of the dignity of innocent persons. So too with the high seas. The nations of the world could renounce their right to be the final arbiter of what constitutes proper whaling regulations. They would not thereby lose the freedom to navigate anywhere on the world ocean. The best method of achieving this would be to grant to some international body such as the Food and Agricultural Organization of the U.N. the sole authority to harvest the whales of the high seas. A World Whaling Authority could limit the catch of each species to its sustainable yield, and it could license the required number of whaling companies needed to achieve that end. Further, the World Whaling Authority could sell the production to nations with the greatest food shortage and limit the profit of the licensed companies to a fair and reasonable level of return on investment. Any excess profits could be used to support research into better food production methods or added to the operating budget of the U.N. itself.[2] Only under the protection of some such international authority can the remaining whales of the high seas be secure from the threat of extinction and constitute a perpetual source of food in a world increasingly plagued with hunger.

A couple of years ago, I inquired of a State Department official the reason for American participation in the International Whaling Commission. He replied: "The United States is a member of a dozen or so important international fisheries commissions. We are a member of the International Whaling Commission primarily because if it should fail we will want to know why in order to prevent the same from happening to the others." But for the marble halls of the State Department I would have used profanity. "The humpback and the blue whale have been slaughtered to the point of biological extinction! Don't you consider the Whaling Commission a failure?" "Why, no. It still exists doesn't it?" The aim of this book is understanding and mercy and therefore that spokesman for the United States of America will remain nameless. His ignorance of the failures of the Whaling Commission is not typical, however, of government officials of many nations associated with that organization. Many influential administrators are well aware of the failures of the Whaling Commission, yet they have made no serious effort to change its basic structure. Why? Most of them believe that somehow the Whaling Commission can yet be made to function as successfully as several almost identical international fisheries commissions. The present International Whaling Commission can never be as successful as the fisheries commissions because of the quite different legal framework of whales and fish. The difference is as misunderstood by diplomats as by conservationists. They should not be criticized too harshly because the difference has never been clarified.

Under Roman law the term *res communis* was used to describe such things as air, rivers, and the sea which by their very nature could not be privately owned. The idea that a *res communis* belonged to no one, but could be used and enjoyed by all, has survived to the present day and is now referred to as a *common property resource*. The modern term has been modified, however, to include not only things such as animals like whales and rabbits that can be individually owned but also things which come within the jurisdictional framework of a nation state. This is illustrated by a specific definition given by Justice Riley of the Supreme Court of Oklahoma. "What is meant by a thing that is common property? It is when the thing involved belongs to the body of the citizenship."[3]

There are obviously many things, animal as well as mineral, that can be considered common property but only so long as they are found within the legal boundaries of a nation state. The high seas and their resources beyond all national boundaries cannot be considered common property belonging to a body of citizenship. To assume that the world ocean belongs to the body of the world citizenship is erroneous for two reasons. First, to state the obvious, the oceans are uninhabited by any permanent human population. Second, and more important, the nations of the world support the principle of the freedom of the seas that grants to all the right to use the sea but denies to all the right of ownership. Only when an oceanic animal such as a whale or a fish is killed or captured may ownership be acquired. Roman law made a clear distinction between such animals and the sea itself and classified them as a *res nullius*.

The Roman legal term *res nullius* referred to wild animals because they had no owner but could by their very nature be captured and then subject to ownership. The Roman distinction between resources such as air and wild animals was a useful one which should be revived today, but revived in the light of modern legal concepts. The buffalo, for example, may be considered a common property resource of the United States whose government may regulate ownership and use of the animal. Animals like the blue whale that inhabit the high seas must be given a modern classification akin to the Roman *res nullius*. Such animals are extraterritorial in both a legal and a geographic sense and the term should be applied to them. They live beyond the territorial limits of all nations in a region of the earth which cannot come under the jurisdiction of any state. The extra-territorial status of a blue whale resembles in essence the extraterritoriality enjoyed by diplomats, namely, the right to live temporarily in a foreign country without being subject to its laws.

Most conservationists are aware of the different legal problems involved in the struggle to protect buffalo and whales even though they consider both types of animals a common property resource. Conservationists must recognize the very clear difference between a common property resource and an extraterritorial resource. Until they do they will not achieve outstanding success in preserving many valuable resources of the world because the existence of a third type of resource will continue to confuse them. It is precisely the third type of resource that misled many to believe that somehow the International Whaling Commission could operate as successfully as similar international fisheries commissions.

There are many animals, such as buffalo, kangaroos, and panda bears, that spend their entire life within the territorial limits of one nation and are therefore common property resources. There are others, such as blue, fin, sei, and sperm whales, that spend their entire life on the high seas and are therefore extraterritorial resources. There is a third type of animal that spends part of its life cycle in one country and part of it on the high seas. Among them, for example, are green turtles, anadromous salmon and shad, seals, shrimp, halibut, lobster, and cod. These are transient common property resources because they spend part of their life cycle, often a critical one, within the territorial limits of some nation state. Several international commissions have been established to protect many of those animals from overexploitation. On the whole they have been quite successful. Compared to the International Whaling Commission they have been eminently successful. Why? Some writers have tried to explain that success by the higher rate of reproductivity of those animals compared to whales. That is a contributing factor but it is not the explanation. The reason for their success derives from the legal framework of the species involved and the potential threat of preemptive ownership by one nation.

Salmon spawn far from the sea in shallow headwaters of fresh water rivers; halibut spawn in shallow protected coastal waters; and shrimp must pass the early stages of their life cycle in the brackish waters of mangrove swamps. In all cases some nation has jurisdiction over those animals during a critical phase of their life cycle. Those and similar transient common property animals can therefore receive effective protection from overexploitation during part of their life cycle and enjoy a much reduced threat of extermination. It is necessary, of course, that the nation in question adopt rational conservation policies for their protection.

The locale where most transient common property animals are harvested usually contributes significantly to their survival chances. The main food source for the adult animals is often in the shallow offshore waters of continental shelves. The rich fishing grounds of the Grand Banks are a typical example. All regulations governing the catch of several species of fish on the Grand Banks have been adopted by the Northwest Atlantic Fisheries Commission. Those regulations apply to over a dozen nations, all of which have exhibited a cooperative attitude in formulating those regulations and in obeying them. In 1969, for example, the Northwest Atlantic Fisheries Commission, meeting in Warsaw, Poland, took effective action to protect the declining stock of haddock. On several occasions inspectors from the United States and the Soviet Union have changed places and inspected each other's vessels operating on the Grand Banks. In view of the spirit of cooperation that made possible those mutual inspections it is not surprising that no serious infractions were found. The reproductivity of fish cannot explain the cooperation by many nations that is responsible for the relative success of the Northwest Atlantic Fisheries Commission. That cooperation and success are due to the legal framework of the fish as transient common property animals of the United States and Canada.

What would happen if some nation refused to cooperate in conserving the stocks of fish of the Grand Banks and threatened the very existence of a valuable species? The United States or Canada or both could simply extend its territorial waters out to the limits of the continental shelf or 200 miles, whichever would grant more protection to the fish. There is ample precedence for such a unilateral declaration and the nations that fish there are well aware of it. They are aware also that many American fishermen now advocate such a move.

The American fishermen claim that Europeans are taking more of their fish than they are and that the supply is diminishing. The American fishermen are not altogether wrong when they claim the fish are theirs. The fish of the Grand Banks may be caught in international waters but their lives are in large measure dependent on the American continent. The food that sustains them is a product of the complex ecological relationship between the waters of the continental shelf, shallow coastal waters, and the land itself. Some species depend directly on the coastal waters for spawning grounds; some species when immature find protection from predators among the rocks and weeds of countless bays and inlets.. What the American fishermen are trying to say is that the fish of the Grand Banks are transient common property resources that the United States and Canada have a greater right to harvest and protect than does any other nation.

Diplomats and conservationists must recognize that the blue whale, like other large cetacean species, was an extraterritorial animal. As such, it could never receive protection from any nation. Every stage of its life cycle was spent on the high seas where no nation had to submit to any conservation regulation it deemed restrictive. When blue whales congregated to feed in Arctic and Antarctic waters they were subjected to a slaughter that the International Whaling Commission was powerless to restrain. Representatives of a nation with an enlightened conservation policy, like Norway, could not protect the blue whale from extinction. They could talk, argue, cajole, or preach, but they could not act. Nations like Japan and the Netherlands do cooperate in the efforts to preserve the resources of the offshore fisheries near their home waters. But on the high seas they could display a deplorable lack of concern for conservation and a crass indifference to the threat of biological extinction of the blue whale. On the high seas they could neither be punished nor denied access to any of its resources. The freedom of the seas dealt a cruel fate to the blue whale.

What is the future of the remaining whales of the world? They have no more protection than the blue whale had. Those species that are useful to man are still in danger and are being hunted too intensively. The International Whaling Commission still exists and is still powerless. No species is safe from extermination and will not be until the nations of the world accept a limitation to the freedom of the seas. The extraterritorial status of the whales must end. Ownership of the whales of the world must be granted to some international authority that has the power to regulate all whaling activities. Until that occurs there can be no hope that the tragedy of the blue whale will not be repeated.

The tragedy of the blue whale is the reflection of an even greater one, that of man himself. What is the nature of a species that knowingly and without good reason exterminates another? How long will man persist in the belief that he is the master of this Earth rather than one of its guests? When will he learn that he is but one form of life among countless thousands, each one of which is in some way related to and dependent on all others? How long can he survive if he does not? It might be easier for man to acknowledge his dependence on other life forms if he could recognize his kinship with them. Whatever the nature of the Creator he surely did not intend that the forms on which he bestowed the gift of life should be exterminated by man. Survival chances for the human race will be greatly enhanced when man concedes to the Earth and all its life forms the right to exist that he wants for himself. The only homage he can now pay to the blue whale is to learn the lessons of dependence on and kinship with all life. If he does not learn them the great blue whale will have died in vain—having taught nothing to his only mortal enemy.

NOTES

I: INTRODUCTION TO TRAGEDY

1. J. C. Moore and E. Clark, "Discovery of Right Whales in the Gulf of Mexico," *Science* (July, 1963), p. 269.

2. J. Norman and F. Fraser, in *Giant Fishes, Whales, and Dolphins* (New York, 1938), were of the opinion that the Greenland Right Whale was all but biologically extinct. E. Slijper, in *Whales* (London, 1962), was of the opinion that the species is showing a comeback and presumably is not facing imminent extinction.

3. R. M. Gilmore, "A census of the California gray whale," *Special Scientific Report: Fisheries,* U.S. Fish and Wildlife Service, #342, pp. 1–30.

4. S. F. Harmer, "History of Whaling," *Proceedings of the Linnaen Society,* CXL (1928), 51–95.

5. R. C. Andrews, "Monographs of the Pacific Cetacea. I. The California Gray Whale," *Memoirs of the American Museum of Natural History,* I (5), 229–87.

6. L. Adams, "Census of the Gray Whale, 1966–67," *Norsk Hvalfangst Tidende* (March/April, 1968), pp. 41–43. See also D. H. Ramsey, "Diurnal Fluctuations in Censuses of Migrating California Gray Whales," *Norsk Hvalfangst Tidende* (September/October, 1968), pp. 101–5.

7. *International Whaling Statistics,* Det Norske Hvalråds Statistiske Publikasjoner, Oslo, XVI (1942), p. 12.

8. *Ibid.,* p. 54.

9. *International Whaling Statistics,* XVI (1942), 86, and LIII (1964), 24–25.

10. *Ibid.,* LXI (1968), 26–28.

11. An exhaustive four-volume history of modern Norwegian whaling entitled *Den Moderne Hvalfangsts Historie* by Professor J. N. Tønnessen is being readied for publication.

12. *International Whaling Statistics,* XVI (1942), 81. Note: all data on catch and catching material cited henceforth are taken from this annual source.

13. J. N. Tønnessen, "Discovery II in the Antarctic," *Norsk Hvalfangst Tidende* (henceforth cited as *NHT*) (October, 1965), pp. 225–26.

II: THE BLUE WHALE

1. Johan T. Ruud, "The Blue Whale," *Scientific American,* Vol. CLXXXXV, No. 6, pp. 46–50.

2. F. W. True, "The Whalebone Whales of the Western North Atlantic," *Smithsonian Contributions to Knowledge,* Vol. XXXIII (Washington, D.C., 1904). For additional discussion on the taxonomy of the blue whale see A. Brinkmann, Jr., "The Identification and Names of Our Fin Whale Species," *NHT* (May/June, 1967), pp. 49–56.

3. V. A. Zemsky and V. A. Boronin, "On the Question of the Pygmy Blue Whale Taxonomic Position," *NHT* (November, 1964), pp. 306–11.

4. A. Brinkmann, "Studies on Female Fin and Blue Whales," *Hvalrådets Skrifter,* XXXI (1948), 36.

5. E. J. Slijper, *Whales* (London: Hutchinson & Co., 1962), pp. 363, 384–85.

6. J. T. Ruud, Å. Jonsgård, and P. Ottestad, "Age Studies on Blue Whales," *Hvalrådets Skrifter,* XXXIII (1950), 39–40.

7. S. Risting, "Whales and Whale Foetuses," *Rapports et Procès-Verbaux des Réunions,* Conseil Permanent International pour l'Exploration de la Mer, L (1928), 54.

8. J. T. Jenkins, *Whales and Modern Whaling* (London, 1932), pp. 138–40.

9. A. Brinkmann, pp. 14–17.

10. Ruud, Jonsgård, and Ottestad, pp. 6–7, 33–34.

11. Reference here is to the fin whale, *Balaenoptera physalus,* a rorqual that resembles the blue whale in many ways. A fin whale in terms of oil production was only half as valuable as a blue, a ratio that will be discussed in a later chapter.

12. Risting, pp. 114–18.

13. N. A. Mackintosh and J. F. E. Wheeler, "Southern Blue and Fin Whales," *Discovery Reports,* I (1929), 436–46.

14. Ruud, Jonsgård, and Ottestad, pp. 1–66.

15. *Ibid.,* pp. 67–72.

16. M. Nishiwaki and T. Oye, "On the Age Determination of Mystacoceti, Chiefly Blue and Fin Whales," *Scientific Reports* (Whales Research Institute, Tokyo), VII (1952), 125–88.

17. Risting, p. 27.

18. S. Risting, *Av Hvalfangstens Historie* (Kristiania [Oslo]: J. W. Cappelens Forlag, 1922), p. 3.

19. E. F. Heyerdahl, *Hvalindustrien I, Råmaterialet* (Komm. Chr. Christensens Hvalfangstmuseum, Sandefjord, 1932), pp. 44–58, 83–87.

20. For details of this temperature rise, see E. F. Heyerdahl, "On the Treatment of the Whale," *NHT* (August, 1938), pp. 339–41.

21. A. B. Holt, "Rendering Plants on Board Factory Ships Considered from the Point of View of Investment," *NHT* (July, 1954), pp. 254–55.

22. Average whale-oil price was calculated by me from information published in the annual reports of the Norwegian pelagic whaling companies.

23. Based on data supplied to my Japanese assistant by Chief of the Accounting Section, Nippon Suisan, Inc.; Chief of the Fishery Section,

Kyokuyo Hogei, Inc.; and Vice Chief of the Whaling Department, Taiyo Gyogyo Inc. Note: Japanese oil sold in Europe measured in long tons; whale meat sold on home market measured in metric tons.

24. W. E. Schevill, W. A. Watkins, and R. H. Backus, "The 20 Cycle Signals and Balaenoptera (Finwhales)," in W. N. Tavogla, ed., *Marine Bio-Acoustics* (Pergammon Press, 1964), pp. 147–52.

25. P. E. Purves, "The Wax Plug in the External Auditory Meatus of the Mysteceti," *Discovery Reports*, XXVII (1956), 293–302. Another interesting but largely ineffective method of age determination was based on the change in translucency of the eye lens with increasing age. See M. Nishiwaki, "Determination of the Age of Antarctic Blue and Fin Whales by the Colour Changes in Crystalline Lens," *Scientific Reports* (Whales Research Institute, Tokyo), IV, 115–61.

26. J. W. S. Marr, "*Euphasia superba* and the Antarctic Surface Currents," *NHT* (March, 1956), pp. 127–34. Marr treats this subject in great detail in his "The Natural History and Geography of the Antarctic Krill (*Euphasia superba*)," *Discovery Reports*, XXXII (1962), 32–464.

27. Mackintosh and Brown, 1956, pp. 469–80. The whales referred to in the graph are blues, fins, and humpbacks, the proportion of blues being about 15 percent. The quantities shown are approximate rather than precise. Scientists on the population research vessel, *Discovery II*, made fewer and less precise observations after the start of the Antarctic winter, and the apparent increase shown for May is almost surely an error.

28. N. A. Mackintosh, "The Southern Stock of Whalebone Whales," *Discovery Reports*, XXII (1942), 209–13.

29. J. T. Ruud, "Om Hvalfangstens Naturgrunnlag," *NHT* (June, 1938), p. 243.

30. S. Risting, "Whales and Whale Foetuses," *Rapports et Procès-Verbaux des Réunions*, L (1928), 93–95.

31. N. A. Mackintosh, "The Southern School of Whalebone Whales," *Discovery Reports*, XXII (1942), 223.

32. R. M. Laws, "Reproduction, Growth and Age of Southern Fin Whales," *Discovery Reports*, XXXI (1961), 456–59.

33. J. T. Ruud, "Blåhvalen," *NHT* (January, 1937), pp. 19–20. Some of the American bomb fragments are on display at the Hvalfangstmuseum in Sandefjord, Norway.

34. "Kongofeltet, Kort Historisk," *NHT* (April, 1936), pp. 109–10.

35. R. Clark, "Migrations of Marine Animals," *NHT* (November, 1957), pp. 616–17.

36. J. Hjort, J. Lie, and J. T. Ruud, "Norwegian Pelagic Whaling in the Antarctic," *Hvalrådets Skrifter*, III (1932), 1–37.

37. S. F. Harmer, "Southern Whaling," *Proceedings of the Linnaean Society* (London), Session 142 (1931), pp. 85–163.

38. S. E. Brown, "The Movements of Fin and Blue Whales Within the Antarctic Zone, *"Discovery Reports,* xxv (1953), 33.

39. J. Lund, "Charting of Whale Stocks in the Antarctic in the Season of 1949/50 on the Basis of Iodine Values," *NHT* (July, 1950), pp. 298–305.

III: DECIMATION

1. *"International Whaling Statistics,* LIII (1964), 14. All data on catch and catching materiel presented in subsequent figures are from this source or *Norsk Hvalfangst Tidende.* In a few instances data for the seasons 1931 through 1933 are incomplete. In all cases rudimentary data for the years of World War II are omitted.

2. For a discussion of the problems involved in trying to adjust the unit of effort to changes in catcher efficiency and weather conditions, see International Whaling Commission, Sixteenth Meeting (1964), "Final Report—Special Committee of Three Scientists," pp. 41–42, 87–92.

3. International Whaling Commission, Eighteenth Meeting (1966), "Report of the IWC/FAO Joint Working Party on Whale Stock Assessment," Doc. No. IWC/18/7, pp. 1–2.

4. International Whaling Commission, Fifteenth Meeting (1963), "Provisional Report, Meeting of the Scientific Committee and the Committee of Three Scientists," Doc. No. IWC/15/6, pp. 37–38.

5. International Whaling Commission, Fifteenth Meeting (Plenary Session of July 1, 1963), Doc. No. IWC/15/17, p. 12.

6. T. Ichihara and T. Doi, "Stock Assessment of Pygmy Blue Whales in the Antarctic," *NHT* (June, 1964), p. 146.

7. Slijper, pp. 272–74.

8. International Whaling Commission, Fifteenth Meeting (1963), "Final Report, Special Committee of Three Scientists," Doc. No. IWC/15/9, pp. 15–16.

IV: ANTARCTIC PELAGIC WHALING

1. For a detailed description of the layout of a factory ship see K. Brandt, "Whaling and Whale Oil During and After World War II," *War-Peace Pamphlets* (Food Research Institute, Stanford University, 1948), XI, 15–18. For the details of the functioning of the rendering apparatuses see E. F. Heyerdahl, "On the Treatment of the Whale," *NHT* (August, 1938), pp. 339–50; (September, 1938), pp. 392–407; and (October, 1938), pp. 440–58.

2. The name and tonnage of all ships used in an Antarctic whaling season were published during the course of the season in *NHT*.

3. W. C. MacKenzie, "The Whaling Industry: Economic Aspects," *Canadian Geographical Journal* (March, 1949), p. 142.

4. "The New Floating Factory *Willem Barendsz* Delivered from the Shipyard," *NHT* (August, 1955), p. 473. (Less than ten years later the Dutch company that operated the *Willem Barendsz* failed and had to sell the ship for a reported price of $2.9 million.)

5. M. Kravanja, "A Short History of Soviet Whaling Activities," unpublished memorandum compiled for the Branch of Foreign Fisheries, Bureau of Commercial Fisheries, U.S. Department of Interior, p. 6.

6. *Beretning og Regnskap,* 1950–51, Aksjeselskapet Kosmos, Sandefjord, Norway. Note: Annual reports of Norwegian corporations are limited in scope; their pages rarely total more than 8 or 10 and are not usually numbered.

7. "Dutch Whaling Operations," *NHT* (December, 1951), pp. 629–30.

8. *Beretning og Regnskap,* Globus, Hvalfangerselskapet, Larvik, Norway, 1951, 1952, 1953.

9. A British whaling chemist was able to show that these values were only approximate. He found that the ideal values should be blue whale, 1; fin whale, 1.7; humpback, 2.5; and sei whale, 3.8. See D. T. Crisp, "The Tonnages of Whales Taken by Antarctic Pelagic Operations During Twenty Seasons, and an Examination of the Blue-Whale Unit," *NHT* (October, 1962), pp. 389–93.

10. Negotiations for a reduction in the number of catchers were private, and no records of them are available. For the best discussion of the problems involved, see "Whale Catcher Restrictions," *NHT* (June, 1956), pp. 297–98. and "Position of the Whaling Industry at the Turn of the Year," *NHT* (January, 1957), pp. 14–19.

11. It should not be assumed that the sperm whale was not hunted excessively elsewhere. On the contrary, there is evidence that the animal has been hunted much too heavily in many low-latitude regions.

12. MacKenzie, p. 141.

13. "Whale Oil Prices in the Years 1888–1939," *International Whaling Statistics,* XVI (1942), 54.

14. M. K. Schwitzer, *Margarine and Other Food Fats* (New York: Interscience Publishers, 1956), p. 79.

15. "The Japanese Whaling Industry," *NHT* (November, 1954), pp. 625–32.

16. Y. Arai and S. Sakai, "Whale Meat in Nutrition," *Scientific Reports* (Whales Research Institute, Tokyo), VII (1952), 54–57.

17. *Beretning og Regnskap* for the following companies: Rosshavet A/S, Sandefjord; Ørnen A/S, Sandefjord; and Polaris A/S, Larvik, 1961–1965. All fiscal data on Norwegian whaling companies henceforth cited in the text are from the annual reports of these companies unless otherwise stated.

18. T. Pedersen, "Oil From the Meat of Sperm Whales," *NHT* (June, 1952), p. 296.

19. G. Borgstrom, *Japan's World Success in Fishing* (London: Fishing News Ltd., 1964), p. 37.

20. *Business Week,* February 9, 1952, p. 23; and, November 30, 1957, pp. 100-7.

21. K. Brandt, *Whale Oil: An Economic Analysis* (Food Research Institute, Stanford University, 1940), p. 134.

V: INDUSTRIAL ECONOMICS AND EXTERMINATION

1. *Beretning og Regnskap* (annual reports) of all Norwegian publicly owned whaling companies. (Prices converted from pounds and kroner to dollars by me.) All whaling companies received the same price for their oil. Prior to World War II they formed a Selling Pool (De Norske Hvalfangstselskapers Salgsring) to market their oil in Western Europe to avoid bargaining against each other. The Selling Pool sold the oil, often at different prices during a given year, and reimbursed the companies according to their production.

2. The final results of those negotiations may be found in the Autumn issues of the *Norsk Hvalfangst Tidende.* Discussion of the differences of opinion between unions and management may only be found in local newspapers, especially the *Sandefjords Blad* and the *Vestfold Fremtid,* both of Sandefjord, Norway.

3. Oppgaver som viser antall norske mannskaper samt gjennomsnittsfortjeneste pr. mann pr. sesong og pr. måned. (Unpublished document of the Bureau of Whaling Statistics, Sandefjord, Norway.)

4. Calculated by me from data used in the construction of Figure 17 taken from *Beretning og Regnskap* of the Norwegian whaling companies listed.

5. Personal communication from C. E. Ash.

6. Personal communication from Kontorsjef Thor Gulliksen, Hvalfangeraktieselskapet Rosshavet, Sandefjord, Norway. For reasons unknown the Rosshavet company, which ceased whaling after the 1965 season, was the only company to offer any assistance to me in this and related matters.

7. Personal interview, July, 1966.

8. Personal communication from C. E. Atkinson, Fisheries Attaché, American Embassy, Tokyo, September, 1967.

9. "Estimated Value of Japan's Antarctic Whale Production 1963-64 Season," unclassified document Tokyo A-844, submitted to the Bureau of Commercial Fisheries by the Fisheries Attaché, U.S. Embassy, Tokyo.

10. J. Walsh, "Whales: Decline Continues Despite Limitations on Catch," *Science,* CLVII (September 1, 1967), 1025.

11. The names of the ships used by the Japanese companies in the North Pacific may be found in annual articles in *NHT*, usually about a year after the close of the season.

VI: NATIONAL WHALING POLICIES

1. K. Eckstrøm, "Main Features in the Development of the Norwegian Whaling Control," *NHT* (February, 1953), pp. 560–62.

2. J. Lie, "Whaling Problems and the Norwegian Whaling Council," *NHT* (October, 1952), pp. 529–33.

3. "Whale Measurements, Season 1936–37," *NHT* (March, 1938), pp. 78–83.

4. "Den Britiske Hvallov," *NHT* (September, 1935), p. 156.

5. "The Norwegian Whaling Act," *NHT* (June, 1939), pp. 232–35.

6. J. Lie, pp. 533–36.

7. "Regulations for Distribution of the Assets of the Whaling Industry's Security Fund," *NHT* (April, 1948), pp. 151–52.

8. Personal communication from J. Lie, Secretary of the Whaling Council, Oslo, Norway.

9. H. Th. Knudtzon, "Concerning Paragraph 5a of the Whaling Act," *NHT* (November, 1953), pp. 621–25. See also, F. Bettum, "Some Observations on the Development of Whaling and Its Central Problem Today," *NHT* (June, 1960), pp. 254–57.

10. Personal communication from Judge H. Th. Knudtzon, former chairman, Norwegian Whaling Council, who represented Norway in most of the discussions with officials of Argentina and Italy.

11. "Lov om endring i lov om fangst av hval av 16 juni, 1939," *NHT* (August, 1946), pp. 184–94.

12. *Norsk Retstidende,* Oslo, 1954, pp. 478–82.

13. This explanation of the reasoning of a majority of the members of the government and the Whaling Council was furnished by Judge H. Th. Knudtzon, former chairman of the Norwegian Whaling Council.

14. Translation from the Norwegian by me from "Fangstsesongen 1960–61," *Beretning og Regnskap,* 31 Driftsår (1959–60), Aksjeselskapet Kosmos, Sandefjord, p. 4.

15. International Whaling Commission, Seventh Meeting, Document No. XXIC (Plenary Session of July 22, 1955), p. 46.

16. J. Lie, "Whaling Problems and the Norwegian Whaling Council," *NHT* (October, 1952), p. 529. Italics are mine.

17. C. D. Carus and C. L. McNichols, *Japan: Its Resources and Industries* (New York: Harper and Bros. Co., 1944), pp. 68–70. See also J. T. Ruud, "International Regulation of Whaling," *NHT* (September, 1956), pp. 376–80.

18. W. M. Terry, "The Japanese Whaling Industry Prior to 1946," Re-

port No. 126, Natural Resources Section, General Headquarters, Supreme Commander for Allied Powers, Tokyo, March 1, 1950, pp. 9–10.

19. *Ibid.*, pp. 132–39.

20. Article 52, Chapter III, *The Fisheries Law*, Ministry of Agriculture and Forestry, Fisheries Agency (reprinted with amendments in 1963), p. 45. Future references to the Fisheries Law will relate to the specific articles and chapters of the law itself.

21. U.S. Bureau of Commercial Fisheries, *Foreign Fishery Information Release No. 62–31*, October 24, 1962, p. 1. (Based on information in *Minato Shimbun*, October 17, 1962; translated by J. H. Shohara.)

22. *Ibid.*, *Release No. 62–25*, October 25, 1965, p. 1. (Compiled from *Suisan Keizai Shimbun*, October 8, 1965 by L. M. Nakatsu and J. H. Shohara.)

23. *Ibid.*, *Release No. 67–38*, November 14, 1967, p. 2. (Compiled by J. H. Shohara from *Shin Suisan Shimbun Sokuko*, November 4, 1967.) Also *Release No. 67–39*, November 20, 1967, p. 2. (Compiled by J. H. Shohara from *Shin Suisan Shimbun*, November 13, 1967.)

24. A recent amendment to the Fishery Law granted to the Minister of Agriculture and Forestry power to prohibit Japanese ships from entering or fishing in waters that the minister might delimit around a foreign country. (Article 92–2, Ordinance 52, Ministry of Agriculture and Forestry, October, 1966.) Japan could also have prevented its whalers from operating off Chile in violation of Whaling Commission regulations by applying its Passport Law, which permits the government to forbid travel outside the country. This law was applied at the insistence of the fishing/whaling companies to prevent skilled fishermen from aiding the development of a South Korean pelagic fishing industry.

25. U.S. Bureau of Commercial Fisheries, *Foreign Fishery Information Release No. 63–17*, August 8, 1963, pp. 1–4.

26. By contrast, only once in the history of the Whaling Commission did a spokesman for the Norwegian whaling companies have the opportunity to address the Commission, and even then he had to obtain permission from the Norwegian commissioner before doing so. See International Whaling Commission, Eighth Meeting (1956), Doc. No. XIIIC, pp. 98–99.

27. U.S. Department of State, Report of the U.S. Commissioner to the Fifteenth Annual Meeting of the International Whaling Commission (London, England, July 1–5, 1963), p. 43.

28. Oral communication, July, 1965, from a State Department official who wishes to remain anonymous because he is still a member of the U.S. delegation to the International Whaling Commission. In August, 1966, I received nearly identical comments from two Norwegian officials who expressed the wish to remain anonymous for the same reason.

29. H. R. Lillie, "Whales Could Be Saved at Trivial Cost," *The Daily Telegraph*, London, July 8, 1966, p. 21.

30. Written communication from Dr. H. R. Lillie, December 15, 1966. Note: the Nippon Suisan company was the only one to offer cooperation to the Japanese investigators engaged by me. Despite the similarity of names it should not be associated with the company owned by the Manchurian Heavy Industries Corporation.

31. U.S. Bureau of Commercial Fisheries, *Foreign Fishery Information Release No. 66–4,* January 28, 1966, p. 1. (Compiled by L. M. Nakatsu and J. H. Shohara from *Suisan Keizai Shimbun,* January 24, 1966.)

32. *Ibid., Release No. 66–11,* May 13, 1966, p. 3. (Compiled by L. M. Nakatsu and J. H. Shohara from *Suisan Tsushin,* April 30, 1966, and other sources not listed.)

33. International Whaling Commission, Sixteenth Meeting (1964), "Report of the Scientific Committee," Doc. No. IWC/16/3, p. 3.

34. The practice related here cannot be documented. It was explained to me by Norwegian whalingmen who were obviously chagrined at being subject to a strict interpretation of the regulations while whalingmen of other nationalities were not.

35. International Whaling Commission, Fifteenth Meeting (1963), "Report of the Scientific Committee," Doc. No. IWC/15/3, p. 3.

36. "*Olympic Challenger,*" *NHT* (1950), pp. 152–54 (some bound copies of the *Norsk Hvalfangst Tidende* have no reference to month of publication; there are also a few bound volumes without advertising, and page numbers do not correspond with other bound copies).

37. "Illegal Operation of the *Olympic Challenger* Factory Ship of Panama Registry," special report submitted by the Japanese Delegation to the Seventh Meeting (1955) of the International Whaling Commission. Document No. XXIV, pp. 1–2.

38. *America,* XCV (April 28, 1956), 94.

39. Details of the illegal whaling practices of the *Olympic Challenger* were reported in numerous articles in several Norwegian newspapers. The following articles cover the infractions cited: *a*) "Norges Hvalfangstforbund bringer bevisene for *Olympic Challengers* ulovlige hvalfangst," *Sandefjords Blad,* Sandefjord, January 16, 1956. *b*) "Bevisene mot Onassis," *Aftenposten,* Oslo, January 17, 1956. *c*) "Onassis ulovlige hvalfangst avsløres," *Norges Handels og Sjøfarts Tidende,* Oslo, March 6, 1956. *d*) "Denne gangen skyr man ingenting," *Tønsbergs Blad,* Tønsberg, March 6, 1956. *e*) "Ikke noen gang har jeg sett de panamanske kontrollørene i verksomhet på flensplan," *Tønsbergs Blad,* March 8, 1956.

Infractions not covered by the preceding Norwegian articles may be found in English in: *a*) "*Olympic Challenger* has not observed the Regulations of the International Whaling Convention," *NHT* (November, 1955), pp. 381–98; continued in January, 1956, pp. 1–37. *b*) "*Olympic Challenger's* catch in relation to the provisions of the International Whaling Convention," *NHT* (April, 1956), pp. 172–208.

40. "Norsk aksjon mot Onassis," *Haugesunds Avis,* Haugesund, March 26, 1956.

41. "Norske hvalredere er gått til ny aksjon mot Onassis," *Arbeiderbladet,* Oslo, April 22, 1956.

42. "Beslagleggelsene i Rotterdam for retten," *Norges Handels og Sjøfarts Tidende,* Oslo, April 24, 1956.

43. "Hvorfor reduserte Hvalfangstforbundet kravet mot Onassis?" *Vestfold Arbeiderblad,* May 24, 1956.

44. "*Olympic Challenger,*" *Tønsbergs Blad,* February 18, 1956.

45. "Onassis—forliket seier for Norge," *Morgonbladet,* Oslo, May 28, 1956.

46. "Intet svar på Norges protest hos Panama?" *Sandefjords Blad,* October 29, 1956.

VII: INTERNATIONAL WHALING CONTROL

1. J. T. Ruud, "International Regulation of Whaling," *NHT* (September, 1956), pp. 376–77.

2. "Whaling Conference 4th & 5th October 1935," *Hvalrådets Skrifter,* XII (1935), 15–16. This article contains the best analysis of the problems of limiting production and whaling control in the 1930s.

3. "Hvalfangerforeningen Årsberetning," *NHT* (February, 1937), pp. 67–68.

4. "The International Negotiations Respecting Limitation of Whaling, and the London Conference," *NHT* (July, 1937), pp. 225–26.

5. "International Whaling Conference in London, 14th June–29th June, 1938," *NHT* (July, 1938), pp. 287–300.

6. This was the first official use of the blue-whale unit. The blue-whale unit was originally adopted by the whaling companies in the 1930s in their production limitation agreements. Each company was allotted so many barrels of production, 110 being the equivalent of 1 blue-whale unit. If a company could extract more than 110 barrels per blue-whale unit, it was allowed to increase its total production. This compensation for efficiency was demanded by certain companies before agreeing to limit production.

7. International Whaling Conference, "United States Proposals for a Whaling Convention," Doc. No. IWC/3, Washington, D.C., October 29, 1946, pp. 1–29.

8. International Whaling Conference, "Minutes of the Tenth Session," Doc. No. IWC/47, pp. 9–13.

9. For a discussion of the problem of nonmembership in the Commission by land-based whaling nations, see International Whaling Commission, Second Meeting (1950), Document No. 13, "Report of the Special Sub-Committee on the Chilean Proposals."

10. International Whaling Conference, "Minutes of the Second Session," Doc. No. IWC/12, p. 29.

11. International Whaling Commission, "Resolutions from Organizations Concerned about the Preservation of the Whale Stocks," Doc. No. IWC/16/13. Note: on occasion an observer from an organization interested in conservation was permitted to attend the plenary sessions of the Commission, but he was never permitted to speak.

12. J. T. Ruud, "International Regulation of Whaling," *NHT* (September, 1956), p. 385.

13. International Whaling Commission, Special Meeting, May, 1965, "Proposal of the Japanese Delegation," Doc. No. IWC/SM/12.

14. *NHT* (March, 1950), p. 108. See also R. Kellogg, "What is Known of the Migrations of Some of the Whalebone Whales?" *Annual Report of the Smithsonian Institution for 1928*, pp. 467-94.

15. For a more detailed discussion of the debates of the International Whaling Commission at annual meetings from 1950 to 1965, see G. L. Small, *The Virtual Extinction of an Extraterritorial Pelagic Resource—the Blue Whale* (Ph.D. dissertation; New York, Columbia University, 1968).

16. International Whaling Commission, Fifth Meeting (1953), "Report of the Scientific Subcommittee," Doc. No. 2, pp. 1-3; and Appendix, pp. 1-6. Note: henceforth references to events at annual meetings of the Whaling Commission are not footnoted; the material in the text is based on the pertinent committee reports and records of plenary sessions of the years in question.

17. "Memorandum of the Dutch Delegation on the Reduction of 16,000 Blue-Whale Units," *NHT* (October, 1953), pp. 560-64.

18. S. G. Brown, "Dispersal in Blue and Fin Whales," *Discovery Reports*, XXVI (January, 1954), 355-84.

19. "The International Whaling Convention," *NHT* (January, 1959), pp. 1-3.

20. The British commissioner by advocating a 4,000 blue-whale-unit quota was voting the death of the British whaling industry. Great Britain's share (9 percent) of 4,000 units would have been 360 units, and that would not have been enough to sustain even 1 floating-factory expedition.

21. T. Ichihara, "Identification of the Blue Whale in the Antarctic," *NHT* (May, 1963), pp. 128-31; and, "Blue Whales in the Waters Around Kerguelen Island," *NHT* (January, 1961), pp. 1-20.

22. Personal communication from Dr. Kellogg. Similar ideas were expressed to me by a noted Norwegian cetologist who wishes to remain anonymous because he still occasionally is a member of the Norwegian delegation to the International Whaling Commission.

23. Ruud, Jonsgård, and Ottestad, p. 31; and, Risting, p. 37.

24. E. Mayr, E. Linsley, and R. Usinger, *Methods and Principles of Systematic Zoology* (New York: McGraw-Hill, 1953), p. 30.

VIII: EPILOGUE OR EPITAPH?

1. J. A. Gulland, "The Effect of Regulations on Antarctic Whale Catches," *Journal du Conseil Permanent International pour l'Exploration de la Mer,* xxx, No. 3 (November, 1966), 308–15.

2. For the most comprehensive article on this subject see J. A. Gulland, "The Management of Antarctic Whaling Resources," *Journal du Conseil International pour l'Exploration de la Mer,* xxxi, No. 3 (1968), 330–41.

3. *Oklahoma Reports,* Initiative Petition No. 112, CLIV (1932), p. 259.

BIBLIOGRAPHY

BOOKS & ARTICLES

Andrews, R. C. *Whale Hunting with Gun and Camera.* New York: Appleton & Co., 1916.

—— "Monographs of the Pacific Cetacea. I. The California Gray Whale," *Memoirs of the American Museum of Natural History,* Vol. I, No. 5, pp. 229–87.

"The Antarctic Baleen Whale Stocks," *Norsk Hvalfangst Tidende* (December, 1963), pp. 350–54.

"The Antarctic Baleen Whale Stocks," *Norsk Hvalfangst Tidende* (September, 1964), pp. 259–66.

"Antarctic Expedition Weighs 46 Whales," *Norsk Hvalfangst Tidende* (December, 1948), pp. 500–4.

Arai, Y., and S. Sakai. "Whale Meat in Nutrition," *Scientific Reports.* Whales Research Institute, Tokyo, VII (1952), 51–68.

Ash, Christopher. *Whaler's Eye.* New York: Macmillan Co., 1962.

—— "On the Body Weights of Whales," *Norsk Hvalfangst Tidende* (July, 1952), pp. 364–74.

—— "Comparing the Fatness of Whales," *Norsk Hvalfangst Tidende* (January, 1955), pp. 20–24.

—— "Weights and Oil Yields of Antarctic Humpback Whales," *Norsk Hvalfangst Tidende* (October, 1957), pp. 569–73.

Bagshawe, T. W. *Two Men in the Antarctic.* Cambridge, England: University Press, 1939.

Barnard, K. H. *A Guide Book to South African Whales and Dolphins.* Cape Town: South African Museum, 1954.

Bell, J. J. *The Whale Hunters.* London: T. Nelson & Sons Ltd., 1929.

Bennett, A. G. *Whaling in the Antarctic.* Edinburgh: Wm. Blackwood & Sons Ltd., 1931.

Bergersen, B. "The International Whaling Convention," *Norsk Hvalfangst Tidende* (November, 1952), pp. 593–602.

—— "The Condition of the Antarctic Whale Stocks," *Norsk Hvalfangst Tidende* (August, 1953), pp. 305–14.

"Beslagleggelsene i Rotterdam for retten," *Norges Handels og Sjøfarts Tidende* (Oslo), April 24, 1956.

Bettum, F. "The Position of the Whaling Companies at the Turn of the Year," *Norsk Hvalfangst Tidende* (January, 1957), pp. 14–19.

—— "The Development of Whaling and the Present Position," *Norsk Hvalfangst Tidende* (October, 1958), pp. 485–502.

—— "Some Observations on the Development of Whaling and on Its Central Problem Today," *Norsk Hvalfangst Tidende* (June, 1960), pp. 245–65.

"Bevisene mot Onassis," *Aftenposten* (Oslo), January 17, 1956.

"Blue Whale Stocks in the Antarctic," *Norsk Hvalfangst Tidende* (March, 1950), pp. 106–15.

Borgstrom, Georg. *Japan's World Success in Fishing*. London: Fishing News Ltd., 1964.

Bowett, D. W. "The Second United Nations Conference on the Law of the Sea," *International and Comparative Law Quarterly*, IX (1960), 415–35.

Brandt, K. *Whaling and Whale Oil During and After World War II*. War-Peace Pamphlets No. 11, Food Research Institute, Stanford University, 1948.

Brinkmann, A. "Studies on Female Fin and Blue Whales," *Hvalrådets Skrifter*, XXXI (1948), 1–38.

British Museum (Natural History). *Handbook of R. H. Burne's Cetacean Dissections*. London: 1952.

Brown, S. G. "Dispersal in Blue and Fin Whales," *Discovery Reports*, XXVI (1954), 355–84.

—— "The Movements of Fin and Blue Whales in Antarctic Waters," *Norsk Hvalfangst Tidende* (June, 1954), pp. 301–9.

—— "Whale Marks Recovered During the Antarctic Whaling Season 1957/1958," *Norsk Hvalfangst Tidende* (October, 1958), pp. 503–7.

—— "The Movements of Fin and Blue Whales Within the Antarctic Zone," *Discovery Reports*, XXXVII (1962), 1–54.

Burke, W. T. "Some Comments on the 1958 Convention," *Proceedings of the American Society of International Law*, LIII (1959), 197–206.

Clark, Robert. "Migration of Marine Animals," *Norsk Hvalfangst Tidende* (November, 1957), pp. 609–29.

"Concerning the Oil Output in Pelagic Antarctic Whaling," *Norsk Hvalfangst Tidende* (February, 1954), pp. 57–67.

Crisp, D. T. "The Tonnage of Whales Taken by Antarctic Pelagic Operations During Twenty Seasons, and an Examination of the Blue-Whale Unit," *Norsk Hvalfangst Tidende* (October, 1962), pp. 389–93.

Crutchfield, James A. "Common Property Resources and Factor Allocation," *Canadian Journal of Economics and Political Science*, XXII (August, 1956), 292–300.

Dean, A. H. "The General Conference on the Law of the Sea; What Was Accomplished," *American Journal of International Law*, LII (1958), 606–28.

—— "Achievements at the Law of the Sea Conference," *Proceedings of the American Society of International Law*, LII (1959), 186–97.

—— "The Geneva Conference on the Law of the Sea; What Was Accomplished," *American Journal of International Law*, LIV (1960), 751–89.

"Denne gangen skyr man ingenting," *Tønsbergs Blad* (Tønsberg), March 6, 1956.

"Dutch Whaling Operations," *Norsk Hvalfangst Tidende* (December, 1951), pp. 629–30.

Eckstrøm, K. "Main Features in the Development of Norwegian Whaling Control," *Norsk Hvalfangst Tidende* (February, 1953), pp. 72–85.

"Expansion of the Pelagic Whaling Fleet in the Antarctic," *Norsk Hvalfangst Tidende* (January, 1950), pp. 13–14.

"Factory Ship *Antarctic* Sold for Breaking Up," *Norsk Hvalfangst Tidende* (December, 1954), pp. 708–10.

"Fangststatistisk," *Norsk Hvalfangst Tidende* (February, 1931), pp. 53–56; (May, 1931), pp. 135–37; (June, 1931), pp. 145–46, 147–49, 151, 163.

Friant, Madeleine. "Un Stade de l'Evolution Cérébrale du Rorqual *(Balaenoptera musculus L.),*" *Hvalrådets Skrifter,* Vol. xlii (1958).

Gambell, R. "A Pygmy Blue Whale at Durban," *Norsk Hvalfangst Tidende* (March, 1964), pp. 66–68.

Gulland, J. A. "The Effect of Regulation on Antarctic Whale Catches," *Journal du Conseil Permanent Internationale pour l'Exploration de la Mer,* xxx, No. 3 (1966), 308–15.

Harmer, S. F. "Cervical Vertebrae of a Gigantic Blue Whale from Panama," *Proceedings of the Zoological Society,* London (1923), p. 1085.

—— "History of Whaling," *Proceedings of the Linnaean Society,* cxl (1928), 51–95.

—— "Southern Whaling," *Proceedings of the Linnaean Society,* cxlii (1931), 85–163.

Heyerdahl, E. F. *Hvalindustrien I, Råmaterialet.* Sandefjord: Kommandør Chr. Christensens Hvalfangst Museum, 1932.

—— "Hvalkjøttets Utnyttelse til Oljefremstilling," *Norsk Hvalfangst Tidende* (August, 1929), pp. 229–33.

—— "On the Treatment of the Whale," *Norsk Hvalfangst Tidende* (August, 1938), pp. 339–50; (September, 1938), pp. 392–407; (October, 1938), pp. 440–58.

Hjort, J., J. Lie, and J. T. Ruud. "Norwegian Pelagic Whaling in the Antarctic II," *Hvalrådets Skrifter,* vii (1933), 128–52.

"Hvalfangerforeningen-Årsberetning," *Norsk Hvalfangst Tidende* (February, 1937), pp. 67–69.

"Hvorfor reduserte Hvalfangstforbundet kravet mot Onassis?" *Vestfold Arbeiderblad,* May 24, 1956.

Ichihara, Tadayoshi. "Blue Whales in the Waters Around Kerguelen Island," *Norsk Hvalfangst Tidende* (January, 1961), pp. 1–20.

—— "Identification of the Pigmy Blue Whale in the Antarctic," *Norsk Hvalfangst Tidende* (May, 1963), pp. 128–31.

"Ikke noen gang har jeg sett de panamanske kontrollørene i verksomhet på flensplan," *Tønsbergs Blad* (Tønsberg), March 8, 1956.

"The International Negotiations Respecting Limitation of Whaling and the London Conference," *Norsk Hvalfangst Tidende* (July, 1937), pp. 225–54.

"International Whaling Conference in London, 14th June–24th June, 1938," *Norsk Hvalfangst Tidende* (July, 1938), pp. 287–300.

"The International Whaling Convention," *Norsk Hvalfangst Tidende* (January, 1959), pp. 1–3.

"The International Whaling Convention of 1946," *Norsk Hvalfangst Tidende* (October, 1953), pp. 549–60.

International Whaling Statistics, Det Norske Hvalråds Statistiske Publikasjoner, Vols. I–LVIII (1930–66).

"Intet svar på Norges protest hos Panama?" *Sandefjords Blad* (Sandefjord), October 29, 1956.

Isachsen, Gunnar. *Jorden Rundt Efter Blåhvalen.* Sandefjord: Kommandør Chr. Christensens Hvalfangst Museum, 1927.

Jacobsen, Alf P. "Endocrinological Studies in the Blue Whale *(Balaenoptera musculus L.),*" *Hvalrådets Skrifter,* XXIV (1941), 1–84.

Japan Whaling Association. *Japanese Whaling Industry.* Tokyo: Fisheries Agency, Ministry of Agriculture and Forestry, 1950.

Japanese Fisheries. Tokyo: Asia Kyokai, 1960.

"The Japanese Whaling Industry," *Norsk Hvalfangst Tidende* (November, 1954), pp. 625–31.

Jenkins, J. T. *Whales and Modern Whaling.* London: H. F. & G. Witherby Co., 1932.

Johnsen, A. O. "Karl Brandt, *Whale Oil,*" *Norsk Hvalfangst Tidende* (June, 1941), pp. 101–20.

Jonsgård, Å. "The Stocks of Blue Whales in Northern Atlantic Ocean and Adjacent Waters," *Norsk Hvalfangst Tidende* (September, 1955), pp. 297–311.

Kellogg, R. "What Is Known of the Migrations of Some of the Whalebone Whales?" *Annual Report,* Smithsonian Institution (1928), pp. 467–94.

Kirschenbauer, H. G. *Fats and Oils: An Outline of Their Chemistry and Technology.* New York: Reinhold Publishing Corp., 1960.

Klem, Alf. "The Milk Fat of the Blue Whale," *Hvalrådets Skrifter,* XI (1935), 56–62.

Knudtzon, H. Th. "Concerning Paragraph 5a of the Whaling Act," *Norsk Hvalfangst Tidende* (November, 1953), pp. 621–25.

Kravanja, Milan. "Soviet Far East Fisheries Expansion," *Commercial Fisheries Review,* XXVI, No. 11a (1964), 1–14.

Laurie, A. H. "Some Aspects of Respiration in Blue and Fin Whales," *Discovery Reports,* VII (1933), 363–406.

—— "The Age of Female Blue Whales and the Effect of Whaling on the Stock," *Discovery Reports,* XV (1937), 223–84.

Laws, R. M. "Reproduction, Growth, and Age of Southern Fin Whales," *Discovery Reports,* XXXI (1961), 327–486.

Leonard, L. L. "Recent Negotiations Toward the International Regulation of Whaling," *American Journal of International Law,* XXXV (1941), 90–113.

Lie, J. "Whaling Problems and the Norwegian Whaling Council," *Norsk Hvalfangst Tidende* (October, 1952), pp. 529–39.

Lillie, Harry R. "Whaling and Its Antarctic Problems Today," *Canadian Geographic Journal,* xxxviii, No. 3 (1949), 104–13.

"Lov om Endring i Lov om Fangst av Hval av Juni 16, 1939," *Norsk Hvalfangst Tidende* (August, 1946), pp. 184–94.

Lund, J. "Whale Tribes in the Antarctic—Iodine Value Determination," *Norsk Hvalfangst Tidende* (June, 1938), pp. 251–61.

—— "Charting of Whale Stocks in the Antarctic in the Season of 1949–50 on the Basis of Iodine Values," *Norsk Hvalfangst Tidende* (July, 1950), pp. 289–305.

McDougal, M. S., and W. T. Burke. *The Public Order of the Oceans.* New Haven: Yale University Press, 1962.

MacKenzie, W. C. "The Whaling Industry: Economic Aspects," *Canadian Geographic Journal,* xxxviii, No. 3 (1949), 140–44.

Mackintosh, N. A. *The Stocks of Whales.* London: Fishing News Ltd., 1965.

—— "The Southern Stock of Whalebone Whales," *Discovery Reports,* xxii (1942), 197–300.

—— "The Natural History of Whalebone Whales," *Annual Report,* Board of Regents of the Smithsonian Institute (1946), pp. 235–64.

—— "Biological Problems in the Regulation of Whaling," *Norsk Hvalfangst Tidende* (August, 1959), pp. 395–404.

—— and S. G. Brown. "Preliminary Estimate of the Southern Populations of the Larger Baleen Whales," *Norsk Hvalfangst Tidende* (September, 1956), pp. 469–80.

—— and J. F. G. Wheeler. "Southern Blue and Fin Whales," *Discovery Reports,* i (1929), 259–540.

Marr, J. W. S. "*Euphasia Superba* and the Antarctic Surface Currents," *Norsk Hvalfangst Tidende* (March, 1956), pp. 127–34.

—— "The Natural History and Geography of the Antarctic Krill *(Euphasia Superba),*" *Discovery Reports,* xxxii (1962), 32–464.

Matthews, L. Harrison. "The Biology of Whales," *The New Scientist,* iv, No. 107 (December, 1958), 1426–27.

"Memorandum of the Dutch Delegation on the Reduction of 16,000 Blue-Whale Units," *Norsk Hvalfangst Tidende* (October, 1953), pp. 560–64.

"Minimum Size of Blue Whales," *Norsk Hvalfangst Tidende* (June, 1938), p. 242.

"Minutes of the Whaling Conference Held at the Norwegian Ministry of Commerce, Oslo, on the 4th and 5th of October, 1935," *Hvalrådets Skrifter,* xii (1935), I–XVI.

Moore, J. C., and E. Clark. "Discovery of Right Whales in the Gulf of Mexico," *Science* (July, 1963), p. 269.

Nemoto, T. "Food of Baleen Whales with Reference to Whale Movements," *Scientific Reports*, xiv (1959), 149–290.

"New Catching Boats under Construction," *Norsk Hvalfangst Tidende* (October, 1952), pp. 562–64.

"The New Floating Factory *Willem Barendsz* Delivered from the Shipyard," *Norsk Hvalfangst Tidende* (August, 1955), pp. 473–75.

"1962 Whale Catch a White Elephant: Industry May Die," New York *Times*, April 8, 1963.

Nishiwaki, M. "On the Body Weight of Whales," *Scientific Reports*, iv (1950), 184–209.

—— "On the Coloration of Crystalline Lens Available for Age Determination of the Antarctic Blue and Fin Whale," *Scientific Reports*, iv (1950), pp. 115–61.

—— "On the Age Determination of Mystacoceti, Chiefly Blue and Fin Whales," *Scientific Reports*, Whales Research Institute, Tokyo, vii (1952), 87–120.

—— "Age Characteristics of Ear Plugs of Whales," *Scientific Reports*, xii (1957), 23–32.

—— and K. Hayashi. "Biological Survey of Fin and Blue Whales Taken in the Antarctic Season 1947–48 by the Japanese Fleet," *Scientific Reports*, iii (1950), 132–90.

—— and T. Oye. "Biological Investigations on Blue Whales and Fin Whales Caught by the Japanese Antarctic Whaling Fleets," *Scientific Reports*, v (1951), pp. 91–167.

"Norges Hvalfangstforbund bringer bevisene for *Olympic Challengers* ulovlige hvalfangst," *Sandefjords Blad* (Sandefjord), January 16, 1956.

Norman, J. R., and F. C. Fraser. *Giant Fishes, Whales, and Dolphins*. New York: W. W. Norton Co., 1938.

Norris, K. S., ed. *Whales, Dolphins, and Porpoises*. Berkeley: University of California Press, 1965.

"Norsk aksjon mot Onassis," *Haugesunds Avis* (Haugesund), March 26, 1956.

"Norske hvalredere er gått til ny aksjon mot Onassis," *Arbeiderbladet* (Oslo), April 22, 1956.

"Norway and the International Whaling Commission," *Norsk Hvalfangst Tidende* (December, 1956), pp. 664–65.

"Norway's Position with Regard to the International Whaling Convention," *Norsk Hvalfangst Tidende* (February, 1963), pp. 33–38.

Oda, Shigeru. *International Control of Sea Resources*. Leyden: A. W. Sythoff Co., 1963.

—— "New Trends in the Regime of the Seas," *Zeitschrift für Ausländisches Öffentliches Recht und Völkerrecht*, xviii (1957), 61–102; 261–86.

Ohno, M., and K. Fujino. "Biological Investigations on the Whales Caught by the Japanese Antarctic Whaling Fleets, Season 1950/51," *Scientific Reports*, VII (1952), 125–88.

"Olympic Challenger," *Norsk Hvalfangst Tidende* (1950), pp. 152–54.

"Olympic Challenger," *Tønsbergs Blad* (Tønsberg), February 18, 1956.

"Olympic Challenger has not observed the Regulations of the International Whaling Convention," *Norsk Hvalfangst Tidende* (November, 1955), pp. 381–98; (January, 1956), pp. 1–37.

"Olympic Challenger's Catch in relation to the provisions of the International Whaling Convention," *Norsk Hvalfangst Tidende* (April, 1956), pp. 172–208.

"Onassis—forliket seier for Norge," *Morgenbladet* (Oslo), May 28, 1956.

"Onassis ulovlige hvalfangst avsløres," *Norges Handels og Sjøfarts Tidende* (Oslo), March 6, 1956.

Ottestad, P. "On Age and Growth of Blue Whales," *Hvalrådets Skrifter*, XXXIII (1950), 67–72.

Pedersen, Torbjørn. "Content of Saturated Fatty Acids in Oil from Different Strata of Blue Whale Blubber," *Hvalrådets Skrifter*, XXXIV (1950), 44ff.

—— "Oil from the Meat of Sperm Whales," *Norsk Hvalfangst Tidende* (June, 1952), pp. 296–98.

Purves, P. E. "The Wax Plug in the External Auditory Meatus of the Mysticeti," *Discovery Reports*, XXVII (1956), 293–302.

Rayner, G. W. "Whale Markings II. Distribution of Blue Fin and Humpback Whales Marked from 1932–1938," *Discovery Reports*, XXV (1953), 31–38.

"Regulations for Distribution of the Assets of the Whaling Industry's Security Fund," *Norsk Hvalfangst Tidende* (April, 1948), pp. 151–52.

Risting, S. *Av Hvalfangstens Historie*. Sandefjord: Kommandør Chr. Christensens Hvalfangst Museum, 1922.

—— "Whales and Whale Foetuses," *Rapports et Procès-Verbaux des Réunions*, Conseil Permanent Internationale pour l'Exploration de la Mer, L (1928), 1–122.

—— "Blåhvalens Parringstid i Sydhavet," *Norsk Hvalfangst Tidende* (1929), pp. 114–24.

Ruud, J. T. "Blåhvalen," *Norsk Hvalfangst Tidende* (January, 1937), pp. 18–32.

—— "Om Hvalfangstens Naturgrunnlag," *Norsk Hvalfangst Tidende* (June, 1938), pp. 243–50.

—— "The Surface Structure of the Baleen Plates as a Possible Clue to Age in Whales," *Norsk Hvalfangst Tidende* (February, 1941), pp. 21–30; 40.

—— "Investigations of the Age of Blue Whales," *Norsk Hvalfangst Tidende* (February, 1950), pp. 80–89.

—— "Investigations of the Age of Blue Whales in the Antarctic Pelagic Catches 1945/46–1948/49," *Norsk Hvalfangst Tidende* (June, 1950), pp. 245–60.

—— "Modern Whaling and Its Prospects," *Norsk Hvalfangst Tidende* (December, 1952), pp. 649–60.

—— "International Regulation of Whaling," *Norsk Hvalfangst Tidende* (September, 1956), pp. 374–87.

—— "The Blue Whale," *Scientific American,* cxcv, No. 6 (December, 1956), 46–50.

—— Å. Jonsgård, and P. Ottestad. "Age Studies on Blue Whales," *Hvalrådets Skrifter,* xxxiii (1950), 1–66.

"Sale of Catching Material to Japan," *Norsk Hvalfangst Tidende* (January, 1957), pp. 23–24.

"Sale of *Kosmos III* and Five Catching Boats to Japan," *Norsk Hvalfangst Tidende* (August, 1961), p. 342.

Schubert, K. "Hvalbestanden i Sydishavet," *Die Fischwirtschaft* (Hamburg), 1952; translated to the Norwegian in *Norsk Hvalfangst Tidende* (February, 1953), pp. 91–92.

Schwitzer, M. K. *Margarine and Other Food Fats.* New York: Interscience Publishers, 1956.

Scott, Anthony. "The Fishery: The Objectives of Sole Ownership," *Journal of Political Economy,* lxiii (April, 1955), 116–24.

Scott, Gordon. "The Economic Theory of a Common Property Resource: The Fishery," *The Journal of Political Economy,* lxii (April, 1954), 124–42.

Simon, Noel. "Of Whales and Whaling," *Science* (August 27, 1965), pp. 943–46.

Simpson, Frank A. *The Antarctic Today.* Sydney: Halstead Press, 1952.

Slijper, E. J. *Whales.* London: Hutchinson Co. Ltd., 1962.

Small, G. L. *The Virtual Extinction of an Extraterritorial Pelagic Resource—The Blue Whale.* Ph.D. Thesis, Columbia University. New York: 1968.

"Statement from the Federation of Norwegian Whaling Companies," *Norsk Hvalfangst Tidende* (November, 1961), pp. 447–52.

"Syd-Georgia Saesongen," *Norsk Hvalfangst Tidende* (November, 1930), pp. 321–36.

Symons, H. W. "The Foetal Growth Rate of Whales," *Norsk Hvalfangst Tidende* (September, 1956), pp. 519–25.

Taubenfell, H. J. "A Treaty for Antarctica," *International Conciliation,* Carnegie Endowment for International Peace, No. 531 (1961), pp. 245–322.

Tavogla, William N., ed. *Marine Bio-Accoustics.* Long Island City: Pergamon Press, 1964.

Tveraaen, I. "Chemical Analyses of Samples of Blue Whale Oils," *Hvalrådets Skrifter,* xi (1935), 5–48.

"Weight of Whales," *Norsk Hvalfangst Tidende* (January, 1953), pp. 16–17.

Wetlesen, C. U. "Whale Liver," *Norsk Hvalfangst Tidende* (June, 1938), pp. 262–63.

"Whale Catcher Restriction 1956–1957," *Norsk Hvalfangst Tidende* (June, 1956), pp. 297–98.

"Whale Oil and Meat Production, 1962–1963 Season," *Commercial Fisheries Review*, xxvi, No. 3 (March, 1964), 61.

"Whaling Factory Ship Sold to Japan," *Commercial Fisheries Review*, xxvi, No. 10 (October, 1964), 73.

White, Gilbert F. "Toward an Appraisal of World Resources: New Views of Conservation Problems," *Geographical Review*, xxxix (1949), 625–39.

Wilson, Charles. *The History of Unilever.* 2 vols. London: Cassell & Co. Ltd., 1954.

"Working Conditions and Earnings on the Japanese Expeditions in the Antarctic," *Norsk Hvalfangst Tidende* (July, 1955), pp. 406–8.

DOCUMENTS AND OTHER SOURCES

Aksjeselskapet Kosmos, Sandefjord, Norway, *Beretning og Regnskap*, 1950–65.

Aktieselskabet Odd, Sandefjord, Norway, *Driftsberetning og Regnskap*, 1950–65.

Aktieselskabet Ørnen, Sandefjord, Norway, *Driftsberetning og Regnskap*, 1950–65.

Bureau of Whaling Statistics, Sandefjord, Norway, "Oppgaver som viser antall norske mannskaper samt gjennomsnittsfortjeneste pr. mann pr. sesong og pr. måned" (unpublished document compiled in 1965).

Hvalfangeraktieselskapet Rosshavet, Sandefjord, Norway, *Beretning og Regnskap*, 1950–65.

Hvalfangerselskapet Globus, Larvik, Norway, *Driftsberetning og Regnskap*, 1950–65.

Hvalfangerselskapet Pelagos, Tønsberg, Norway, *Beretning og Regnskap*, 1950–65.

Hvalfangerselskapet Polaris, Larvik, Norway, *Driftsbereting og Regnskap*, 1950–65.

International Whaling Commission, Office of the Commission, London, from annual meetings held in several world cities, 1949 through 1965: "Income and Expenditure Account"; "Minutes of Plenary Sessions"; "Press Release"; "Report of Ad Hoc Scientific Committee"; "Report of Committee of Three (Scientists)"; "Report of Scientific Committee"; "Report of Scientific Subcommittee"; "Report of Technical Committee"; "Report on Infractions"; and occasional miscellaneous documents.

Japan, Fisheries Agency, Ministry of Agriculture and Forestry, *The Fisheries Law,* Tokyo, 1963 printing with amendments.

Norway, Hvalrådet, financial statement supplied by the Secretary, September 6, 1966, on the income and expenditures of Hvalkonsesjonsavgiftsfondet, Hvalfangstbedriftens Kontrollavgiftsfondet, and Hvalfangstbedriftens Sikringsfondet, 1950–65.

U.S., Bureau of Commercial Fisheries, Fish and Wildlife Service, *Taiyo Fishing Company's Foreign-Based Fishing Operations and Business Enterprises (as of September, 1962)*, memorandum, based on private sources, from Acting Area Director, Terminal Island, California, July 3, 1963.

U.S., Bureau of Commercial Fisheries, Market News Service, Pacific Southwest Region, Terminal Island, California, *Foreign Fishery Information Release Numbers: 65–25*, October 25, 1965; *66–2*, January 14, 1966; *66–4*, January 28, 1966; *66–11*, May 13, 1966; *67–5*, February 16, 1967; *67–6*, February 24, 1967; *67–21*, June 16, 1967; *67–29*, September 1, 1967; *67–30*, September 11, 1967; *67–38*, November 14, 1967; *67–39*, November 20, 1967.

U.S., Department of State, *Official Report of the United States Delegation to the Nineteenth Meeting of the International Whaling Commission*, Washington, D.C., July 28, 1967.

U.S., Department of State, *Report of the United States Commissioner to the Annual Meeting of the International Whaling Commission*, Washington, D.C., sixteen annual reports, from 1949 through 1965.

INDEX